Praise for Thomas Moore's pre̶̶̶̶̶̶̶̶̶

CARE OF THE SOUL

"There is the depth and originality of Mr. Moore's observations . . . and a deeply consoling intelligence . . . that should draw many readers." —*New York Times*

"Thoughtful, eloquent, inspiring." —*San Francisco Chronicle*

"Invigorating, demanding, and revolutionary." —*Publishers Weekly*

SOUL MATES

"I devoured *Soul Mates* like some comfort food for the spirit. . . . Moore moves love off the fast track and into the realm of mystery and imagination where it belongs." —*New Woman*

"An eloquent, passionate, often mystical exploration of how we mere mortals might better understand ourselves and others in a late-20th century society in which so much emphasis is placed on interpersonal dynamics and so little on introspection, care, grace, gratitude and honor." —*Detroit News*

MEDITATIONS

"[Moore] is a literate, informed, and careful participant observer, and his meditations are full of practical insights for life. . . . The collection is as much about the poetry and music of our lives together as about overly religious discipline." —*Booklist*

THE RE-ENCHANTMENT OF EVERYDAY LIFE

"Every so often a book comes along that is perfect for its time. Thomas Moore's *The Re-Enchantment of Everyday Life* is just such a book. . . . This book is an absolute joy to read and re-read."

—*Parabola*

"[A] profound yet practical sequel to Moore's massive bestseller *Care of the Soul*. . . . [T]his important book will dare many to believe that life really is full of enchantment."

—*Publishers Weekly* (starred review)

"[A] worthy sequel to *Care of the Soul* and *Soul Mates*."

—*New Age Journal*

THE
EDUCATION
OF THE
HEART

Also by Thomas Moore

The Re-Enchantment of Everyday Life

Meditations

Soul Mates

Care of the Soul

Rituals of the Imagination

The Planets Within

Dark Eros

A Blue Fire: The Essential Writings of James Hillman *(editor)*

The EDUCATION *of the* HEART

READINGS AND SOURCES FOR

CARE OF THE SOUL, SOUL MATES, AND

THE RE-ENCHANTMENT OF EVERYDAY LIFE

EDITED BY

THOMAS MOORE

HarperPerennial

A Division of HarperCollins*Publishers*

Since this page cannot legibly accommodate all the copyright notices, pages 343–348 constitute an extension of this copyright page.

A hardcover edition of this book was published in 1996 by HarperCollins Publishers.

THE EDUCATION OF THE HEART. Copyright © 1996 by Thomas Moore. All rights reserved. Printed in the United States of America. No part of this book may be used or reproduced in any manner whatsoever without written permission except in the case of brief quotations embodied in critical articles and reviews. For information address HarperCollins Publishers, Inc., 10 East 53rd Street, New York, NY 10022.

HarperCollins books may be purchased for educational, business, or sales promotional use. For information please write: Special Markets Department, HarperCollins Publishers, Inc., 10 East 53rd Street, New York, NY 10022.

First HarperPerennial edition published in 1997.

Designed and electronically produced by David Bullen

The Library of Congress has catalogued the hardcover edition as follows:

Moore, Thomas, 1940–
The education of the heart : readings and sources from Care of
the soul, Soul mates, and The re-enchantment of everyday life /
Thomas Moore. — 1st ed.
p. cm.
Includes bibliographical references and index.
ISBN 0-06-017410-2
1. Conduct of life—Literary collections. 2. Soul—Literary
collections. 3. Spiritual life—Literary collections. I. Title.
PN6014.M35 1997
158—dc20 96–38276
ISBN 0-06-092860-3 (pbk.)

00 01 ❖/RRD 10 9 8 7 6 5 4

TO ABRAHAM
AND SIOBHÁN

CONTENTS

ACKNOWLEDGMENTS

I would like to thank the following talented, dedicated, and hard-working people for their part in piecing together this manual for the heart: Paul DuBois Jacobs, Michael Katz, Hugh Van Dusen, Kate Ekrem, David Bullen, Anne Hayes, and Jerriann Boggis.

THE
EDUCATION
OF THE
HEART

INTRODUCTION

EDUCATION IS AN eduction, the art of educing or bringing out what is latent in a person. In its early forms, the word was used of basic physical nurturing, bringing out the undeveloped powers of the physical body, and could even be applied to animals. In its deepest form, education is the art of enticing the soul to emerge from its cocoon, from its coil of potentiality and its cave of hiding. Education is not the piling on of learning, information, data, facts, skills, or abilities—that's training or instructing—but is rather a making visible what is hidden as a seed.

Deep education entails an emergence of character and personality, and often takes the form of initiation. In this sense, a person can be educated by the death of a relative or friend, as, in one of the earliest recorded tales, the proud Gilgamesh was educated and profoundly transformed by witnessing the death of his friend Enkidu. To be educated, a person doesn't have to know much or be informed, but he or she does have to have been exposed vulnerably to the transformative events of an engaged human life.

One of the great problems of our time is that many are schooled but few are educated. True to our modern values and vision, we tend to the instruction of the mind and the training of the body, while we generally neglect the soul. It's not surprising that as our culture advances in information and technology, we seem to become more inarticulate about matters of the heart. We quantify "human behavior" and develop programs of therapy and treatment, and yet this Procrustean trimming of the soul to fit our programs of science doesn't have much effect. We still encounter the soul chiefly as a set of intractable problems rather than as a creative and constructive source of life.

The spirit of instruction is mesmerized by the future, by the latest developments in machinery and language, and by fantasies of a golden era yet to come. The soul is more enticed by the past, especially by the beauty and wisdom that is our world heritage. Spirit-driven modernism sees our culture as an evolutionary achievement, but the soul appreciates the eternal insights of the past. The elders of a people teach the traditional stories and rites that hold a community together, but modern instruction favors the fresh, young product of an up-to-date school over the old professor types who live in the past and whose ideas are outmoded.

Peruse a few pages of a new technical manual and you will probably find many tables and statistics, a volume organized on a precise grid of numbers, and many acronyms and abbreviations used as if they were real words. Together, these methods create an abstract fantasy of the subject at hand and perhaps the illusion of control over the material. Now look at an older volume on almost any subject, and you may find more poetic speech, less obvious organization of ideas, and attention to the beauty of language. Eternal ideas, beauty of expression, a concern for values, and a human scale all give education a soul and soul an education. They allow it to address the heart and not only the mind.

In my three books *Care of the Soul, Soul Mates,* and *The Re-Enchantment of Everyday Life,* I have tried to write about the soul in the style of the soul, especially by appealing to past wisdom and avoiding technical jargon. Although these books are sometimes placed in the category of self-help, my purpose has been to educate rather than to provide therapy. I have wanted to discuss the basic issues of human life, not with the aim of helping people deal with personal problems but with the hope that thoughtful discussion might deepen our reflection on the human condition.

I could add a footnote to almost every sentence in these books, so indebted am I to my contemporaries and my ancestors. And so it seems quite natural to present an anthology of my sources, not merely as a study guide, which it can be, or as a reference work or reader's tool, but for the most part as a manual for the education of the heart.

I recommend not taking a purely mental approach to the selections presented here. Many readers have told me how they studied literature and mythology in school without ever considering the relevance and importance of that literature to their lives. We can read these selections on the soul with heart, not just mind. Just as we recite poems "by heart," we can read by heart. I don't intend to provide any information on these sources or interpretations; I merely want to offer a selection of readings, artfully chosen and arranged, that speak for themselves.

A reader can browse through these passages and read them at random, or go from beginning to end, treating this collection as a course on soul. I have designed the book to serve both these purposes, choosing selections for their individual merit and beauty, arranging them by theme to link them to my books, and weaving them together to make a tapestry image of the soul.

The reader can begin the process of shifting from a mechanical to a soul-centered world in the very reading of this book by giving up the intrusive quest for information, clarity, definition, and answers. Instead, enter into the beauty of language and thought. Meditate on the book, read passages aloud, write them down for future reference, tell them to friends, commit them to memory—these are all ways of educating the heart.

Without an education, the heart presents itself as a cauldron of raw emotions, suspicious desires, and disconnected images. Dreams appear stupefying, longings inappropriate, and relationships confounding. Without an animating, educated heart, the intellect appears superior, and we give too much attention and value to it. Our institutions and ideas then lack the humanizing breath of the soul. Education of the proper kind brings into view the order and sense in matters of the heart that otherwise seem elusive, and position the heart to play a significant role in affairs of the mind.

After contemplating the many passages, long and short, gathered here, a reader might realize how much ingenuity and meditation has gone into issues of the soul over hundreds and even thousands of years. It might become apparent how much we have to learn from our ancestors. We might discover that we can imitate the premodern society, turning to its elders for life-sustaining wisdom, and regard our forebears as teachers and guides. We can find comfort in our traditions of storytelling, philosophy, and theology and guidance that is grounded in long traditions and in many generations of reflection.

We might also appreciate how the beauty of language and imagery animates an idea and how much is lost when we focus only on meaning. From the soul perspective, meaning is less important than meaningfulness. Ideas that move us with the grace of their presentation penetrate the heart and serve purposes that go beyond understanding, as they foster passion, interest, and decision.

Writers of the past still speak and have a presence; we can hear their voices in the words, phrases, and sentences of their books. In their literary style we can sense their inflections, emphases, and concerns. As we read their words, we engage their personalities and imaginations. We are present to them, as they present themselves to us. This book, then, is a collection of dialogues in which you, the reader, are among the cast of characters. You have an opportunity to enter many conversations here, expanding your own community as you engage these voices of the past with your heart and soul.

In order to live with more soul in a culture dedicated to a materialistic and mechanistic worldview, we have to do everything from a deeper, more reflective position. As we discuss these selections, we might accent memory, reverie, story, and association instead of interpretation, correctness, and understanding. We might try to educate our hearts and imaginations rather than our minds.

A writer concerned about the soul will lead us deep into a subject, where clarity may be elusive and certainty grounded in poetry rather than fact. The language will be more evocative than explanatory, and the test of our reading will be insight or sensibility rather than understanding.

As we educate our hearts, we may spend a lifetime contemplating certain phrases and ideas, never fully grasping their meanings, but becoming more intimate with their mysteries. Gradually they may be woven into our own ways of thinking and living as the basic themes of our own mythology and philosophy.

The many and varied selections that follow, then, are to be meditated upon, discussed, written, and repeated—or perhaps in the spirit of magic, simply kept physically close. The soul deepens by a process like osmosis, an almost imperceptible growth in love and attachment for the words and personalities of the authors. Reading can be an exercise in eros as well as logos, an intimate act with, as many authors have commented, sexual overtones. Love, desire, and pleasure are the chief signals of the presence of soul. Bring them to this reading, and chances are, soul will be called out from hiding and we readers in the deepest sense will be educated.

THE REDISCOVERY OF THE SOUL

The soul enjoys the body in its pleasures
and takes over to heal it in its illnesses.

MARSILIO FICINO

"Soul" is a *strange word. We use it in everyday speech, and you can find it in almost every newspaper, as when a headline says: "The City Has Been Shaken to Its Soul!" Yet we don't know exactly what it means, and our first impulse might be to look for a definition. But the soul, as mysterious as life itself, is beyond definition. We have to be satisfied with descriptions, ancient and modern, that help us meditate on the nature of the soul. Over time, we may develop a strong sense of what the soul is, and then how to take care of it.*

Many associate the soul with religion and belief. They may imagine the soul as a thing, as a part of one's being, perhaps the part that survives after death. But we may also understand the soul as a dimension of our experience as a person, or even as a quality in a community, place, or thing. Heraclitus, the ancient Greek philosopher, emphasizes the depth of the soul, while James Hillman, a contemporary philosopher and psychologist, associates the soul with death and beauty.

Perhaps we have become interested in the soul once again—it has been seriously discussed by theologians, philosophers, and poets for centuries—because we know there is more to life than what the sciences can grasp. We may like the word "soul" precisely because it is beyond definition and keeps the mystery element in life intact.

For centuries, the work of the Christian priest has been called "care of the soul," and, in fact, the priest is sometimes called a curate. But in modern times, when the soul is in trouble, we bring it to the psychologist or psychotherapist. Like almost every aspect of modern life, concern for the soul finds its way into the arena of the expert and specialist, the scientifically trained professional, who generally gives the impression that the psyche—we prefer the clinically sounding Greek word for soul—is an organ that is sometimes in need of repair, a problem to be solved.

But psychotherapy, too, has shown signs in recent decades of expanding beyond its clinical image, at first looking for a spiritual dimension in various transpersonal approaches, and recently considering that its real concern might be the soul. Therapy of the soul takes seriously the medieval philosophical notion that the soul is what makes us human, and it doesn't easily dismiss human problems and foibles as diseases to be cured, but sees them as necessary, if painful, ingredients in a fully human life.

Ancient literature makes a distinction between the soul and the spirit, and this important consideration, foreign in many ways to common thinking, has been developed in creative ways by C. G. Jung and especially James Hillman. Although the issue is subtle and complicated, in general terms we can see the spirit as focused on transcending the limits of our personal, time-bound, concrete life. The spirit is fascinated by the future, wants to know the meaning of everything, and would like to stretch, if not break altogether, the laws of nature through technology or prayer. It is full of ideals and ambition, and is a necessary, rewarding, and inspiring aspect of human life.

The soul is, as Jung says, the "archetype of life," embedded in the details of ordinary, everyday experience. In the spirit, we try to transcend our humanity; in the soul, we try to enter our humanity fully and realize it completely. Egged on by spiritual ambition, a person might imitate the old saints and go into the desert or the forest to be cleansed and discover a high level of consciousness. Full of soul, a person might endure the highs and lows of family life, marriage, and work, motivated by a compassionate and hungry heart.

Wondering about the soul, seeking adequate language for it, wanting definition and insight, all mark the beginning of the process of bringing soul to life. Care of the soul begins in a felt acknowledgment of its reality and importance. The soul becomes more present as we consider it in our conversation, writing, meditating, and the thoughtful living of our everyday lives.

In a culture largely driven in spirited directions—evolving, growing, changing—the concerns of the soul may well appear slight and soft. Giving genuine attention to the soul, we may find ourselves somewhat at odds with the world around us. The soul finds value in dependency, the past, intimacy, a slow pace, and sometimes even regression. Introducing soul to modern life may appear at first glance to be a quiet, unobtrusive work, but because the soul has such deep roots in personal and social life and its values run so contrary to modern concerns, caring for the soul may well turn out to be a radical act, a challenge to accepted norms.

The soul is deep and attention to it often simple, and yet it is the source of our passions, our identity, and our vitality. Acknowledging its primacy for the first time, we may find that we have opened Pandora's box and let loose all the debris of a fully engaged, vibrant human life.

1.

WHAT IS THE SOUL?

Those who have written about the soul, both in the distant past and in the present, give the impression that the soul is something intimate, known to us more directly than anything else, and yet at the same time elusive, indescribably profound, not entirely knowable, not within our control, and not completely our personal possession. While it is tempting to define and sketch the structures of the soul, in the end it may be better to speak directly from our experience and intuitions. The descriptions that follow require meditation, not argument, and they invite us never to end our speculating, our search for language that might convey something of the qualities of this elusive aspect of our very being.

You could never arrive at the limits of the soul, no matter how many roads you traveled, so deep is its mystery.

HERACLITUS

Since the soul animates the body, just as the soul is animated by the spirit, she tends to favor the body and everything bodily, sensuous, and emotional. She lies caught in "the chains" of Physis, and she desires "beyond physical necessity." She must be called back by the "counsel of the spirit" from her lostness in matter and the world. This is a relief to the body too, for it not only enjoys the advantage of being animated by the soul but suffers under the disadvantage of having to serve as the instrument of the soul's appetites and desires.

C. G. JUNG, *Mysterium Coniunctionis*

If there were only two things in the world, mind and body, but no soul, then the mind would not be involved with the body, because it is fixed and emotionless and very distant from physical life. Nor would the body have anything to do with the mind, because by itself it is inept and powerless. It is also far removed from the mind. But if soul is placed between these two, adjusted to the nature of each, then one will easily become involved with the other.

MARSILIO FICINO, *Book of Life*

For the sense of being which in calm hours rises, we know not how, in the soul, is not diverse from things, from space, from light, from time, from man, but one with them and proceedeth obviously from the same source whence their life and being also proceedeth.

RALPH WALDO EMERSON, *Self-Reliance*

But in order that a man's soul should quit his body, it is not necessary that he should be asleep. It may quit him in his waking hours, and then sickness or (if the absence is prolonged) death will be the result. Thus the Mongols sometimes explain sickness by supposing that the patient's soul is absent, and either does not care to return to its body or cannot find the way back. To secure the return of the soul it is therefore necessary on the one hand to make its body as attractive as possible, and on the other hand to show it the way home. To make the body attractive all the sick man's best clothes and most valued possessions are placed beside him; he is washed, incensed, and made as comfortable as possible; and all his friends march thrice round the hut calling out the sick man's name and coaxing his soul to return. To help the soul to find its way back a coloured cord is stretched from the patient's head to the door of the hut. The priest in his robes reads a list of the horrors of hell and the dangers incurred by souls which wilfully absent themselves from their bodies. Then turning to the assembled friends and the patient he asks, "Is it come?" All answer Yes, and bowing to the returning soul throw seed over the sick man. The cord which guided the soul back is then rolled up and placed round the patient's neck, who must wear it for seven days without taking it off. No one may frighten or hurt him, lest his soul, not yet familiar with its body, should again take flight.

JAMES G. FRAZER, *The Golden Bough*

By *soul* I mean, first of all, a perspective rather than a substance, a viewpoint toward things rather than a thing itself. This perspective is reflective; it mediates events and makes differences between ourselves and everything that happens. Between us and events, between the doer and the deed, there is a reflective moment—and soul-making means differentiating this middle ground.

It is as if consciousness rests upon a self-sustaining and imagining substrate—an inner place or deeper person or ongoing presence— that is simply there even when all our subjectivity, ego, and consciousness go into eclipse. Soul appears as a factor independent of the events in which we are immersed. Though I cannot identify soul with anything else, I also can never grasp it by itself apart from other things, perhaps because it is like a reflection in a flowing mirror, or like the moon which mediates only borrowed light. But just this peculiar and paradoxical intervening variable gives one the sense of having or being a soul. However intangible and indefinable it is, soul carries highest importance in hierarchies of human values, frequently being identified with the principle of life and even of divinity.

In another attempt upon the idea of *soul* I suggested that the word refers to that unknown component which makes meaning possible, turns events into experiences, is communicated in love, and has a religious concern. These four qualifications I had already put forth some years ago. I had begun to use the term freely, usually interchangeably with *psyche* (from Greek) and *anima* (from Latin). Now I am adding three necessary modifications. First, *soul* refers to the *deepening* of events into experiences; second, the significance *soul* makes possible, whether in love or in religious concern, derives from its special *relation with death.* And third, by *soul* I mean the imaginative possibility in our natures, the experiencing through reflective speculation, dream, image, and *fantasy*—that mode which recognizes all realities as primarily symbolic or metaphorical.

JAMES HILLMAN, *Re-Visioning Psychology*

Some Questions You Might Ask

Is the soul solid, like iron?
Or is it tender and breakable, like
the wings of a moth in the beak of the owl?
Who has it, and who doesn't?
I keep looking around me.
The face of the moose is as sad
as the face of Jesus.
The swan opens her white wings slowly.
In the fall, the black bear carries leaves into the darkness.
One question leads to another.
Does it have a shape? Like an iceberg?
Like the eye of a hummingbird?
Does it have one lung, like the snake and the scallop?
Why should I have it, and not the anteater
who loves her children?
Why should I have it, and not the camel?
Come to think of it, what about the maple trees?
What about the blue iris?
What about all the little stones, sitting alone in the moonlight?
What about roses, and lemons, and their shining leaves?
What about the grass?

MARY OLIVER

As our body is a part of the universe, so also our soul is a part of the
Soul of the universe. . . . Souls are responsive to one another because
they all come from the same soul.

PLOTINUS, *Enneads*

It is the soul that bears man's burdens and joys. It has reason, foresight, and wisdom as companions. These three are intended to rule
over the body and to lead it, lest the soul's yoke prove too burden-
some. But over them the spirit has been appointed, and the spirit
governs reason as well as wisdom and foresight. Then arises the order
of life, and thus do all things spring from the light of the spirit.

The seat and home of the soul is in the heart, the center of the
person; it is the heart that nourished the spirits which know of good
and evil. It dwells within the person in the place where life is, against
which death fights.

PARACELSUS

We are a psychic process which we do not control, or only partly
direct. Consequently, we cannot have any final judgment about ourselves or our lives. If we had, we would know everything—but at
most that is only a pretense. At bottom we never know how it has all
come about. The story of a life begins somewhere, at some particular
point we happen to remember; and even then it was already highly
complex. We do not know how life is going to turn out. Therefore the
story has no beginning, and the end can only be vaguely hinted at.

The life of man is a dubious experiment. It is a tremendous phenomenon only in numerical terms. Individually, it is so fleeting, so
insufficient, that it is literally a miracle that anything can exist and
develop at all. I was impressed by that fact long ago, as a young medical student, and it seemed to me miraculous that I should not have
been prematurely annihilated.

Life has always seemed to me like a plant that lives on its rhizome. Its true life is invisible, hidden in the rhizome. The part that appears above ground lasts only a single summer. Then it withers away—an ephemeral apparition. When we think of the unending growth and decay of life and civilizations, we cannot escape the impression of absolute nullity. Yet I have never lost a sense of something that lives and endures underneath the eternal flux. What we see is the blossom, which passes. The rhizome remains.

In the end the only events in my life worth telling are those when the imperishable world irrupted into this transitory one. That is why I speak chiefly of inner experiences, amongst which I include my dreams and visions. These form the *prima materia* of my scientific work. They were the fiery magma out of which the stone that had to be worked was crystallized. . . .

Similarly, other people are established inalienably in my memories only if their names were entered in the scrolls of my destiny from the beginning, so that encountering them was at the same time a kind of recollection.

Inner experiences also set their seal on the outward events that came my way and assumed importance for me in youth or later on. I early arrived at the insight that when no answer comes from within to the problems and complexities of life, they ultimately mean very little. Outward circumstances are no substitute for inner experience. Therefore my life has been singularly poor in outward happenings. I cannot tell much about them, for it would strike me as hollow and insubstantial. I can understand myself only in the light of inner happenings. It is these that make up the singularity of my life, and with these my autobiography deals.

C. G. JUNG, *Memories, Dreams, Reflections*

People whose desire is solely for self-realization never know where they are going. They can't know. In one sense of the word it is of course necessary, as the Greek oracle said, to know oneself: that is the nrst achievement of knowledge. But to recognize that the soul of a man is unknowable, is the ultimate achievement of wisdom. The final mystery is oneself. When one has weighed the sun in the balance, and measured the steps of the moon, and mapped out the seven heavens star by star, there still remains oneself. Who can calculate the orbit of his own soul?

OSCAR WILDE, *De Profundis*

The soul, that glancing, Aeolian* thing, elusive as a butterfly (anima, psyche).

*Soul, from Old German *saiwalo,* may be cognate with *aiolos,* "quick-moving, changeful of hue, shifting." It also has the meaning of "wily" or "shifty."

C. G. JUNG, *Archetypes and the Collective Unconscious*

When a carpenter builds a house, it first lives in him as an idea; and the house is built according to this idea. Therefore, from the form of the house, one can make inferences about the carpenter's ideas and images. What nature has in mind . . . no one can know until it has acquired form and shape. . . . Now note well that virtue forms the shape of a man, just as the carpenter's ideas become visible in his house; and a man's body takes shape in accordance with the nature of his soul. . . . Nature acts no differently. She gives man an outward appearance that is in keeping with his inner constitution. . . . And each man's soul can be recognized, just as the carpenter can be known by his house.

PARACELSUS

2.

THERAPY WITH SOUL

We live in a mechanistic age, a time of unimagined technological achievement. It is understandably tempting to carry over to matters of the heart the principles and attitudes that have made modern life so functional. When marriages are tottering, when depression sets in, when fantasy dominates reality, and when we lose a sense of direction, we turn to experts in human behavior to repair the problem. But the danger in this application of modern thought to our daily problems is that we will lose sight entirely of the soul.

The passages gathered here under the rubric of therapy may not seem directly related to therapy at all. They emphasize simply living the full range of human emotions and experience, and they even suggest that the many negative challenges we endure have a place in the unfolding of a human life. They suggest that therapy with soul asks for yielding and openness, that the material of our lives is the raw material from which the soul is made and manifested.

The soul sees by means of affliction. Those who are most dependent upon the imagination for their work—poets, painters, fantasts—have not wanted their pathologizing degraded into the "unconscious" and subjected to clinical literalism. ("The unconscious," and submitting the pathologized imagination to therapy, found favor with less imaginative professions: nurses, educationalists, clinical psychologists, social workers.) The crazy artist, the daft poet and mad professor are neither romantic clichés nor antibourgeois postures. They are metaphors for the intimate relation between pathologizing and imagination. Pathologizing processes are a source of imaginative work, and the work provides a container for the pathologizing processes. . . .

The wound and the eye are one and the same. From the psyche's viewpoint, pathology and insight are not opposites—as if we hurt because we have no insight and when we gain insight we shall no longer hurt. No. Pathologizing is itself a way of seeing; the eye of the complex gives the peculiar twist called "psychological insight."

JAMES HILLMAN, *Re-Visioning*

The Soul should always stand ajar
That if the Heaven inquire
He will not be obliged to wait
Or shy of troubling Her

Depart, before the Host have slid
The Bolt unto the Door—
To search for the accomplished Guest,
Her Visitor, no more—

EMILY DICKINSON

While you are working with the soul, keep the body quiet. Fatigue of the body is bad, fatigue of the soul is worse, but worst of all is fatigue of both, with opposite motions distracting a person and destroying his life. Let meditation walk no further than pleasure, and even a little behind.

MARSILIO FICINO, *Book of Life*

I remember when I was at Oxford saying to one of my friends as we were strolling round Magdalen's narrow bird-haunted walks one morning in the year before I took my degree, that I wanted to eat of the fruit of all the trees in the garden of the world, and that I was going out into the world with that passion in my soul. And so, indeed, I went out, and so I lived. My only mistake was that I confined myself so exclusively to the trees of what seemed to me the sun-lit side of the garden, and shunned the other side for its shadow and its gloom. Failure, disgrace, poverty, sorrow, despair, suffering, tears even, the broken words that come from lips in pain, remorse that makes one walk on thorns, conscience that condemns, self-abasement that punishes, the misery that puts ashes on its head, the anguish that chooses sackcloth for its raiment and into its own drink puts gall:—all these were things of which I was afraid. And as I had determined to know nothing of them, I was forced to taste each of them in turn, to feed on them, to have for a season, indeed, no other food at all.

   I don't regret for a single moment having lived for pleasure. I did it to the full, as one should do everything that one does. There was no pleasure I did not experience. I threw the pearl of my soul into a cup of wine. I went down the primrose path to the sound of flutes. I lived on honeycomb. But to have continued the same life would have been wrong because it would have been limiting. I had to pass on. The other half of the garden had its secrets for me also.

OSCAR WILDE, *De Profundis*

So, dear Sir, I can't give you any advice but this: to go into yourself and see how deep the place is from which your life flows; at its source you will find the answer to the question of whether you must create. Accept that answer, just as it is given to you, without trying to interpret it. Perhaps you will discover that you are called to be an artist. Then take that destiny upon yourself, and bear it, its burden and its greatness, without ever asking what reward might come from outside. For the creator must be a world for himself and must find everything in himself and in Nature, to whom his whole life is devoted.

RAINER MARIA RILKE, *Letters to a Young Poet*

A complex must be laid at the proper altar, because it makes a difference both to our suffering and perhaps to the God who is there manifesting, whether we consider our sexual impotence, for example, to be the effect of the Great Mother's Son who may be served thereby, or Priapus who, neglected, is taking revenge, or Jesus whose genitality is simply absent, or Saturn who takes physical potency and gives lascivious fantasy. Finding the background for affliction calls for familiarity with an individual's style of consciousness, with his pathologizing fantasies, and with myth to which style and fantasy may revert.

JAMES HILLMAN, *Re-Visioning*

Mistress, is your mind suddenly possessed
because Pan floods it with madness?
Is this Hekate's fury at work?
Should we accuse those holy Korybantes
or the Great Mother of beasts
glowering in her mountains?
Did you forget to provide
a smooth honeyed sacrifice, and that lapse
offends the huntress—
Artemis!—who sickens you,
spiriting your vigor away?

EURIPIDES, *Hippolytos*

Yield and overcome;
Bend and be straight;
Empty and be full;
Wear out and be new;
Have little and gain;
Have much and be confused.

LAO TZU, *Tao Te Ching*

If the physician understands things exactly and sees and recognizes all illnesses in the macrocosm outside man, and if he has a clear idea of man and his whole nature, then and only then is he a physician. Then he may approach the inside of man; then he may examine his urine, take his pulse, and understand where each thing belongs. This would not be possible without profound knowledge of the outer man, who is nothing other than heaven and earth.

PARACELSUS

To A. Tjoa and R.H.C. Janssen
[original in English]

27 December 1958

Dear Sirs,

Your questions remind me of a very wonderful discussion I once attended at a joint session of the Mind Association and the Aristotelian Society in London about the question: are the individual minds contained in God or not? I must call your attention to the fact that I cannot possibly tell you what a man who has enjoyed complete self-realization looks like, and what becomes of him. I never have seen one, and if I did see one I could not understand him because I myself would not be completely integrated. Thus far your question is a scholastic one, rather like the famous "how many angels can stand on the point of a needle?" Integration in the empirical sense of this word means completion and not perfection. Being a doctor I have seen much of the profound misery of man in our days and of his dissociation. I had to help innumerable people to get a bit more conscious about themselves and to consider the fact that they consist of many different components, light and dark. That's what one calls integration: to become explicitly the one one has been originally. As Japanese Zen says: "Show me thine original face."

C. G. JUNG, *Letters*

But this is human life: the war, the deeds,
The disappointment, the anxiety,
Imagination's struggles, far and nigh,
All human; bearing in themselves this good,
That they are still the air, the subtle food,
To make us feel existence.

JOHN KEATS, "Endymion"

The prima materia, . . . as the raw material of the opus, provides ample occasion for wearisome trials of patience. The prima materia is, as one can so aptly say in English, "tantalizing": it is cheap as dirt and can be had everywhere, only nobody knows it; it is as vague and evasive as the lapis that is to be produced from it; it has a "thousand names." And the worst thing is that without it the work cannot even be begun. The task of the alchemist is obviously like shooting an arrow through a thread hung up in a cloud, as Spitteler says. The prima materia is "saturnine," and the malefic Saturn is the abode of the devil, or again it is the most despised and rejected thing, "thrown out into the street," "cast on the dunghill," "found in filth." These epithets reflect not only the perplexity of the investigator but also his psychic background, which animates the darkness lying before him, so that he discovers in the projection the qualities of the unconscious. This easily demonstrable fact helps to elucidate the darkness that shrouds his spiritual endeavours and the *labor Sophiae:* it is a process of coming to terms with the unconscious, which always sets in when a man is confronted with its darkness.

C. G. JUNG, *Alchemical Studies*

———

The reader must forgive my temerity in expressing the profound effect that some lines from Rafael Cadenas' poem have had on me, but in so doing, I believe I am communicating the great joy I felt when I came across *Fracaso:* joy that is affirmed and lived in a state of higher consciousness, which comes to us from the profound consciousness of failure. It is difficult to find another line that expresses our reality so accurately as Cadenas': "I don't praise you for what you are, but for what you've kept me from becoming. For not giving me another life. For having limited me."

RAFAEL LOPEZ-PEDRAZA, *Cultural Anxiety*

———

Man is split within himself. Life moves against itself through aggression, hate, and despair. We are wont to condemn self-love; but what we really mean to condemn is contrary to self-love. It is that mixture of selfishness and self-hate that permanently pursues us, that prevents us from loving others, and that prohibits us from losing ourselves in the love with which we are loved eternally. He who is able to love himself is able to love others also; he who has learned to overcome self-contempt has overcome his contempt for others. But the depth of our separation lies in just the fact that we are not capable of a great and merciful divine love towards ourselves. On the contrary, in each of us there is an instinct of self-destruction, which is as strong as our instinct of self-preservation. In our tendency to abuse and destroy others, there is an open or hidden tendency to abuse and to destroy ourselves. Cruelty towards others is always also cruelty towards ourselves.

Thus, the state of our whole life is estrangement from others and ourselves, because we are estranged from the Ground of our being, because we are estranged from the origin and aim of our life. And we do not know where we have come from, or where we are going. We are separated from the mystery, the depth, and the greatness of our existence. We hear the voice of that depth; but our ears are closed. We feel that something radical, total, and unconditioned is demanded of us; but we rebel against it, try to escape its urgency, and will not accept its promise.

PAUL TILLICH, "You Are Accepted"

Where prohibition reinforces inhibition, instinct may get split against itself. This split may heal in analytical treatment ("the return of the repressed") but the original inhibition returns too, manifest in such forms as a re-awakened fantasy life, a sense of autonomy, and conscience.

. . . Conscience and imagination are furthered by this inhibition; this fosters intrapsychic tension which may lead to increasing introverted development.

JAMES HILLMAN, Loose Ends

When we call something intolerable we often mean little more than disapproval or a reluctance to endure the irritations of the daily round. What the word really means, however, might be better understood in the image of a torture that goes beyond the endurance of consciousness. It compels some change in the state of being, as becomes evident when the victim faints or dies. This is no petty discomfort, but an affect that is unendurable. So, too, with psyche the word intolerable means unendurable to the point where some change is compelled.

NIEL MICKLEM, "The Intolerable Image"

Freud viewed symptoms as compromise solutions. He meant that symptoms act as safeguards, giving a partial expression to unconscious contents, thereby assuring their continued repression. Imagined physically, this mechanism is like letting some steam from a pot escape so that it doesn't blow its cover entirely. In other words, repression is maintained by relieving some of its pressure in the form of symptoms.

Symptoms are defenses. So, for our purposes, let us hypothesize that *a defense expresses something of the unconscious content from which it would defend itself.* As I put it elsewhere, like not only cures like but like also *defends* against like.

Further, defenses are most effective the more closely they simulate the enemy (from which they would defend themselves). This implies that, if taken far enough, a defense could become indistinguishable from its enemy. By simulating ever more closely, the defense becomes more like that content from which it is, with increasing effectiveness, defending itself.

By stressing the content of the defense, we have been moving from a Freudian to a more Jungian attitude. We have said that the defense expresses that content from which it would defend itself. Now to take the Jungian leap: each content has telos. If a defense expresses unconscious contents (Freud), and if unconscious contents are purposeful (Jung), then, as our title suggested, "defense and telos in dreams" have an inherent relation; in fact the defense is one face of the dream's purpose and necessary to the dream's just-so nature. *The defense is as purposeful as the telos itself.*

Our model has allowed us to discover a telos in the dream ego's defense. Recognition of the purpose in the defense frees it of the values it has had to protect. But for a defense to be so freed, it must first be dismantled with a critical eye to its pathological structure, its too-easy way and secondary gains. Assuredly the defense, invented by Freud, deserves a Freudian treatment. It needs severe reduction and must be brought home as an ego-defense mechanism. But the dream is more than the ego's defense; it is also the psyche's purpose. And this purposefulness may be discovered even in the ego's pathology. For the ego's pathology is inherently in sympathy with the psyche's individuation.

PATRICIA BERRY, *Echo's Subtle Body*

———————

L.P. *Talking about therapy; then. . . .*

J.H. It's so many different things, isn't it? . . . It's a practice of religion, a practice of magic, a practice of teaching, a practice of political brainwashing, it's a practice of change of consciousness, it's a practice of terror even; there are just an incredible variety of things happening in therapy; it's a form of love, there is coupling, there is complicity—all these things are going on in therapy. People have tried to understand why it came when it did in our historical context, other people are concerned with when is it going to be finished. I brought lots of these questions into *The Myth of Analysis*. For me therapy is basically the evocation of imagination: it's training, working, struggling with imagination. If I were to say that it has to do with healing, I'd have to say healing the imagination or healing the relationship to the imagination. If I want to say therapy has to do with raising or deepening the levels of consciousness or intensifying it, I'll still put therapy in connection with imagination as the development of a psychological sense of imagination.

JAMES HILLMAN, *Interviews*

———————

Call the world if you Please "The vale of Soul-making" Then you will find out the use of the world (I am speaking now in the highest terms for human nature admitting it to be immortal which I will here take for granted for the purpose of showing a thought which has struck me concerning it) I say 'Soul making' Soul as distinguished from an Intelligence—There may be intelligences or sparks of the divinity in millions—but they are not Souls till they acquire identities, till each one is personally itself. I[n]telligences are atoms of perception—they know and they see and they are pure, in short they are God—How then are Souls to be made? How then are these sparks which are God to have identity given them—so as ever to possess a bliss peculiar to each ones individual existence? How, but by the medium of a world like this? This point I sincerely wish to consider because I think it a grander system of salvation than the chrysteain religion—or rather it is a system of Spirit-creation— This is effected by three grand materials acting the one upon the other for a series of years. These three Materials are the *Intelligence*— the *human heart* (as distinguished from intelligence or Mind) and the *World* or *Elemental space* suited for the proper action of *Mind and Heart* on each other for the purpose of forming the *Soul* or *Intelligence destined to possess the sense of Identity*. I can scarcely express what I but dimly perceive. . . . —and yet I think I perceive it—that you may judge the more clearly I will put it in the most homely form possible—I will call the *world* a School instituted for the purpose of teaching little children to read—I will call the *human heart* the *horn Book* used in that School—and I will call the *Child able to read, the Soul* made from that *school* and its *hornbook*. Do you not see how necessary a World of Pains and troubles is to school an Intelligence and make it a soul? A Place where the heart must feel and suffer in a thousand diverse ways! Not merely is the Heart a Hornbook, It is the Minds Bible, it is the Minds experience, it is the teat from which the Mind or intelligence sucks its identity— As various as the Lives of Men are—so various become their souls, and thus does God make individual beings, Souls, Identical Souls of the sparks of his own essence—

JOHN KEATS, *Letters*

3.

SPIRIT AND SOUL

There was a time when people reflected deeply on the nature of the "interior life," as they called it, and the meaning of the cosmos. Today, we surrender most of this reflection to scientists. Not having thought much about their inner lives, people are often confused when faced with the traditional distinction between the soul and the spirit, but distinguishing these two dimensions of experience can be helpful. We might notice, for instance, how much we are motivated by the spirit in our concentration on the future, on understanding, and on achievement. We might then see how we neglect the soul, which has complementary but very different values, such as slowness, the past, inaction, feeling, mystery, and imagination.

The pages that follow do not all speak directly to the intellectual task of distinguishing spirit from soul, but they offer many different images that imply how we might experience these two directions. We may sense spirit as eternity or as vast nature finding their way into our lives. We may become aware of a daimonic presence within ourselves, another personality that is part of our makeup and yet somehow other at the same time.

To suggest a distinction between soul and spirit is not to advocate a separation of the two. On the contrary, it seems best to arrive at a place where in effect the two work together, as in a marriage or partnership.

Who is going up the mountain? . . . Is the one ascending the spiritual impetus of the puer aeternus, the winged godlike imago in us each, the beautiful boy of the spirit—Icarus on the way to the sun, then plummeting with waxen wings; Phaethon driving the sun's chariot out of control, burning up the world; Bellerophon, ascending on his white winged horse, then falling onto the plains of wandering, limping ever after? These are the puer high climbers, the heaven stormers, whose eros reflects the torch and ladder of Eros and his searching arrow, a longing for higher and further and more and puer and better. Without this archetypal component affecting our lives, there would be no spiritual drive, no new sparks, no going beyond the given, no grandeur and sense of personal destiny.

So, psychologically, and perhaps spiritually as well, the issue is one of finding connections between the puer's drive upward and the soul's clouded, encumbering embrace. . . .

The anima, "the archetype of life," as Jung has called her, is that function of the psyche which is its actual life, the present mess it is in, its discontent, dishonesties, and thrilling illusions, together with the whitewashing hopes for a better outcome. The issues she presents are as endless as the soul is deep, and perhaps these very endless labyrinthine "problems" *are* its depth. . . .

The spirit asks that the psyche help it, not break it or yoke it or put it away as a peculiarity or insanity. And it asks the analysts who act in psyche's name not to turn the soul against the puer adventure but rather to prepare the desire of both for each other.

JAMES HILLMAN, "Peaks and Vales"

———————

Without soul, spirit is as dead as matter, because both are artificial abstractions; whereas man originally regarded spirit as a volatile body, and matter as not lacking in soul.

C. G. JUNG, *Alchemical Studies*

———————

It sometimes happens that I feel "foreign to myself," and at such times I feel completely happy. This "other" whom I discover in myself seems to have come from elsewhere. I then "listen to myself" with emotion, and with the badly contained impatience to discover this unknown life of "another" who is, however, myself, a "new life," perhaps.

MIRCEA ELIADE, *Journals*

Tzu Sang-hu, Meng Tzu-fan, and Tzu Ch'in-chang were friends. They said to each other, "Who can live together without any special effort to live together and help each other without any special effort to help each other? Who can ascend to heaven, roam through the clouds, revolve in the realm of the infinite, live without being aware of it, and pay no attention to death?" The three looked at each other and smiled, completely understood each other, and thus became friends.

CHUANG TZU, *The Mystical Way*

You can see the beauty of Christ in each individual person, in that which is most his, most human, most personal to him, in things which an ascetic might advise you sternly to get rid of.

THOMAS MERTON, *Conjectures of a Guilty Bystander*

Soul is at home in the deep, shaded valleys. Heavy torpid flowers saturated with black grow there. The rivers flow like warm syrup. They empty into huge oceans of soul.

Spirit is a land of high, white peaks and glittering jewel-like lakes and flowers. Life is sparse and sounds travel great distances. . . .

Desolation is of the depths, as is brooding. At these heights, spirit leaves soul far behind.

FOURTEENTH DALAI LAMA OF TIBET

[Apollo chasing the nymph Daphne]
I tell futures, pasts, presents;
I tune songs; best shot in the world, except
for the arrow that got my heart; invented medicine!
famous doctor! all drugs are in my power!
though no drug to cure love; my skills
help everyone but they don't help me!

& more: but Daphne rushes off, scared,
cutting him short; even then seeming beautiful:
winds baring body, clothes blown back,
light breeze in hair: chase enhancing beauty

young god can't wait, wasting words:
moved by love, he moves faster: as hound
spotting hare down field runs for prey
& hare runs for life; one's held—almost—
in snout, one's unsure if caught, slips out
bite of open mouth: so god & girl

OVID, *Metamorphoses*

———————

What for the soul is Allure, for the spirit is Beauty.

NOVALIS, *Pollen and Fragments*

———————

The power I possess is sex, passion, love,
which you mortals, in honoring me,
celebrate in your diverse ways.
I'm no less the darling of heaven.
I am the goddess Aphrodite . . .
Now this young man, alone
among his contemporaries,
says freely I am a despicable goddess.

Marriage is anathema to him,
he goes to bed with no girl.
The goddess he adores is Artemis, a virgin,
Apollo's sister, the daughter of Zeus.
Our young friend thinks *her*
kind of divinity the most exhilarating.
In the pale green forest they are inseparable,
they drive their killer hounds until the wild life,
squirrels as well as stags, is extinct.
Such a friendship between human and god
is a remarkable even—
I would not deny him this happiness.
I have no reason to.
                    It's purely his
offenses against me which I resent
and will punish—today.

EURIPIDES, *Hippolytos*

Another odd thing happened. The river and everything I remembered about it became a possession to me, a personal, private possession, as nothing else in my life ever had. Now it ran nowhere but in my head, but there it ran as though immortally. I could feel it—I can feel it—on different places on my body. I pleases me in some curious way that the river does not exist, and that I have it. In me it still is, and will be until I die, green, rocky, deep, fast, slow, and beautiful beyond reality. I had a friend there who in a way had died for me, and my enemy was there.

JAMES DICKEY, *Deliverance*

There is as much worship in good workmanship done in the right spirit, as in any other act; the spirit of the thing done and not the act itself is the key to tell whether anything done be worship or not, but God, the master workman, who has made the minutest insect with as much care as the mammoth elephant, sets us the example of good works. Imitation is the sincerest praise.

THE SHAKER MANIFESTO

Now it is time that gods came walking out
of lived-in Things . . .
Time that they came and knocked down every wall
inside my house. New page. Only the wind
from such a turning could be strong enough
to toss the air as a shovel tosses dirt:
a fresh-turned field of breath. O gods, gods!
who used to come so often and are still
asleep in the Things around us, who serenely
rise and at wells that we can only guess at
splash icy water on your necks and faces,
and lightly add your restedness to what seems
already filled to bursting: our full lives.
Once again let it be your morning, gods.
We keep repeating. You alone are source.
With you the world arises, and your dawn
gleams on each crack and crevice of our failure . . .

RAINER MARIA RILKE

Therefore, we ascend from the Body to the Soul, from this to the Angel, and from this to God. God is above eternity. The Angel is completely in eternity. Clearly its operation as well as its being remains stable. But stability is characteristic of eternity. The Soul is partly in eternity, partly in time for its substance always remains the same, and without any change either of increase or decrease. But its operation, as we showed a little while ago, runs through intervals of time. The Body is entirely subject to time. For its substance is subject to change and all of its functions require the space of time. Therefore, the One itself is above stability or motion, the Angel is in stability, the Soul is equally in stability and in motion, and the Body is only in motion. Again, the One remains above number, motion, and place; the Angel is placed in number, above motion and place; the Soul is in number and motion, but above place; the Body is subject to number, motion, and place. Although the One itself has no number, is not composed of parts, is not changed in any way from what it is, and is not enclosed in any place, the Angel certainly has a number of parts, or forms, but it is free from motion and place. The Soul has multiplicity of parts and passions, and is subject to change, both in the process of thinking and in fluctuations of mood, but it is exempt from limits of place. The Body, however, is subject to all of these.

MARSILIO FICINO, *Commentary on Plato's Symposium*

For Spirit is first of all power, the power that drives the human spirit above itself towards what it cannot attain by itself, the love that is greater than all other gifts, the truth in which the depth of being opens itself to us, the holy that is the manifestation of the presence of the ultimate.

You may say again—"I do not know this power. I have never had such an experience. I am not religious or, at least, not Christian and certainly not a bearer of the Spirit. What I hear from you sounds like ecstasy; and I want to stay sober. It sounds like mystery, and I try to illuminate what is dark. It sounds like self-sacrifice and I want to fulfill my human possibilities." To this I answer—Certainly, the Spiritual power can thrust some people into an ecstasy that most of us have never experienced. It can drive some towards a kind of self-sacrifice of which most of us are not capable. It can inspire some to insights into the depth of being that remain unapproachable to most

of us. But this does not justify our denial that the Spirit is also working in us. Without doubt, wherever it works, there is an element,
possibly very small, of self-surrender, and an element, however weak,
of ecstasy, and an element, perhaps fleeting, of awareness of the mystery of existence. Yet these small effects of the Spiritual power are
enough to prove its presence.

PAUL TILLICH, *The Eternal Now*

I find you, lord, in all Things and in all
my fellow creatures, pulsing with your life;
as a tiny seed you sleep in what is small
and in the vast you vastly yield yourself.

The wondrous game that power plays with Things
is to move in such submission through the world:
groping in roots and growing thick in trunks
and in treetops like a rising from the dead.

RAINER MARIA RILKE

And then our good Lord opened my spiritual eye, and showed me
my soul in the midst of my heart. I saw the soul as wide as if it were
an endless citadel, and also as if it were a blessed kingdom, and from
the state which I saw in it, I understood that it is a fine city. In the
midst of that city sits our Lord Jesus, true God and true man, a
handsome person and tall, highest bishop, most awesome king, most
honorable lord. And I saw him splendidly clad in honors. He sits
erect there in the soul, in peace and rest, and he rules and guards
heaven and earth and everything that is. The humanity and divinity
sit at rest.

JULIAN OF NORWICH, *Showings*

As the body stands in conjunction with the world, so stands the soul in conjunction with the spirit. Both paths course out from humanity and end in God. Both circumnavigations are required in corresponding points of their path. Both must think of the means— despite the distance—to remain together and to make both journeys commonplace.

NOVALIS, *Pollen and Fragments*

THE ART AND CRAFT OF LIVING

Mouth on fire . . . stream of words . . . in her ear . . .
practically in her ear . . . not catching the half . . .
not the quarter . . . no idea what she's saying! . . .
imagine! . . . no idea what she's saying! . . .
and can't stop . . .

SAMUEL BECKETT, *Not I*

I N MODERN LIFE *we place our trust in machines and in under-standing. In our physical work, the need for craft has diminished considerably as we continue to invent sophisticated technologies, while in our personal lives we seem to think that if we could only under-stand what we're going through, our problems would be solved. But the soul is more deeply affected by imagination than by clever and expert coercions. It is moved by good words and images. A stirring story may have more effect than a reasoned argument. A picture may truly say more than a million words. A poem may depict the soul more accurately than a long, footnoted treatise. A simple song may linger in the memory and affect our mood.*

In recent decades our language has become brittle and abstract. We use abbreviations as though they were words, we use a common jargon for our subtle emotional experiences, and we prefer tables, graphs, num-bers, and step-by-step procedures over lengthy reflection. All of this is the result of the spirited bias of the times. But the soul takes things in slowly and piecemeal, savoring the details and the qualities of expression. A good phrase may inspire meditation for many years, and a good tune may stay with us for a lifetime.

It makes a difference what kind of language we use to express our feel-ings and thoughts. Some words are more evocative than others, some fresher than those that immediately come to mind. Choosing the right word may make all the difference, and that choice requires art.

Words becomes sentences, and sentences paragraphs, as our language takes form, and although the form may look rational and straightfor-ward, there may be a wealth of fantasy and story beneath it. Words have their rich histories, which are always to some extent present in every usage. A dictionary may give the impression that a word can be defined simply and definitively, but the etymology and history of a word suggest that words are alive and can't be stuffed once and for all into a defini-tion.

In a similar way, our ordinary statements also have stories buried deep within them. The evident purpose and content of our words have one kind of effect, while the underlying story, the soul of the text, has an added impact. Becoming sensitive to the stories embedded in everyday discourse is a useful way to stay in tune with the soul, and a good way to remain sensitive is to read, listen to, tell, write, and illustrate stories of all kinds.

It's a short step, then, to an appreciation of other arts. In our modern context, we tend to see the arts as forms of self-expression or as encoded messages, but the soul of the arts is to be found again in the underlying dimensions. The arts present the deep stories and themes, the archetypal patterns and figures, that are directly tied to emotion and meaning. The absence of meaningfulness and a corresponding aimlessness in life are characteristic of our times and stem from our being disconnected from our archetypal roots.

Artists and writers often confess that they are mere scribes, putting into form and material the images they have received. Ancient traditions also speak of objects of art as though they were alive, having presence and true personality. In contrast, we often think of art objects as the exclusive product of the painter or writer. Once again, appreciating the impersonal in the art offers a route toward the soul of the art.

For centuries writers on the soul have claimed music as a particularly important soul art. Plato discussed the impact of music on the soul, Boethius taught that music is foremost an aesthetic structure of the soul, Ficino spelled out ways in which music can temper the soul, and Robert Fludd pictured the cosmos as a musical field.

Ficino considered architecture a primary art because of its considerable influence on the emotions and imagination; theater has close ties to religion in its development, and dance is always ritualistic to some degree. All the arts constitute a school of the imagination and, far from being at the edge of "real life," as they are often treated today, are truly of central importance.

4.

LANGUAGE AND STORYTELLING

The artist admits that when he or she speaks and writes, it's a muse or an angel that is making the utterance. But isn't the same true of all of us, all the time? Whenever we speak, other voices are speaking through us. We never know the full resonance of our words, spoken or written, and it is from those mysterious depths that words take their power. The more we stand back and allow those other voices to be heard, the more fully we speak and the more powerfully we are heard.

It is similar with the stories we tell and the stories we live. We can only glimpse them, and when we try to capture them in a narrative—a conversation or a diary—we feel the inadequacy of our expression. And so our stories are sometimes only attempts at stories, and sometimes they are nonstories, mere grunts of telling that collapse in midsentence in tears, laughter, or silence.

Some stories—perhaps more accurately some storytellers—present themselves as the story to supplant, to superannuate, even to destroy all other stories. The responses solicited by such a story are responses aimed at leading thenceforth to regarding all other stories as false, wrong, misguided, erroneous, incomplete, etc., because this one story is the Truth of the matter. But a story to end all other stories must ultimately fail on the grounds that it appeals to criteria of judgment which emanate from other than narrative modes of thinking, which is to say, such a story finally defeats itself. A story of real importance is not an argument so much as it is a presentation and an invitation. It presents a realm of experience accessible through the imagination and invites participation in imaginative responses to reality, indeed to respond to reality as imaginative. A story invites one to tell one's own personal and collective stories in response. Stories evoke other stories. The importance of stories lies ultimately less in what is told than in how whatever is told gets told. The temptation is always to stop—to stop listening, to stop responding, to stop storying—but premature death (and what other kind is there, at least from life's point of view?) is always to be mourned. Any story purporting to kill other stories and the storytelling impulse will lead, sooner or later, to its own demise.

First, there were stories. Then, there were no stories. Now, there are stories. For those who have ears attuned to stories, there *are* now stories. And there will be new stories, no matter how old they may sound to those whose hearing is either committed only to particular old stories or to those who have willfully deafened themselves to all stories, not noticing that by now that too is a story in a state of rigor mortis.

JAMES WIGGINS, *Religion As Story*

———

Stories are medicine. I have been taken with stories since I heard my first. They have such power; they do not require that we do, be, act anything—we need only listen. The remedies for repair or reclamation of any lost psychic drive are contained in stories. Stories engender the excitement, sadness, questions, longings, and understandings that spontaneously bring the archetype, in this case Wild Woman, back to the surface.

Stories are embedded with instructions which guide us about the complexities of life. Stories enable us to understand the need for and the ways to raise a submerged archetype.

CLARISSA PINKOLA ESTÉS, *Women Who Run with the Wolves*

———

A colleague once told me about a new patient walking out on her when she challenged the thematic mode of the patient's story. The patient presented himself as a rather sick case, having been more or less steadily in therapy for fifteen of his thirty-six years; things had not much changed (alcohol, homosexuality, depressions, money worries), and he had tried many kinds of therapy. My colleague said: "For me, you are a new case, and I don't accept that you are as sick as you believe you are. Let's begin today." By refusing his web of constructions, she also cut him off from his supporting fiction. He did not return. His story still made sense to him: an incurable, but still a dues-paying member of the therapeutic traffic. He wanted analysis and the analyst to fit into his story.

A second case, this one from my practice: psychotic episodes, hospitalizations with medical abuses, seductions, and violations of rights, shock treatments and 'helpful drugs.' I took this story like a past another woman might tell of: falling in love in high school and marrying the boy next door, having a loving husband, children, and a spaniel, a story of making it. In other words both are consistent accounts exposing a thematic motif which organizes events into experience. Both of these women, this one from her percale sheets and the other from her canvas strait jacket—to put the fantasy figuratively—might come in to therapy, desperate, saying precisely the same thing: "It doesn't make any sense; I've wasted the best years of my life, I don't know where I am, or who I am." The senselessness derives from a breakdown in the thematic motif: it no longer holds events together and gives them sense, it no longer provides the mode of experiencing. The patient is in search of a new story, or of reconnecting with her old one.

I believed her story to be her sustaining fiction, but that she had not read it for its hermetic possibilities, its covert meanings. She had taken her story literally in the clinical language in which it had been told her, a tale of sickness, abuse, wastage of the best years. The story needed to be doctored, not her: it needed reimagining. So I put her years of wastage into another fiction: she knew the psyche because she had been immersed in its depths. Hospital had been her finishing school, her initiation rites, her religious confirmation, her rape, and her apprenticeship with psychological realities. Her pedigree to survival and diploma was her soul's endurance through, and masochistic enjoyment of, these psychological horrors. She was indeed a victim, not of her history but of the story in which she had put her history.

JAMES HILLMAN, *Healing Fiction*

If one is to learn theology on oneself, one expects to discover religion's images to be precise metaphoric expressions of that which one thinks and feels: thrown into a world where things need naming; expulsed from Edenic sense; towering Babel; flooding in life; bondage; walking dry through the midst of seas; wandering in wildernesses; drawn to gold idols; wanting a king like the others; exiled; on an ash heap; whirlwind; something sacred getting born out of a virginal place in the self; nailed; betrayed; miraculously going on; waiting for the spirit to come; apocalypse now; my God, why hast thou forsaken me. Every image and story of religion, every doctrinal and creedal idea, becomes stunningly connected with the soul's sense of things when one looks and listens with the eyes and ears of a depth theology.

Of course there will always be those who think of such an approach to religion as psychologizing, subjective, solipsistic, or gnostic. But this would be to continue to imagine that such senses of self—moods, dreams, illnesses—are under the will's control or are susceptible to an analysis or explanation by the ego's intellect and reason. If one were to note, as did Freud and Jung, that it is precisely at these moments that the ego is *un*conscious, then this approach would seem not a psychologizing of religion but a theologizing of the self, an amplification rather than a reduction, mythos rather than logos, story and poetry rather than logic.

DAVID MILLER, *Three Faces of God*

The Sibyl with raving mouth utters solemn, unadorned, unlovely words, but she reaches out over a thousand years with her voice because of the god in her.

HERACLITUS

I dare not pretend to be any other than the Secretary the Authors are in Eternity

WILLIAM BLAKE

Freud, on investigating the psychogenesis of the pleasure afforded by wit, recognised the significance of the child's *play with words.* "Children," he says, "treat words as objects."

The distinction, not yet rigorously carried out, between what is only imagined and what is real (i.e., the tendency of the mind to relapse into the primary, regressive mode of functioning), may also make the special character of obscene words comprehensible, and justify the surmise that at a certain stage of development this concreteness, and with it probably a strong tendency to regression, applies still to all words. On this, indeed, rests Freud's explanation of dream images; in sleep we fall back on the original mode of mental functioning, and once more regressively revive the perceptual system of consciousness. In dreams we no longer think in words, but hallucinate.

SANDOR FERENCZI, "On Obscene Words"

We make out of the quarrel with others, rhetoric, but of the quarrel with ourselves, poetry.

W. B. YEATS, "Anima Hominis"

Meaningful art, music, literature are not new, as is, as must strive to be, the news brought by journalism. Originality is antithetical to novelty. The etymology of the word alerts us. It tells of "inception" and of "instauration," of a return, in substance and in form, to beginnings. In exact relation to their originality, to their spiritual-formal force of innovation, aesthetic inventions are "archaic." They carry in them the pulse of the distant source.

GEORGE STEINER, *Real Presences*

A person ought to describe threefold in his soul the meaning of divine letters, that is, so that the simple may be edified by, so to speak, the body of the Scriptures; for that is what we call the ordinary and narrative meaning. But if any have begun to make some progress and can contemplate something more fully, they should be edified by the soul of Scripture. And those who are perfect are like those concerning whom the Apostle says, "Yet among the perfect we do impart wisdom, although it is not a wisdom of this world or of the rulers of this world, who are doomed to pass away. But we impart a secret and hidden wisdom of God, which God decreed before the ages for our glorification" (1 Cor. 2:6–7). Such people should be edified by that spiritual Law (cf. Rom. 7:14) which has a shadow of the good things to come (cf. Heb. 10:1), edified as by the spirit of Scripture. Thus, just as a human being is said to be made up of body, soul, and spirit, so also is sacred Scripture, which has been granted by God's gracious dispensation for man's salvation.

ORIGEN, "On First Principles"

Language has been traditionally imagined as that which distinguishes us from the beasts. Even Jung saw symbols as a means by which the animal instincts may be transformed. We have understood culture to be a Herculean way of taming the wilderness. But text, language, and culture may be imagined as Artemis' web as well—reversing our heroic fantasy of language as civilized. Longinus says, "Above all, we must learn from art that there are some things in language that depend on nature alone." A text may be read not only according to the civilized Athena-fantasy, but as wild imaginings; as Plato insists, every *logos* ought to be a *zoon,* an animal. And as Aristotle says, an animal does not think, but can only imagine.

Orpheus, we are told, charmed the animals with his singing. It is as if only the animal ear can hear language poetically, the words themselves dangerous and unpredictable, living by desire and hunger and fear. The poet John Haines has recently written:

> Dear friend at the continent's end:
> Wilderness survives at the camp
> we have made within us,
> a forest filled up with night,
>
> its ancient sounds
> and floating, starlit images.

We frequently see complexes through the fantasy of Alexander the Great, as problems to be solved, as Gordion knots to be loosened by means of heroically incisive, analytic (*analuo:* "to loosen") insight. But in the fantasy of Artemis, the complex is the wilderness itself, filled with night: an irritating entanglement to the civilized ego, but one which keeps us untamed. The complex in this fantasy is not something to be heroically loosened; rather, it is always loosening us, releasing the animal, the wildness. In terms of language this wildness is that aspect of words which stubbornly refuses to be reduced to the useful, domesticated concepts of civilization, an ancient instinct within language which keeps it poetic and free. This wildness is the "friend at the continent's end." The continent ends: language is incontinent, uncontained, a voice crying from the wilderness.

STEPHEN SIMMER, *The Net of Artemis*

The word is made flesh. To recover the world of silence, of symbolism, is to recover the human body. "A subterranean passage between mind and body underlies all analogy." The true meanings of words are bodily meanings, carnal knowledge; and the bodily meanings are the unspoken meanings. What is always speaking silently is the body.

NORMAN O. BROWN, *Love's Body*

———————

There is no Frigate like a Book
To take us Lands away
Nor any Coursers like a Page
Of prancing Poetry—
This Traverse may the poorest take
Without oppress of Toll—
How frugal is the Chariot
That bears the Human soul.

EMILY DICKINSON

———————

By locating the holy in the spiritual depths rather than the heights—in the quotidian rather than the supernatural—the form and imagery, not the substance, of the religious consciousness is changed. If the promises that redeem us spring from mundane soil rather than from an authorized covenant with God, history is, nevertheless, experienced as the story of promise and fulfillment. Human existence is still sanctified by sacrifice, and we may appropriately face the mysterious givenness of life and personality with gratitude and reverence. This change in language from images of height to depth represents the religious response of the twentieth-century mind to the loss of the traditional metamundane myths. If God is gone from the sky, he must be found in the earth. Theology must concern itself not only with the Wholly Other God but with the sacred "Ground of Being" (Tillich)—not with a unique incarnation in past history but with the principles, powers, and persons which are presently operative to make and keep human life luminous and sacred.

Whether such a subterranean theology will allow us to weather the crisis in spiritual identity through which we are passing is still unknown. For those who no longer find in the stories and myths of orthodox religion the power to inform life with creative meaning, it may, at least, point to a locality and a method which may be useful in discovering a sacred dimension of life. And, perhaps, if each of us learns to tell his own story, even if we remain ignorant of the name of God or the form of religion, it will be sufficient.

SAM KEEN, *To a Dancing God*

To start with the ordinary and the everyday, with personal life, with corporate stories, with "our times" in their political and social agony, is the bold business of theology. But it is exactly where Jesus' parables start. Daniel Berrigan insists that few if any will be able to understand Jesus' parables until they have become skilled at reading the text of the events of their own lives—and ordering their lives accordingly; Augustine knew he would not fully understand the language of Christian faith until he could read it in the familiar events of his own life—and attempt to embody it there anew. A theology that takes its cues from the parables has no other course than to accept what may appear to be severe limitations—limitations imposed by never leaving behind the ordinary, the physical, and the historical. But these limitations are the glory of parabolic, metaphoric movement, for they declare that human life in all its complex everydayness will not be discarded, but that it is precisely the familiar world we love and despair of saving that is on the way to being redeemed. The central Christian affirmation, the belief that somehow or other God was in and with Jesus of Nazareth, is the ground of our hope that the ordinary is the way to the extraordinary, the unsurprising is the surprising place.

A theology that is informed by parables is necessarily a risky and open-ended kind of reflection. It recognizes not only the inconclusiveness of all conceptualization when dealing with matters between God and human beings (an insight as old as religion itself), but also the pain and scepticism—the dis-ease—of such reflection. Theology of this sort is not neat and comfortable, but neither is the life with and under God of which it attempts to speak. The parables accept the complexity and ambiguity of life as lived here in this world and insist that it is in *this* world that God makes his gracious presence known. A theology informed by the parables can do no less—and no more. Such theology never reaches its object, but in language, belief, and life as metaphor, story, and living engagement we are sent off in its direction. We make the leap not with our minds alone but with our total selves—our words, our stories, and our life engagement—and wager that we are on the way, that the metaphor sees in a glass darkly what we do not see and cannot know.

SALLIE MCFAGUE TESELLE, "Parable, Metaphor, and Theology"

———————

Long before writing was invented, human beings read their world. They interpreted their dreams and the flights of birds. They read the intestines of sacrificial animals and the memories of their ancestors. They read the things that surprised them, or the things that reminded them of something else. Most of all, they read in the places where there were holes—spaces—gaps. They filled up the blanks of the universe, as though they were pages, with writing. Leonardo advised aspiring artists to "discover" the pictures to be found in the cracks in walls; Chinese sages were conceived as their mothers stepped into the footprints of unicorns; all of us make up our lives out of the cracks in the walls of our past memories and the unicorn footprints of our futures. The making of a life is similar to the making of a text. We live by reading our own stories. We read by recall and imagination. A sacred text is made by making up what is felt to be already there, just like a life. A sacred text is an impression in stone, or imagination filling up the maker of the space.

LYNDA SEXSON, *Ordinarily Sacred*

But, then, what is faith? Consider these two stories.

The noted anthropologist Leo Frobenius tells about a colleague of his at the university:

> A professor is writing at his desk and his four-year-old little daughter is running about the room. She has nothing to do and is disturbing him. So he gives her three burnt matches, saying, "Here, Play!" and, sitting on the rug, she begins to play with the matches, Hansel, Gretel, and the witch. A considerable time elapses, during which the professor concentrates upon his task, undisturbed. But then, suddenly, the child shrieks in terror. The father jumps. "What is it? What has happened?" The little girl comes running to him, showing every sign of great fright. "Daddy, Daddy," she cries, "take the witch away! I can't touch the witch any more!"

The second story is very much like the first. A father was awakened in the middle of the night by the screams of his three-year-old daughter. He rushed to her bedroom and asked what was the matter. Sobbing, she pointed in the direction of her dresser and whispered, "A monster! A monster!" The father looked. The street-light was reflected through trees and windows in such a fashion as to transform the dresser-drawer knobs and mirror into a fearsome sight indeed. So the father simply flicked on the bedroom light, with the reassuring words, "See, Honey, no monster, just your dresser. OK?" She assented. It was OK. The father kissed his daughter good-night and left the room, flicking off the light as he went. No sooner had the light gone out, however, than the screams returned. The monster was back!

The point is simple, as simple as the wisdom of a playful child. Faith is being gripped by a story, by a vision, by a ritual (game). It is being seized, being gripped by a pattern of meaning, a pattern of meaning that affects one's life-pattern, that becomes a paradigm for the way one sees the world. It is not belief. These kids do not believe in this business, at least they do not believe in thoughtful reflection when the mind's light is on. But neither does the efficacy and the meaning-function depend upon their believing in the truth of something. Belief is beside the point. Faith is not belief. It is not intellectual assent. It is not some ritual played *so that* something will happen. Faith is being turned on by an incredible vision. It is make-believe. Questions of truth and falsity remain irrelevant. Belief and disbelief are transcended in authentic faith.

Faith is make-believe. It is playing as if it were true. It is not that the religious story is not true. It is simply that questions of truth are irrelevant while in the midst of make-believe, while in the midst of faith.

DAVID MILLER, *Gods and Games*

───────────

As Jorge Luis Borges says, God is not a theologian. Neither is he a metaphysician. There are those who have said he is an artist, a maker, a poet. But this language is difficult, at least so against the background of the crisis in the mythological consciousness that we have been tracing. Theological language, still edging its way into the question as to how the Word "means" in a time which presupposes "a radical change in all the forms as they existed on the old plane," has yet to face its dilemma squarely. It has yet to come to terms with the Primary Imagination and the transfer of its terms (1) from contexts of dualistic transcendence to those of radical immanence, and (2) from the systematics of theo-logic to the open centers of theopoietics. Meanwhile, it runs the risk that its mythos will lapse, if it has not already done so, into a pseudomythology. This is why Eastern religions have, at the moment, so relevant an appeal. "He who believes in something does not believe." "To know it is to live it." "Tao is disclosed only to the depth of man . . . [It is] One with the source." These, and other like maxims, stand nearer to the archetypal consciousness than to the intellectualistic doctrines of the Western religious consciousness. Only the mystical tradition in the West stands closer. "Thou wert with me, but I was not with Thee" (Augustine). "God is nearer to me than I am to myself" (Meister Eckhardt).

But scriptural art is parable art, and that is very close to the archetypal consciousness indeed. The quest motif, so evident in most contemporary literature, is as biblical as it is modern. And a doctrine of the Word, if understood in its paradoxical mode both of revealing and concealing, is precisely that metaphor for meaning that the poet most ardently desires. Nothing is more desirable or more dangerous for the poet than his relation to the word.

But we are in the position of that poet, who—in Stefan George's poem called "Das Wort"—took his dreams to the gray Norn who sat by a deep well. From the well the Norn would draw out names for the poet's dreams. With these names the poet wrote his easy poems. But one day the poet brought a jewel in his hand. The goddess of fate sought long after the name for the jewel. At last she said to the poet: "For such there sleep nothing (no thing, no name) in the deep ground." Sadly the poet returned from his journey. "I learned, he said sadly, No thing is where the Word is broken."

Like the poet, we manipulate words, control our meaning, contrive our patterns. But when we ask for the essence of speech (the jewel), the deep well does not comply: there is no name for it, it cannot be converted to a thing, it is not subject to my manipulation. The Word is given, it is not at our disposal. My words today are broken symbols. We know, after our fashion, that no thing is where the Word is broken. We must learn again, this time from the depth, to hear the Word that resounds through our words.

Or like the young man of the East who came to the monk in the marketplace and asked the way to the city: all those within hearing distance laughed. He was already there. So, with us, we have only to let Being be (to let God God in us). Thence all is transformed: what was projected in the dualistic mythological world pictures, falls back to the deep psyche and sustains us as a Presence there.

STANLEY ROMAINE HOPPER, "Myth, Dream and Imagination"

Sometimes I think that one day, Muslims will be ashamed of what Muslims did in these times, will find the "Rushdie affair" as improbable as the West now finds martyr burning. One day they may agree that—as the European Enlightenment demonstrated—freedom of thought is precisely freedom from religious control, freedom of accusations of blasphemy. Maybe they'll agree, too, that the row over *The Satanic Verses* was at bottom an argument over who should have control over the grand narrative, the Story of Islam, and that the power must belong equally to everyone. That even if my novel were incompetent, its attempt to retell the story would still be important. That if I've failed, others must succeed, because those who do not have the power over the story that dominates their lives, power to retell it, rethink it, deconstruct it, joke about it, and change it as times change, truly are powerless, because they cannot think new thoughts.

SALMAN RUSHDIE, *Lecture*

The use of story as a heuristic device to construe the meaning of existence has the danger of our substituting a syntactical order of necessity, either logical, causal, or teleological, for the surprising disorder of lived possibilities. . . .

Religionists concerned with the hermeneutical possibilities of story often imply that life is like a well-integrated plot. It may be that life is more often like a loose-leaf novel, the parts of which do not have a necessary arrangement, or like a series of short stories, which do not link together in an ordered sequence. One sometimes receives the impression that instead of literature imitating life, the religionists interested in story want life to imitate literature. This tendency recalls the practice of Alfred Jarry, the founder of the Pataphysicians, who sauntered about Paris with a pair of revolvers on his belt and a lobster on a leash. A favorite sardonic expression of Jarry's was, "Isn't that beautiful. Just like literature." Like Beckett's character who wants his life to be as in the story his father read to him, the religionists seem to want life to have the order of resolute adventure, "just like literature.". . .

Life alone may not be enough, for we "have to talk about it." But we talk about life in a multiplicity of ways, not through story alone. As Beckett writes, "The forms are many in which the unchanging seeks relief from its formlessness." Or, as I tend to prefer, the forms are many in which the changing displays itself.

TED L. ESTESS, "The Inenarrable Contraption"

Intercourse is what goes on in the sentence. In every sentence the little word "is" is the copula, the penis or bridge; in every sentence magically, with a word, making the two one flesh. The little word "is" is the hallmark of Eros, even as, Freud said, the little word "no" is the hallmark of Death. Every sentence is dialectics, an act of love.

NORMAN O. BROWN, *Love's Body*

Only the words break the silence, all other sounds have ceased. If I were silent I'd hear nothing. But if I were silent the other sounds would start again, those to which the words have made me deaf, or which have really ceased. But I am silent, it sometimes happens, no, never, not one second. I weep too without interruption. It's an unbroken flow of words and tears. With no pause for reflection. But I speak softer, every year a little softer. Perhaps. Slower too, every year a little slower. Perhaps. It is hard for me to judge. If so the pauses would be longer, between the words, the sentences, the syllables, the tears, I confuse them, words and tears, my words are my tears, my eyes my mouth. And I should hear, at every little pause, if it's the silence I say when I say that only the words break it. But nothing of the kind, that's not how it is, it's for ever the same murmur, flowing unbroken, like a single endless word and therefore meaningless, for it's the end gives the meaning to words.

SAMUEL BECKETT, *Texts for Nothing*

5.

MUSIC OF THE SOUL

An ordinary life is full of musical rhythms, episodes, and cadences. The themes of our work, play, families, and geographies are like melodies that come and go as though in an elaborate fugue. And yet when we feel ill in body or spirit, we speak of our malaise in wooden and metallic terms: We've run out of steam, our batteries are low, we're not functioning well, nothing is working right. We could say instead that life has lost its music, or an unexpected dissonance or disharmony has entered.

To our physical ears, too, music is everywhere—in the radios and concert halls, in the sounds of nature and daily life, and in the silences that allow subtle sounds to be heard. The modern world often seems deaf to the cacophony that is characteristic of the age, and one wonders if it might discover a large measure of soul simply by becoming more sensitive to sound.

A writer upon music should therefore state at the beginning how many kinds of music those who have investigated the subject are known to have recognized. There are three kinds: the first, the music of the universe; the second, human music; the third, instrumental music, as that of the cithara or the tibiae or the other instruments which serve for melody.

The first, the music of the universe, is especially to be studied in the combining of the elements and the variety of the seasons which are observed in the heavens. How indeed could the swift mechanism of the sky move silently in its course? And although this sound does not reach our ears (as must for many reasons be the case), the extremely rapid motion of such great bodies could not be altogether without sound, especially since the courses of the stars are joined together by such mutual adaptation that nothing more equally compacted or united could be imagined. For some are borne higher and others lower, and all are revolved with a just impulse, and from their different inequalities an established order of their courses may be deduced. For this reason an established order of modulation cannot be lacking in this celestial revolution.

Now unless a certain harmony united the differences and contrary powers of the four elements, how could they form a single body and mechanism? But all this diversity produces the variety of seasons and fruits, and thereby makes the year a unity. Wherefore if you could imagine any one of the factors which produce such a variety removed, all would perish, nor, so to speak, would they retain a vestige of consonance. And just as there is a measure of sound in low strings lest the lowness descend to inaudibility, and a measure of tenseness in high strings lest they be broken by the thinness of the sound, being too tense, and all is congruous and fitting, so we perceive that in the music of the universe nothing can be excessive and destroy some other part by its own excess, but each part brings its own contribution or aids others to bring theirs. For what winter binds, spring releases, summer heats, autumn ripens; and the seasons in turn bring forth their own fruits or help the others to bring forth theirs. These matters will be discussed more searchingly later on.

What human music is, anyone may understand by examining his own nature. For what is that which unites the incorporeal activity of the reason with the body, unless it be a certain mutual adaptation and as it were a tempering of low and high sounds into a single consonance? What else joins together the parts of the soul itself, which in the opinion of Aristotle is a joining together of the rational and the irrational? What causes the blending of the body's elements or holds its parts together in established adaptation? But of this I shall treat later.

The third kind of music is that which is described as residing in certain instruments. This is produced by tension, as in strings, or by blowing, as in the tibiae or in those instruments activated by water, or by some kind of percussion, as in instruments which are struck upon certain bronze concavities, by which means various sounds are produced.

BOETHIUS, *De Institutione Musica*

Thus without music no discipline can be perfect, for there is nothing without it. For the very universe, it is said, is held together by a certain harmony of sounds, and the heavens themselves are made to revolve by the modulation of harmony. Music moves the feelings and changes the emotions. In battles, moreover, the sound of the trumpet rouses the combatants, and the more furious the trumpeting, the more valorous their spirit. Song likewise encourages the rowers, music soothes the mind to endure toil, and the modulation of the voice consoles the weariness of each labor. Music also composes distraught minds, as may be read of David, who freed Saul from the unclean spirit by the art of melody. The very beasts also, even serpents, birds, and dolphins, music incites to listen to her melody. But every word we speak, every pulsation of our veins, is related by musical rhythms to the powers of harmony.

ISIDORE OF SEVILLE, *Etymologiarum*

In music also our rule is verified. It is impossible to find two things that are perfectly equal in weight, or length, or thickness; and it is likewise impossible for the various notes of flutes and other instruments, of bells and of the human voice to be so perfectly in concord that they could not be more concordant. As with human voices, so it is with instruments, all are only relatively true and all differ necessarily according to place, time, natural characteristics and so on. Consequently the most perfect, faultless harmony cannot be perceived by the ear, for it exists not in things sensible but only as an ideal conceived by the mind. From this we can form some idea of the most perfect or infinite harmony, which is a relation in equality. No man can hear it while still in the body, for it is wholly spiritual and would draw to itself the essence of the soul, as infinite light would attract all light to itself. Such infinitely perfect harmony, in consequence, would be heard only in ecstasy by the ear of the intellect, once the soul was free from the things of sense. Much of the sweetness of contemplation could be experienced here by a meditation on the immortality of the intellectual and rational soul and on that essential incorruptibility, which enables it to find in music an image of itself that is at once a resemblance and a contrast.

NICHOLAS OF CUSA, *Beyond Ignorance*

Do not be surprised, Francesco, that we combine medicine and the lyre with the study of theology. Since you are dedicated to philosophy, you must remember that within us nature has bonded body and spirit with the soul. The body is indeed healed by the remedies of medicine; but spirit, which is the airy vapour of our blood and the link between body and soul, is tempered and nourished by airy smells, by sounds, and by song. Finally, the soul, as it is divine, is purified by the divine mysteries of theology. In nature a union is made from soul, body and spirit. To the Egyptian priests medicine, music and the mysteries were one and the same study. Would that we could master this natural and Egyptian art as successfully as we tenaciously and wholeheartedly apply ourselves to it!

MARSILIO FICINO, *Letters*

The faculty of creating is never given to us all by itself. It always goes hand in hand with the gift of observation. And the true creator may be recognized by his ability always to find about him, in the commonest and humblest thing, items worthy of note. He does not have to concern himself with a beautiful landscape; he does not need to surround himself with rare and precious objects. He does not have to put forth in search of discoveries: they are always within his reach. He will have only to cast a glance about him. Familiar things, things that are everywhere, attract his attention. The least accident holds his interest and guides his operations. If his finger slips, he will notice it; on occasion, he may draw profit from something unforeseen that a momentary lapse reveals to him.

One does not contrive an accident: one observes it to draw inspiration therefrom. An accident is perhaps the only thing that really inspires us. A composer improvises aimlessly the way an animal grubs about. Both of them go grubbing about because they yield to a compulsion to seek things out. What urge of the composer is satisfied by this investigation? The rules with which, like a penitent, he is burdened? No: he is in quest of his pleasure. He seeks a satisfaction that he fully knows he will not find without first striving for it. One cannot force one's self to love; but love presupposes understanding, and in order to understand, one must exert one's self.

So we grub about in expectation of our pleasure, guided by our scent, and suddenly we stumble against an unknown obstacle. It gives us a jolt, a shock, and this shock fecundates our creative power.

IGOR STRAVINSKY, *Poetics of Music*

Then may we not say, Glaucon, said I, that those who established an education in music and gymnastics had not the purpose in view that some attribute to them in so instituting, namely to treat the body by one and the soul by the other?

But what? he said.

It seems likely, I said, that they ordained both chiefly for the soul's sake.

How so?

Have you not observed, said I, the effect on the disposition of the mind itself of lifelong devotion to gymnastics with total neglect of music? Or the disposition of those of the opposite habit?

In what respect do you mean? he said.

In respect of savagery and hardness or, on the other hand, of softness and gentleness?

I have observed, he said, that the devotees of unmitigated gymnastics turn out more brutal than they should be and those of music softer than is good for them.

And surely, said I, this savagery is a quality derived from the highspirited element in our nature, which, if rightly trained, becomes brave, but if overstrained, would naturally become hard and harsh.

I think so, he said.

And again, is not the gentleness a quality which the philosophical nature would yield? This if relaxed too far would be softer than is desirable but if rightly trained gentle and orderly?

That is so.

But our requirement, we say, is that the guardians should possess both natures.

It is.

And must they not be harmoniously adjusted to one another?

Of course.

And the soul of the man thus attuned is sober and brave?

Certainly.

And that of the ill-adjusted is cowardly and rude?

It surely is.

Now when a man abandons himself to music, to play upon him and pour into his soul as it were through the funnel of his ears those sweet, soft, and dirgelike airs of which we were just now speaking, and gives his entire time to the warblings and blandishments of song, the first result is that the principle of high spirit, if he had it, is softened like iron and is made useful instead of useless and brittle. But when he continues the practice without remission and is spellbound, the effect begins to be that he melts and liquefies till he completely dissolves away his spirit, cuts out as it were the very sinews of his soul and makes of himself a "feeble warrior."

Assuredly, he said.

And if, said I, he has to begin with a spiritless nature he reaches this result quickly, but if a high-spirited, by weakening the spirit he makes it unstable, quickly irritated by slight stimuli, and as quickly quelled. The outcome is that such men are choleric and irascible instead of high-spirited, and are peevish and discontented.

Precisely so.

On the other hand, if a man toils hard at gymnastics and eats right lustily and holds no truck with music and philosophy, does he not at first get very fit and full of pride and high spirit and become more brave and bold than he was?

He does indeed.

But what if he does nothing but this and has no contact with the Muse in any way? Is not the result that even if there was some principle of the love of knowledge in his soul, since it tastes of no instruction nor of any inquiry and does not participate in any discussion or any other form of culture, it becomes feeble, deaf, and blind, because it is not aroused or fed nor are its perceptions purified and quickened?

That is so, he said.

And so such a man, I take it, becomes a misologist and a stranger to the Muses. He no longer makes any use of persuasion by speech but achieves all his ends like a beast by violence and savagery, and in his brute ignorance and ineptitude lives a life of disharmony and gracelessness.

That is entirely true, he said.

For these two, then, it seems there are two arts which I would say some god gave to mankind, music and gymnastics for the service of the high-spirited principle and the love of knowledge in them—not for the soul and the body except incidentally, but for the harmonious adjustment of these two principles by the proper degree of tension and relaxation of each.

Yes, so it appears, he said.

Then he who best blends gymnastics with music and applies them most suitably to the soul is the man whom we should most rightly pronounce to be the most perfect and harmonious musician, far rather than the one who brings the strings into unison with one another.

PLATO, *Republic*

———————

, we could simply de-cide   not to have a discussion   .   What ever you like.   But
now   there are silences   and the
words   make   help make   the
silences   .
                                    I have nothing to say
            and I am saying it   and that is
poetry   as I need it   .
            This space of time   is organized
.   We need not fear these   silences, —
    we may love them   .
                                        This is a composed
talk   , for I am making it
            just as I make   a piece of music.   It is like a glass
            of milk   .   We need the   glass
and we need the   milk .   Or again   it is like an
empty glass   into which   at any
moment   anything   may be poured
.   As we go along   ,   (who knows?)
            an i-dea may occur in this   talk   .
                            I have no idea   whether one will
        or not.   If one does,   let it.

JOHN CAGE, *Silence*

———————

Remember that all music proceeds from Apollo; that Jupiter is musical to the extent that he is consonant with Apollo; and that Venus and Mercury claim music by their proximity to Apollo [i.e., to the Sun]. Likewise remember that song pertains to only those four; the other three planets have voices but not songs. Now we attribute to Saturn voices that are slow, deep, harsh, and plaintive; to Mars, voices that are the opposite—quick, sharp, fierce, and menacing; the Moon has the voices in between. The music, however, of Jupiter is deep, earnest, sweet, and joyful with stability. To Venus, on the contrary, we ascribe songs voluptuous with wantonness and softness. The songs between these two extremes we ascribe to the Sun and Mercury: if with their grace and smoothness they are reverential, simple, and earnest, the songs are judged to be Apollo's; if they are somewhat more relaxed [than Apollo's or Jupiter's], along with their gaiety, but vigorous and complex, they are Mercury's. Accordingly, you will win over one of these four to yourself by using their songs, especially if you supply musical notes that fit their songs. When at the right astrological hour you declaim aloud by singing and playing in the manners we have specified for the four gods, they seem to be just about to answer you like an echo or like a string in a lute trembling to the vibration of another which has been similarly tuned. And this will happen to you from heaven as naturally, say Plotinus and Iamblichus, as a tremor re-echoes from a lute or an echo arises from an opposite wall. Assuredly, whenever your spirit—by frequent use of Jovial, Mercurial, or Venereal harmony, a harmony performed while these planets are dignified—singing at the same time most intently and conforming itself to the harmony, becomes Jovial, Mercurial, or Venereal, it will meanwhile become Phoebean as well, since the power of Phoebus himself, the ruler of music, flourishes in every consonance. And conversely when you become Phoebean from Phoebean song and notes, you at the same time lay claim to the power of Jupiter, Venus, and Mercury. And again, from your spirit influenced within, you have a similar influence on your soul and body.

Remember, moreover, that a prayer, when it has been suitably and seasonably composed and is full of emotion and forceful, has a power similar to a song. There is no use in reporting what great power Damis and Philostratus tell us certain Indian priests have in their prayers, nor in mentioning the words they say that Apollonius employed to call up the shade of Achilles. For we are not now speaking of worshipping divinities but of a natural power in speech, song, and words. That there is indeed in certain sounds a Phoebean and medical power, is clear from the fact that in Puglia everyone who is stung by the phalangium [meaning one of various kinds of venomous spider] becomes stunned and lies half-dead until each hears a certain sound proper to him. For then he dances along with the sound, works up a sweat, and gets well. And if ten years later he hears a similar sound, he feels a sudden urge to dance. I gather from the evidence that this sound is Solar and Jovial.

MARSILIO FICINO, *Book of Life*

To turn to the compositions, do you think Bernstein felt that he had failed as a composer?

Ah, but *Mon Dieu*, we are all frustrated in life, we all want to do something else than what we do. *West Side Story* or *Candide*, I think these are wonderful works, but maybe he only thought of them as a light music, operetta music. You know, I think with Bernstein, and with all of us, often the thing that we really can do, it's not so interesting. We always want to sing something else, or compose something else, or whatever. Karajan also felt this. Before he died he said: "I have still so much to do."

CHRISTA LUDWIG

Music is not helping much, either . . . I can't finish the two Poe stories, everything is as dull as a hole in the ground. For every bar that has some freedom about it, there are twenty that are stifled by the weight of one particular tradition; try as I may, I'm forced to recognize its hypocritical and destructive influence. The fact that this tradition belongs to me by right is hardly relevant . . . it's just as depressing, because whatever masks you wear, underneath you find yourself. In fact, we ought to destroy what devours the best of our thoughts and reach a position where we love nothing but ourselves, with a fierce attention to detail. But what happens is the opposite: first of all there's the family, which clutters up the path, either with too much kindness or with a blind serenity. Then come the Mistresses or the Mistress, with whom we don't really reckon because we're so happy to lose ourselves in passion. I keep clear of these, and of stronger temptations . . . Truth to tell, there's nothing we can do. We have a soul bequeathed to us by a bunch of totally unknown people who, through the family tree, act upon us very often without our being able to do much about it.

CLAUDE DEBUSSY, *Letters*

First, some observations about Pablo Casals.

I met him for the first time at his home in Puerto Rico just a few weeks before his ninetieth birthday. I was fascinated by his daily routine. About 8 A.M. his lovely young wife Marta would help him to start the day. His various infirmities made it difficult for him to dress himself. Judging from his difficulty in walking and from the way he held his arms, I guessed he was suffering from rheumatoid arthritis. His emphysema was evident in his labored breathing. He came into the living room on Marta's arm. He was badly stooped. His head was pitched forward and he walked with a shuffle. His hands were swollen and his fingers were clenched.

Even before going to the breakfast table, Don Pablo went to the piano—which, I learned, was a daily ritual. He arranged himself with some difficulty on the piano bench, then with discernible effort raised his swollen and clenched fingers above the keyboard.

I was not prepared for the miracle that was about to happen. The fingers slowly unlocked and reached toward the keys like the buds of a plant toward the sunlight. His back straightened. He seemed to breathe more freely. Now his fingers settled on the keys. Then came the opening bars of Bach's *Wohltemperierte Klavier,* played with great sensitivity and control. I had forgotten that Don Pablo had achieved proficiency on several musical instruments before he took up the cello. He hummed as he played, then said that Bach spoke to him here—and he placed his hand over his heart.

Then he plunged into a Brahms concerto and his fingers, now agile and powerful, raced across the keyboard with dazzling speed. His entire body seemed fused with the music; it was no longer stiff and shrunken but supple and graceful and completely freed of its arthritic coils.

Having finished the piece, he stood up by himself, far straighter and taller than when he had come into the room. He walked to the breakfast table with no trace of a shuffle, ate heartily, talked animat-edly, finished the meal, then went for a walk on the beach.

After an hour or so, he came back to the house and worked on his correspondence until lunch. Then he napped. When he rose, the stoop and the shuffle and the clenched hands were back again. On this particular day, a camera and recording crew from public televi-sion were scheduled to arrive in mid-afternoon. Anticipating the visit, Don Pablo said he wished some way could be found to call it off; he didn't feel up to the exertion of the filming, with its innumer-able and inexplicable retakes and the extreme heat of the bright lights.

Marta, having been through these reluctances before, reassured Don Pablo, saying she was certain he would be stimulated by the meeting. She reminded him that he liked the young people who did the last filming and that they would probably be back again. In par-ticular, she called his attention to the lovely young lady who directed the recording.

Don Pablo brightened. "Yes, of course," he said, "it will be good to see them again."

As before, he stretched his arms in front of him and extended his fingers. Then the spine straightened and he stood up and went to his cello. He began to play. His fingers, hands, and arms were in sublime coordination as they responded to the demands of his brain for the controlled beauty of movement and tone. Any cellist thirty years his junior would have been proud to have such extraordinary physical command.

Twice in one day I had seen the miracle. A man almost ninety, beset with the infirmities of old age, was able to cast off his afflictions, at least temporarily, because he knew he had something of overriding importance to do. There was no mystery about the way it worked, for it happened every day. Creativity for Pablo Casals was the source of his own cortisone.

NORMAN COUSINS, *Anatomy of an Illness*

6.

ART AND ARCHETYPE

It's not surprising that in many cultures and in many periods in Western life the arts have been closely tied to religion. The arts are in the business of mystery, conveying in irreducible images the vastness of meaning and the depth of experience. Not self-expression, but the glimpsing of a profound, archetypal realm is the real work of art. Many artists confess how they are the interpreters of images that come to them, the receivers of inspiration, and often mere scribes. They may not understand what they have created, and as a result the objects of their art stand alone, like persons, things with a voice.

Objects of art have been enchanted by their magician-makers, and the onlookers present themselves to the magic and in the best of cases are affected. The power of the object heals and educates, edifies and empowers.

Art is essential to the soul, and it is only a society that has forgotten the soul that could marginalize its art and its artists.

Three specific details have been observed in the Isenheim Altarpiece that link it to the hospital context. One concerns the closed state, whose wings represent Saints Sebastian and Anthony. Sebastian had long been invested with the power to protect against the plague. Outbreaks of this scourge within living memory had turned him into a popular cult figure in the region of Alsace. A prayer to Saint Sebastian formulated in 1516—"Let us be released from this epidemic's pestilence and from every tribulation of the flesh and the spirit!"—further reveals that this saint came to be associated with the repelling and warding off of general bodily harm and of sudden, devastating, and epidemic disease in the broad sense. As for Anthony Abbot, Aymar Falco declared the primary goal of the monastery to be the care of those afflicted with a disease perceived to be like a plague—*ignis plaga, pestilentia ignis*—which often went under the name of this patron: Saint Anthony's Fire, *Feu d'Antoine, Antonius Feuer.* Moreover, inspired by the saint's acts of healing recorded in Athanasius's biography, and specific to the circumstances of the founding of the Antonite order, curative powers came to be identified with Anthony. Sebastian and Anthony are paired in other key examples, such as Roger van der Weyden's Beaune altarpiece, on whose exterior they appear in grisaille. Together they establish the themes of dire illness and miraculous healing as central to the meaning of the altarpiece at Isenheim. . . .

Amulets in general and coral in particular were used in fending off evil spirits and protecting against the evil eye. The common belief in such an unseen force or spell, capable of causing harm to the point of death, must have seemed especially pertinent to the case of disease. In turn, various kinds of amulets and semiprecious and precious stones of different colors came to be credited with the power to ward off or heal diseases, as we find catalogued under *De Lapidibus* in the typical *Hortus Sanitatis* of the period. Grünewald's musical angels wear a variety of gold rings, some mounted with red stones, on different fingers of both hands, which they display through the bowing and fingering of their instruments. One of the headings in Agrippa von Nettesheim's nearly contemporary book on magic is "Of Magical Rings and Their Compositions." In this section he describes rings "inasmuch as they do fortify us against sickness, poisons, enemies, evil spirits, and all manner of hurtful things." Furthermore, red stones, such as rubies and garnets, by suggesting the color of blood, were recommended to arrest hemorrhage and to nullify the effect of wounds.

Several other elements in this stage of the altarpiece support my view of its purpose as a magical catalyst for protection and transformation. Most important are the three music-making angels at the left side of the central section. They, of course, traditionally populate a celestial realm. But there is an equally applicable and age-old tradition of music that the flute would cure sciatica, and Democritus thought its sound could help a victim of the plague. Such speculation has a long history; indeed, today there are many journals of music therapy. Around the time of the Isenheim Altarpiece, discussion of the subject took place in both musical and medical studies. Paracelsus, a trained physician, practiced what he himself called musical medicine. In a late fifteenth-century treatise on the effects of music by Johannes Tinctoris, we learn that music lifts sadness, chases away demonic forces, causes ecstasy, helps in the contemplation of the supernatural, and cures the sick.

Such attitudes depend on two related insights. One is a recognition of the cathartic effects of music; the other is the perceived connection between mind and body in any illness that would admit of such a psychotherapeutic road to healing. Pythagoras had established a theoretical basis for this notion. In his system, music became an aesthetic model for both cosmic and human nature. The human body was compared to an instrument, with the soul as its music. For the Pythagorean doctor, health was the proper attunement of body and soul, and harmony became the conceptual figure for good health. Theoretical and technical handbooks on music during the Renaissance connect different classes of instruments with the essential components of music; drums were related to rhythm, viols to harmony. In depicting three levels of viols—bowable, stringed instruments—Grünewald embodies this aesthetic equivalent for health. Furthermore, in restricting his instruments to three, he displays the basis of a tripartite harmony that had just emerged about 1500 as the canonical revision of Pythagoras' fourfold ideal.

ANDRÉE HAYUM, *The Isenheim Altarpiece*

———

When my good friends, Antonio Calderini and Bindaccio da Ricasoli, and I were reading together what you each wrote in praise of Carlo Marsuppini, that child of the Muses, we agreed that Plato was right in his view that poetry springs not from technique but from a kind of frenzy. Although it is not necessary to give reasons where the matter is self-evident, I shall nevertheless mention the reasons Plato gives. In *Phaedrus* and *Ion,* he discusses divine frenzy, of which he claims there are three principal signs.

Firstly, without God, one man can scarcely master a single art, even after a long time; but the true poets, such as he holds Orpheus, Homer, Hesiod and Pindar to have been, included in their poems signs and evidence of every art. Secondly, those who are in a frenzy utter many wonderful things, which a little later, when their frenzy has abated, they themselves do not really understand, as if they had not spoken them, but God had sounded through them, as though through trumpets. Thirdly, neither prudent men nor those learned from their youth have proved to be the best poets. Indeed, some were out of their minds, as Homer and Lucretius were known to have been, or unlettered, as Hesiod testifies of himself, and as Plato describes Ion and Tynnicus of Calchis. Passing beyond the limitations of skill, these men suddenly produced astonishing poetry.

Plato adds that some very unskilled men are thus possessed by the Muses, because divine providence wants to show mankind that the great poems are not the invention of men but gifts from Heaven. He indicates this in *Phaedrus* when he says that no one, however diligent and learned in all the arts, has ever excelled in poetry unless to these other qualities has been added a fiery quickening of the soul.

MARSILIO FICINO, *Letters*

This subject-matter is something I have received from the generations, part of that compact with my fellow men made in my name before I was born. I cannot break from it without breaking from some part of my own nature, and sometimes it has come to me in super-normal experience; I have met with ancient myths in my dreams, brightly lit; and I think it allied to the wisdom or instinct that guides a migratory bird. . . .

Then too I would have all the arts draw together; recover their ancient association, the painter painting what the poet has written, the musician setting the poet's words to simple airs, that the horseman and the engine-driver may sing them at their work.

W. B. YEATS, *Essays and Introductions*

What should these sacred buildings be like; when are their parts properly proportioned and harmonized? Vitruvius supplied the answer. He had introduced his third book on Temples with the famous remarks on the proportions of the human figure, which should be reflected in the proportions of temples. As a proof of the harmony and perfection of the human body he described how a well-built man fits with extended hands and feet exactly into the most perfect geometrical figures, circle and square. This simple picture seemed to reveal a deep and fundamental truth about man and the world, and its importance for Renaissance architects can hardly be overestimated. The image haunted their imagination. . . .

Francesco Zorzi (or Giorgi), a neo-Platonic friar, who was also closely associated with architecture, takes us a step further to his work on Universal Harmony. Here we find an illustration of the Vitruvian text—significantly only the "Homo ad circulum"—in a chapter entitled: "Quod Homo imitatur mundum in figura circulari" ("Why Man in the figure of the Circle is an Image of the World"). The cosmic meaning of this figure could not be made clearer. But the title contains only half of the author's views. Vitruvius' figure holds for him a dual quality: it discloses through the visible, corporeal world ("homo-mundus") the invisible, intellectual relation between the soul and God; for God is the "intelligibilis sphaera." The author interprets the figure derived from Vitruvius in the light of the mystic geometry of neo-Platonism which had reached him through Ficino from Plotinus.

RUDOLF WITTKOWER, *Architectural Principles*

When I am asked, as it often happens in the discussion following a lecture, "Why don't you speak of symbols?", "What's the difference between an image, an archetypal image, and a symbol?", I usually reply with a confession: I come from Zürich; for the past quarter-century I have lived in a world of symbols. They no longer hold my attention. Everyone in Zürich speaks of symbols, looks them up, writes theses on them: the swan, the cave, the arrow, the number five, light-and-dark, the wounded heel, calf, knee, thigh, hip . . . These are symbols, and I too have worked on them. This is because it is said by the Zürich school that one cannot understand psychic materials, dreams especially, without a knowledge of symbols. . . .

There are no symbols as such, only images. Every psychic process is an image, said Jung. Symbols appear, only can appear, in images and as images. They are abstractions from images. (Else we couldn't look them up.) The only swans we can find as such are in a dictionary or index. Every other swan—Swan matches, Swan Lake, swans on the river Coole, or raping Leda, or pulling Aphrodite's chariot—is located in a specific context, mood, and scene. Each symbol is articulated, vivified or deadened, by the image that presents it. A symbol cannot appear at all unless in an image. . . .

Symbols become images when they are particularized by a *specific context, mood,* and *scene,* that is, when they are precisely qualified.

JAMES HILLMAN, "Inquiry into Image"

A few years ago the Venetians celebrated the return of the Virgin *Nicopeia* to S. Marco, from which it had been forcibly removed. In the old republic the icon had been publicly honored as the true sovereign of the state. The prehistory of its cult in Venice leads back to Byzantium, where in 1203 the icon was seized from the chariot of the opposing general. For the Byzantines it was the embodiment of their celestial commander, to whom the emperors gave precedence at victory celebrations. The Venetians took home this palladium, which they gained as a fruit of victory and which in turn brought them vic-

tory, as a part of the "transfer of cults." They placed their community under the icon's protection just as the ancient Greeks had once
done with the image of Athena from Troy.

The icon was soon known in Venice as St. Luke's Madonna. It was
seen as an original from the days of the apostles, and Mary herself
was believed to have posed for it. This "authentic" portrait was naturally preferred by the Virgin, as it showed her "correctly" and had
been made with her cooperation; special grace thus accrued to this
one painting. It led a unique existence, even a life of its own. At state
ceremonies, it was received as if it were an actual person. . . .

Authentic images seemed capable of action, seemed to possess
dynamis, or supernatural power. God and the saints also took up
their abode in them, as was expected, and spoke through them.
People looked to such images with an expectation of beneficence,
which was often more important to the believer than were abstract
notions of God or an afterlife.

HANS BELTING, *Likeness and Presence*

"Are you talking about statues, Trismegistus?"

"Statues, Asclepius, yes. See how little trust you have! I mean statues ensouled and conscious, filled with spirit and doing great deeds;
statues that foreknow the future and predict it by lots, by prophecy,
by dreams and by many other means; statues that make people ill and
cure them, bringing them pain and pleasure as each deserves.". . .

"Our ancestors once erred gravely on the theory of divinity; they
were unbelieving and inattentive to worship and reverence for god.
But then they discovered the art of making gods. To their discovery
they added a conformable power arising from the nature of matter.
Because they could not make souls, they mixed this power in and
called up the souls of demons or angels and implanted them in like-
nesses through holy and divine mysteries, whence the idols could
have the power to do good and evil."

HERMES TRISMEGISTUS, *Asclepius*

Nothing has been created as *ultima materia*—in its final state. Everything is at first created in its *prima materia*, its original stuff; whereupon Vulcan comes, and by the art of alchemy develops it into its final substance. . . . For alchemy means: to carry to its end something that has not yet been completed. To obtain the lead from the ore and to transform it into what it is made for. . . . Accordingly, you should understand that alchemy is nothing but the art which makes the impure into the pure through fire. . . . It can separate the useful from the useless, and transmute it into its final substance and its ultimate essence.

PARACELSUS

In the midst of this period when I was so preoccupied with the images of the unconscious, I came to the decision to withdraw from the university, where I had lectured for eight years as *Privatdozent* (since 1905). My experience and experiments with the unconscious had brought my intellectual activity to a standstill. After the completion of *The Psychology of the Unconscious* I found myself utterly incapable of reading a scientific book. This went on for three years. I felt I could no longer keep up with the world of the intellect, nor would I have been able to talk about what really preoccupied me. The material brought to light from the unconscious had, almost literally, struck me dumb. I could neither understand it nor give it form. At the university I was in an exposed position, and felt that in order to go on giving courses there I would first have to find an entirely new and different orientation. It would be unfair to continue teaching young students when my own intellectual situation was nothing but a mass of doubts.

I therefore felt that I was confronted with the choice of either continuing my academic career, whose road lay smooth before me, or following the laws of my inner personality, of a higher reason, and forging ahead with this curious task of mine, this experiment in confrontation with the unconscious. But until it was completed I could not appear before the public.

Consciously, deliberately, then, I abandoned my academic career. For I felt that something great was happening to me, and I put my trust in the thing which I felt to be more important *sub specie aeternitatis*. I knew that it would fill my life, and for the sake of that goal I was ready to take any kind of risk.

C. G. JUNG, *Memories*

The poem is the cry of its occasion,
Part of the res itself and not about it.
The poet speaks the poem as it is,

Not as it was: part of the reverberation
Of a windy night as it is, when the marble statues
Are like newspapers blown by the wind. He speaks

By sight and insight as they are. There is no
Tomorrow for him. The wind will have passed by,
The statues will have gone back to be things about.

WALLACE STEVENS, "An Ordinary Evening in New Haven"

Another master was having tea with two of his students when he suddenly tossed his fan to one of them, saying, "What's this?" The student opened it and fanned himself. "Not bad," was his comment. "Now you," he went on, passing it to the other student, who at once closed the fan and scratched his neck with it. This done, he opened it again, placed a piece of cake on it, and offered it to the master. This was considered even better, for when there are no names the world is no longer "classified in limits and bounds."

ALAN WATTS, *The Way of Zen*

Far be it from me to attempt yet another detailed interpretation of the figures in the "Primavera." I want only to suggest that in the context of the study of Ficino's magic the picture begins to be seen as a practical application of that magic, as a complex talisman, an "image of the world" arranged so as to transmit only healthful, rejuvenating, anti-Saturnian influences to the beholder. Here, in visual form is Ficino's natural magic, using grouping of trees and flowers, using only planetary images and those only in relation to the "world," not to attract demons; or as shadows of Ideas in the Neoplatonic hierarchy. And, whatever the figures on the right may represent mythologically, is it not the *spiritus mundi* which blows through them, blown from the puffed cheeks of the aerial spirit, made visible in the wind-blown folds of the draperies of the running figure? The *spiritus* which is the channel for the influences of the stars has been caught and stored in the magic talisman.

How different is Botticelli's Alma Venus, with whom, as Ficino advises, we walk in the green and flowery meadows, drinking in the scented air, laden with *spiritus*—how different she is from the prim little talisman Venus, with an apple in one hand and flowers in the other! Yet her function is the same, to draw down the Venereal spirit from the star, and to transmit it to the wearer or beholder of her lovely image.

FRANCES A. YATES, *Giordano Bruno*

One day, in the cinema, some lines jumped onto the screen, just before the film ended. I could barely read them through my tears. The story was about a girl committed to an asylum, her spirit broken by a young man who was unable to value her for her old-fashioned qualities. I later found the film-text in a newspaper review: "He came close to her, very close to her, but did not see her. Because she was one of those souls that never reach out, that you must know how to study and that you must examine with enduring patience. In olden times a painter would have chosen her for a genre picture. She would have been a linen maid, a water-bearer . . . or a lacemaker."

This was the only mention of a "lacemaker" in "La Dentellière," a film by Claude Goretta, made in 1977. I was deeply impressed. Here was a metaphor for a sense of quality in life! If it was possible to convey to an audience the tragedy of a young woman out of step with her time because she patted a lettuce-head dry in a fine tea-towel with patient care, taking time over her chore—instead of flinging it into a fast-whirling, plastic water extractor—then it had to be possible for me to find women with whom to form a group where we could articulate the significance of "lacemaking" and discover ways of becoming "a new lacemaker." The idea was that we would look for ways in which we could achieve a quality of life in our everyday actions as well as in our creative work, over and against the lack of concern and love for things, the blind faith in technology, and the urgent, hypnotic commands of the soul-less media. What we wished to find was the connection between soul-making and lace-making.

EVA LOEWE, *The New Lacemaker*

Humility in the artist is his frank acceptance of all experiences, just as love in the artist is simply the sense of beauty that reveals to the world its body and its soul. In *Marius the Epicurean* Pater seeks to reconcile the artistic life with the life of religion, in the deep, sweet, and austere sense of the word. But Marius is little more than a spectator: an ideal spectator indeed, and one to whom it is given "to contemplate the spectacle of life with appropriate emotions," which Wordsworth defines as the poet's true aim; yet a spectator merely, and perhaps a little too much occupied with the comeliness of the benches of the sanctuary to notice that it is the sanctuary of sorrow that he is gazing at.

I see a far more intimate and immediate connexion between the true life of Christ and the true life of the artist; and I take a keen pleasure in the reflexion that long before sorrow had made my days her own and bound me to her wheel I had written in *The Soul of*

Man that he who would lead a Christ-like life must be entirely and absolutely himself, and had taken as my types not merely the shepherd on the hillside and the prisoner in his cell, but also the painter to whom the world is a pageant and the poet for whom the world is a song. I remember saying once to André Gide, as we sat together in some Paris café, that while metaphysics had but little real interest for me, and morality absolutely none, there was nothing that either Plato or Christ had said that could not be transferred immediately into the sphere of Art and there find its complete fulfilment.

Nor is it merely that we can discern in Christ that close union of personality with perfection which forms the real distinction between the classical and romantic movement in life, but the very basis of his nature was the same as that of the nature of the artist—an intense and flamelike imagination. He realized in the entire sphere of human relations that imaginative sympathy which in the sphere of Art is the sole secret of creation. He understood the leprosy of the leper, the darkness of the blind, the fierce misery of those who live for pleasure, the strange poverty of the rich.

OSCAR WILDE, *De Profundis*

––––––––––

Elsewhere Khunrath says that at the hour of conjunction the blackness and the raven's head and all the colours in the world will appear, "even Iris, the messenger of God, and the peacock's tail." He adds: "Mark the secrets of the rainbow in the Old and New Testament." This is a reference to the sign of God's covenant with Noah after the flood (Gen. 10:12f.) and to the "one in the midst of the four and twenty elders," who "was to look upon like a jasper and a sardine-stone, and there was a rainbow round about the throne, in sight like unto an emerald" (Rev. 4:3f.), and to the vision of the angel with a rainbow on his head (Rev. 10:1). Iris as the "messenger of God" is of special importance for an understanding of the opus, since the integration of all colours points, as it were, to a coming of God, or even to his presence.

The colour green, stressed by Khunrath, is associated with Venus.

The "Introitus apertus" says: "But in the gentle heat the mixture will liquefy and begin to swell up, and at God's command will be endowed with spirit, which will soar upward carrying the stone with it, and will produce new colours, first of all the green of Venus, which will endure for a long time." Towards the end of this procedure, which was known as the regimen of Venus, the colour changes into a livid purple, whereupon the philosophical tree will blossom. Then follows the regimen of Mars, "which displays the ephemeral colours of the rainbow and the peacock at their most glorious." In "these days" the "hyacinthine colour" appears, i.e., blue.

The livid purple that appears towards the end of the regimen of Venus has something deathly about it. This is in accord with the ecclesiastical view of purple, which expresses the "mystery of the Lord's passion." Hence the regimen of Venus leads by implication to passion and death.

C. G. JUNG, *Mysterium Coniunctionis*

The transit from black to white via blue implies that blue always brings black with it. (Among African peoples, for instance, black includes blue; whereas in the Jewish-Christian tradition blue belongs rather than white). Blue bears traces of the *mortificatio* into the whitening. What before was the stickiness of the black, like pitch or tar, unable to be rid of, turns into the traditionally blue virtues of constancy and fidelity. The same dark events feel different. The tortured and symptomatic aspect of mortification—flaying oneself, pulverizing old structures, decapitation of the headstrong will, the rat and rot in one's personal cellar—give way to depression. As even the darkest blue is not black, so even the deepest depression is not the *mortificatio* which means death of soul. The *mortificatio* is more driven, images locked compulsively in behavior, visibility zero, psyche trapped in the inertia and extension of matter. A *mortificatio* is a time of symptoms. These inexplicable, utterly materialized tortures of psyche in physis are relieved, according to the procession of colors, by a movement toward melancholy, which can commence as a mournful regret even over the lost symptom: "It was better when it hurt physically—now I only cry." Blue misery. So, with the appearance of blue, feeling becomes more paramount and the paramount feeling is the mournful plaint (Rimbaud equates blue with the vowel "O"; Kandinsky with the sounds of the flute, cello, double bass and organ). These laments hint of soul, of reflecting and distancing by imaginational expression. Here we can see more why archetypal psychology has stressed depression as the *via regia* in soul-making. The ascetic exercises that we call "symptoms" (and their "treatments"), the guilty despairs and remorse as the *nigredo* decays, reduce the old ego-personality, but this necessary reduction is only preparatory to the sense of soul which appears first in the dark imagination of depression as it blues into melancholy.

JAMES HILLMAN, *Alchemical Blue*

Before you can paint a bamboo, the bamboo must have grown deep inside you. It is then that, brush in hand gazing intently, you will see the vision rise up before you. Capture the vision at once by the strokes of your brush, for it may vanish as suddenly as a hare at the approach of the hunter.

SU DONGPO

EVERYDAY RELIGION

If a Greek is stirred to the remembrance of God
by the art of Pheidias, an Egyptian by paying
worship to animals, another man by a river,
another by fire—I have no anger for their
divergences; only let them know, let them
love, let them remember.

MAXIMUS OF TYRE

M ANY WRITERS SEEM *to have a sense similar to mine that in religion we need a fresh appreciation for the sacred things in ordinary life. Many books on religion have in their titles words such as "ordinary," "everyday," "commonplace," "earthly," "daily," and "personal." For too long religion has implied otherworldly concerns, even though we can find clear statements of the sacredness of creation in the theology and prayers of many traditions.*

At the same time, we have reduced the meaning of "God" to a set of attributes and a personality that we defend passionately, losing sight of traditional notions of divine infinity, namelessness, and mystery. Paul Tillich wrote about "the God beyond theism" and Dietrich Bonhoeffer spoke of a "God beyond God." Both of these remarkable Christian theologians were concerned with a religion embedded in culture and a sense of divinity beyond any human conceptions, biases, and agendas. Perhaps it is a paradox that the more we honor the mystery of divinity, the more tangible and ordinary religion becomes.

When we reduce the very idea of God or the divine to naive and simplistic terms, we soon come up against a barrier dividing our secular culture from religious sentiment. We are at a point in modern life where we believe in ourselves, thinking that we can live satisfying lives and create a humane world at a purely human level. Many religious institutions criticize this limited view, thinking that this is the work of "secular humanism," while those actively involved in humane and humanitarian concerns without a religious base find contemporary religion intellectually weak or neurotically defensive.

In my work on the soul I have tried to find a way out of this modern divisive and antagonistic argument. One way is to study religious traditions from around the world and discover how people who have lived in an enchanted culture have honored the sacred in the everyday. Another is to find ways of describing the presence of divinity without losing the mystery inherent in it.

It is my hope that a new kind of theology might emerge from the re-enchantment of religion, from finding a deeper ground for religion than worried belief or purely mental and moral interpretations. As long as our society conceives religion as something separate from secular life, it will remain stuck in the sterile division of religion from secularity. Understood as full participation in concrete daily life, secularity is as much a gift as religion.

The soul of religion is not always to be found in severe moral statements or extreme rationalistic presentations of doctrine; it is more evident in the ceremonies, traditions, paintings and sculptures, architecture, stories, and biographies. The soul of religion is its base and foundation, and it includes a spiritual life inspired by nature, an appreciation of the invisible depth of commonplace objects and activities, and a profoundly poetic imagination that sees through literal events to their deep stories and motifs.

Religion's soul is a prerequisite for religious institutions and beliefs. Without a foundation in religious sentiments of reverence, piety, ethics, and community, church institutions and personal beliefs have no roots.

I can imagine a renewal of religious institutions based on a fresh appreciation for ancient traditions. Tradition can be a source of rigid rules and limitations, or it can be the inspiration, as it was in Renaissance Europe, for a deepening of values and an increase of vision. Personally, I find endless treasures of wisdom and beauty in the religious traditions of the world, and I try to approach them with the intelligence and sensibility of our own times. Then they become the foundation for a spiritual life and the cultivation of soul.

7.

CONTEMPLATING
THE COMMONPLACE

While many people seem bent on achieving extraordinary levels of consciousness and great powers of spirit, religions also teach the holiness of the commonplace. It isn't easy in our complicated world to enjoy the pleasures of ordinary living—children, family, neighborhood, nature, walking, gathering, eating together. I imagine life not as an ambitious quest, but as an anti-quest, a search for the ordinary and a cultivation of the unexceptional.

In our cult of celebrity, our desire for the latest technology, and our deification of electronic media, I sense a misplaced, diverted longing for enchantment in everyday life. Our hours and days have been flattened by the work ethic, the endless interpretations and explanations, the materialistic goals and rewards. In reaction, we long so for a magical life that we seek it in the wrong places, and the more our entertainments and achievements fail to satisfy, the more desperate we become in our search.

Deus absconditus, the hidden God, is concealed and held more securely in the ordinary than in the extreme. He, It, She is to be found there in the world He created, not in the realm we fantasize.

Do you fast, Jesus?
Do guests fast at a wedding?

JOHN DOMINIC CROSSAN, *The Essential Jesus*

"Those who are introduced into the mysteries," wrote Proclus, "at first meet with manifold and multiform gods, but being entered and thoroughly initiated . . . they participate the very Deity." In *De ludo globi* Cusanus compared this law of regression, from many outward images to the inward One, with a law of nature observed by Aristotle. "Elemental forces, according to Aristotle, have the smallest extension and the greatest power. . . . The force inherent in a spark is that of the whole fire. . . . A small seed has the strength of many grains. . . . The core of the apparent is in the occult, the outward depends on the inward. The skin and crust are there because of the muscles and marrow, and these because of the invisible force that is concealed in them."

Erasmus repeated the argument in the *Adagia*, under the heading *Sileni Alcibiadis*: "Thus the most important is always the least conspicuous. A tree flatters the eye with flowers and foliage, and exhibits the massiveness of its trunk: but the seed, from which these have their strength, what a small thing it is, and how hidden. . . . Gold and gems have been concealed by Nature in the recesses of the earth. . . . What is most divine and immortal in man is inaccessible to perception. . . . And also in the temperament of the physical body, while phlegm and blood are familiar to the senses and tangible, that which contributes most to life is least patent, namely the spirit. And in the Universe the greatest things are invisible, like the so-called separate substances. And the supreme among these is furthest removed. . . . God, unintelligible and unthinkable because He is the unique source of all."

EDGAR WIND, *Pagan Mysteries*

As a Chinese poem says, "I went and I returned. It was nothing special. Rozan famous for its misty mountains; Sekko for its water." People think it must be wonderful to see the famous range of mountains covered by mists, and the water said to cover all the earth. But if you go there you will just see water and mountains. Nothing special.

It is a kind of mystery that for people who have no experience of enlightenment, enlightenment is something wonderful. But if they attain it, it is nothing. But yet it is not nothing. Do you understand? For a mother with children, having children is nothing special. That is zazen. So, if you continue this practice, more and more you will acquire something—nothing special, but nevertheless something. You may say "universal nature" or "Buddha nature" or "enlightenment." You may call it by many names, but for the person who has it, it is nothing, and it is something. . . .

The most important thing is to forget all gaining ideas, all dualistic ideas. In other words, just practice zazen in a certain posture. Do not think about anything. Just remain on your cushion without expecting anything. Then eventually you will resume your own true nature. That is to say, your own true nature resumes itself.

SHUNRYU SUZUKI, *Zen Mind, Beginner's Mind*

This morning, before Prime, in the early morning sky, three antiquated monoplanes flew over the monastery with much noise, followed by a great heron.

THOMAS MERTON, *Conjectures*

Every morning was a cheerful invitation to make my life of equal simplicity, and I may say innocence, with Nature herself. I have been as sincere a worshipper of Aurora as the Greeks. I got up early and bathed in the pond; that was a religious exercise, and one of the best things which I did. They say that characters were engraven on the bathing tub of king Tching-thang to this effect: "Renew thyself completely each day; do it again, and again, and forever again." I can understand that. Morning brings back the heroic ages. I was as much affected by the faint hum of a mosquito making its invisible and unimaginable tour through my apartment at earliest dawn, when I was sitting with door and windows open, as I could be by any trumpet that ever sang of fame. It was Homer's requiem; itself an Iliad and Odyssey in the air, singing its own wrath and wanderings. There was something cosmical about it; a standing advertisement, till forbidden, of the everlasting vigor and fertility of the world.

HENRY DAVID THOREAU, *Walden*

Old Pond
Frog leaps
Splash!

BASHŌ

Today I see Jung. He is in a chaise longue on the terrace, listening through the open window to Scholem's lecture. For a man of seventy-five, he appears in excellent health. From Mme. Corbin I learn some of the rumors that circulate around the great man. Jung has a prodigious appetite and is a great master in culinary matters. Knowing that Mme. Frobe-Kapteyn does not set a very good table, he secretly bought some dainties and treated himself in his room alone at night. But eventually he was found out, and one of his admirers in Ascona sent him yesterday evening, quite surreptitiously, a fried chicken.

MIRCEA ELIADE, *Journals*

(Ashanti, Ghana). In Africa, some important persons develop a close relationship with their wooden stools, as if part of their personality is in them. A man may bring his own stool to a meeting, saving himself and his host the embarrassment of offering someone else's stool to an uninvited but prominent guest. No one may sit on a man's stool except his eldest son after his death. For a king his stool represents his authority over the Earth on which it stands. In English, too, one may refer to "the Throne," meaning the Sovereign.

More than two hundred years ago Osai Tutu was made King of all the Ashanti peoples. This happened as follows. One day there appeared before Osai Tutu a famous medicine man called Anochi who spoke: "Great Chief Osai, it has pleased Nyame (God) to give you the kingdom of Ashanti and all the Akan-speaking peoples. If you convene the Grand Council of all the clan-heads of the realm, I will perform the ceremony that will confirm you as the national sovereign. God wills it."

As soon as the Grand Council was in session, Anochi prayed to God that He show a sign to express His pleasure with Osai Tutu as King. As all the eyes were raised upwards, there descended from the sky a stool made of pure gold, touched the ground and placed itself right in front of Osai Tutu. Anochi spoke: "This stool contains by God's will the soul of the Ashanti nation. No one may ever sit on it, and no one may ever remove it from Ashanti or else great misfortune will happen to all people." The kings of Ashanti defeated all their enemies from that day forth, until the British came a century ago and besieged Kumasi, their capital. After a fierce defence, the Ashanti king surrendered, lest the Golden Stool be damaged by gunfire, since the soul of the nation resided in it.

JAN KNAPPERT, *African Mythology*

Rune of Saint Patrick

At Tara today in this fateful hour
I place all Heaven with its power,
And the Sun with its brightness,
And the snow with its whiteness,

And Fire with all the strength it hath,
And lightning with its rapid wrath,
And the winds with their swiftness along the path,
And the sea with its deepness,
And the rocks with their steepness,
And the Earth with its starkness:
All these I place
By God's almighty help and grace,
Between myself and the powers of Darkness.

TRADITIONAL CELTIC

In front of this wall was a slope in which was embedded a stone that jutted out—my stone. Often, when I was alone, I sat down on this stone, and then began an imaginary game that went something like this: "I am sitting on top of this stone and it is underneath." But the stone also could say "I" and think: "I am lying here on this slope and he is sitting on top of me." The question then arose: "Am I the one who is sitting on the stone, or am I the stone on which *he* is sitting?" This question always perplexed me, and I would stand up, wondering who was what now. The answer remained totally unclear, and my uncertainty was accompanied by a feeling of curious and fascinating darkness. But there was no doubt whatsoever that this stone stood in some secret relationship to me. I could sit on it for hours, fascinated by the puzzle it set me.

C. G. JUNG, *Memories*

Perhaps
The truth depends on a walk around a lake,

A composing as the body tires, a stop
To see hepatica, a stop to watch
A definition growing certain and

A wait within that certainty, a rest
In the swags of pine-trees bordering the lake.

WALLACE STEVENS, "Notes Toward a Supreme Fiction"

He began in 1900, and continued until 1903, to write a series of what, because he was following no one, he declined to call *prose poems* as others would have done. For these he evolved a new and more startling descriptive term, "epiphanies." The epiphany did not mean for Joyce the manifestation of godhead, the showing forth of Christ to the Magi, although that is a useful metaphor for what he had in mind. The epiphany was the sudden "revelation of the whatness of a thing," the moment in which "the soul of the commonest object . . . seems to us radiant." The artist, he felt, was charged with such revelations, and must look for them not among gods but among men, in casual, unostentatious, even unpleasant moments. He might find "a sudden spiritual manifestation" either "in the vulgarity of speech or of gesture or in a memorable phase of the mind itself." Sometimes the epiphanies are "eucharistic," another term arrogantly borrowed by Joyce from Christianity and invested with secular meaning. These are moments of fullness or of passion. Sometimes the epiphanies are rewarding for another reason, that they convey precisely the flavor of unpalatable experiences. The spirit, as Joyce characteristically held, manifested itself on both levels.

RICHARD ELLMAN, *James Joyce*

From Bachelard, we become aware of the interior spaces, the intimate corners, the poetics of spaces. Such spaces are created in and around a bridge. Three such spaces immediately come into view: the centre (the highest point, the crown of a bridge, the desperate leap, the point of reverie, the place of transformation in myths and tales); and the ends (the approach, a sense of initiation, of defence, of entry and of departure). The entrance to a bridge always invites us. How can one pass the entrance to a bridge and resist stepping onto it? And the middle? As a child this point held both fear and fascination. It seemed to evoke both the jump and the reverie from the crown. Like the edge of a cliff it drew both a sweeping overview and a downward pull. In an age before flight or even before easily available flight, standing on the crown of a bridge was the nearest one could get to it: surrounded by space; suspended high in space; supported only by the minimum of matter.

And, of course, there is always the underside of a bridge (the place of secrets, of trolls, tramps, wanderers, the smell of water, earth, stone, concrete, of hasty sex, of faeces and urine). Bridges gather to themselves an underside, they have an underworld. These are places of stillness and exile. They are outside the rush and flow taking place above, over the bridge. . . .

There is the naming of the bridge and then a story about it, some-times set in history and sometimes in legend. We also find multiple images of the bridge's use—to be lingered upon by lovers or in soli-tary reverie, to be defended, triumphed upon, fought upon, as well as just simply crossed. Bridges in medieval time were often locations for tournaments and battles, or were centres for trade and also crime. In the country especially, they were used as public meeting places, for gossip and chatter as well as for official business. Assassinations, executions and the display of severed heads, grace the story of bridges. . . .

The first cloverleaf interchange was built near Woodbridge, New Jersey, in 1928. These interchanges consume bridges. There is no tol-eration of interruption. With the complexities of these interchanges, we can get lost, disorientated, and drive considerable distances. The important criteria is to keep moving. The "aesthetics" demand an "unobstructed flow of space." Once again the bridge is asked to be as invisible as possible to allow maximum traffic speed and flow. Once again the concern is with clean, dynamic space. Intersections and cross-roads were once places where a pause and a meeting could occur, and so eventually shops, shrines, and restaurants gathered there. Now, not only is it dangerous to stop, it is often illegal. It is even less possible to pause on the bridge itself. Many large bridges scarcely have provision for pedestrians to scurry across, let alone linger. Roebling's insistence on a separate walkway for pedestrians across Brooklyn Bridge in 1883, on which they could pause and breathe the clean air, marked the end of an era.

The fantasy of maximum uninterrupted flow is still a dominant one of our age. Concerns with consumerism, cash flow, fast food, fast knowledge, instant enlightenment, the quick return and the quick cure, the arrival and not the journey, are apparent everywhere in our cities, and in our daily lives.

This concern with uninterrupted flow has resulted in a single-minded focus on the axial, longitudinal span of the bridge.

PETER BISHOP, "The Soul of the Bridge"

8.

THEOLOGY IN THE WORLD

We have yet to create a discipline of theology for the new century that is upon us. One hopes it is a world less in love with technology, less divided between materialism and spiritual extravagance, and less removed from the antique virtues of reverence and piety.

This new theology, in my utopian imagination, would be equal in validity and importance to any science. It would be thoroughly nonsectarian, even as it drew upon every imaginable instance of creed, worship, and holy text. It would be an applied discipline, its practitioners guiding governments and individual lives. It would largely replace, or at least modify, the therapeutic culture that developed in the twentieth century, and thus restore, in every aspect of individual and social life, attention to the eternal.

A new theology could address the depth of emotion and imagination that both inspires and deeply troubles the modern person, a depth not accessible to the sciences and to materialistic philosophies.

Let us consider the deepest and most fundamental element in all strong and sincerely felt religious emotion. Faith unto salvation, trust, love—all these are there. But over and above these is an element which may also on occasion, quite apart from them, profoundly affect us and occupy the mind with a wellnigh bewildering strength. Let us follow it up with every effort of sympathy and imaginative intuition wherever it is to be found, in the lives of those around us, in sudden, strong ebullitions of personal piety and the frames of mind such ebullitions evince, in the fixed and ordered solemnities of rites and liturgies, and again in the atmosphere that clings to old religious monuments and buildings, to temples and to churches. If we do so we shall find we are dealing with something for which there is only one appropriate expression, "*mysterium tremendum.*" The feeling of it may at times come sweeping like a gentle tide, pervading the mind with a tranquil mood of deepest worship. It may pass over into a more set and lasting attitude of the soul, continuing, as it were, thrillingly vibrant and resonant, until at last it dies away and the soul resumes its "profane," non-religious mood of everyday experience. It may burst in sudden eruption up from the depths of the soul with spasms and convulsions, or lead to the strangest excitements, to intoxicated frenzy, to transport, and to ecstasy. It has its wild and demonic forms and can sink to an almost grisly horror and shuddering. It has its crude, barbaric antecedents and early manifestations, and again it may be developed into something beautiful and pure and glorious. It may become the hushed, trembling, and speechless humility of the creature in the presence of—whom or what? In the presence of that which is a *mystery* inexpressible and above all creatures.

RUDOLF OTTO, *The Idea of the Holy*

Divine worship is as natural for men almost as neighing is for horses or barking for dogs.

MARSILIO FICINO, *Platonic Theology*

---

7 March

The meaning of Isaac's sacrifice was not evident to Abraham. In appearance it was an infanticide, and for Abraham it was unthinkable that Yahweh could ask him to make such a gesture. The "sacrality" of Isaac's sacrifice was camouflaged, not in the "profane," but in a "crime." To compare with the current situation: In our time religious experience has become unrecognizable, for it is camouflaged in its contrary—in materialism, antireligion, etc. . . .

MIRCEA ELIADE, *Journals*

———————

Study yourselves with unswerving attention, put aside all that is not self, proceed with the sense ever more closely directed to the purely inward. The more you pass by all foreign elements, making your personality appear diminished almost to the vanishing point, the clearer the Universe stands before you, and the more gloriously the terror of annihilating the fleeting is rewarded by the feeling of the eternal.

Look outside again on one of the widely distributed elements of the world. Seek to understand it in itself, and seek it in particular objects, in yourself and everywhere. Traverse again and again your way from centre to circumference, going ever farther afield. You will rediscover everything everywhere, and you will only be able to recognize it in relation to its opposite. Soon everything individual and distinct will have been lost and the Universe be found.

FRIEDRICH SCHLEIERMACHER, *On Religion*

———————

Overcoming a dualistic heritage (however strongly those dualistic presuppositions seem to belong to religious knowledge) brings one into the sphere in which ordinary reality is saturated with the sacred. Religion is made up of nothing special—the ordinary is holy or potentially holy; since the object of the religious is no-thing, its images can be improvised from oatmeal boxes and sand sculpture. The apprehension of the sacred is manifested in an imaginal relationship with the divine—reinventing the *ordinarily sacred*.

Another scan of contents and contours within the temple reveal how the holy is made: from the ephemera and scraps of the ordinary world by means of metaphor.

As Kafka's aphorism tells us,

Leopards break into the temple and drink the sacrificial chalice dry; this occurs repeatedly, again and again: finally it can be reckoned on beforehand and becomes part of the ceremony.

Now we would ask Kafka for a parable in which there is no temple, no established ceremony or sacrificial vessel, but one in which leopards nevertheless surprise us by appearing and drinking from our cups. Leopards breaking in—upon whatever our complacencies—is the nature of religion. We long for a reappearance of Kafka himself to break in and tell us that mysterious thing we need to know about religion: religion as leopards drinking from—if not our sacred vessels—then whatever cups we have in hand.

The shock of leopards, even if they can be reckoned on beforehand, even if they are a part of the ceremony, is religion. The intrusions of the "mundane" become agents of the sublime. They are incorporated—"bodied" into the divine. Thus the containers: the chalices, temples, ceremonies, memories, predictions, words and works, envelop the shock and become associated with the sacred.

LYNDA SEXSON, *Ordinarily Sacred*

———————

We have here the original sense of the word "religious," not referring to a particular religion, but to an attitude of respect, or beyond that, of worship, or more still, a feeling of giddiness on the edge of the abyss, of the Nihil, or "nothingness." This attitude may refer either to a god, who will be addressed as "thou," or to the festal reality of the world—a godly world or a world full of gods—or even to the Nihil in a completely godless world, a *kosmos atheos*. It is the situation which lets nothing be hidden and causes everything essential to come clearly to the fore.

C. KERENYI, *Religion of the Greeks and Romans*

———————

Psychology as religion implies imagining all psychological events as effects of Gods in the soul, and all activities to do with soul, such as therapy, to be operations of ritual in relation to these Gods. Our theories about the soul are then also myths, and the history of depth psychology a kind of Church history: early disciples and tales of martyrs; the search for a prehistory in extraterritorial areas; the struggle with unbelievers and heresies; apologetics and official biographers; the patristic literature, schools of interpretation and commentaries; the ecumenical attempts, the great schism; the holy localities, their legends and their cures; the conversional mission, and above all, depth psychology's impetus to salvation.

That the contemporary ministry is drawn so strongly by psychology toward a new brotherhood of psychology and religion in parish, mental health center, and individual quest reflects the current ecumenical movement, drawing all branches together. It is not a question of religion turning to psychology—no, psychology is simply going home. Whether this home is North or South, monotheistic Reformation or polytheistic Renaissance, we have yet to see. But the wrong way could again be the imprisonment of soul in an imageless universe, the soul again rent between barricades and barbarians.

Also, by means of religion we might become more aware of the nonagnostic aspect of therapy, that it is a work invoking Gods. Little wonder then that it is fraught with magic, charlatanism, and priestly powers. Little wonder, too, that the emotions having to do with beginning therapy and ending it, and with its central experience of transference, have no adequate explanations in psychology books. The level of such accounts is strikingly trivial compared to the depth of the experiences.

Religion would not only give us primary images of soul-making but would open depth psychology's eyes to the religious depth of its activities, to the realization that since its inception it has been actively practising religion. Here we need to psychologize more deeply into Freud's move decrying religion as an "illusion" and considering psychoanalysis to be reality. This step is necessary in the founding of any religion. Also we could reappraise Jung's lifelong effort to reinterpret, not so much science, philosophy, society, or even psychiatry, but theology. Depth psychology is thoroughly involved a priori with religion because it is a psychology of the soul. As such, psychology is driven by the "will to believe" (as James called it), of which its belief in sexuality, or humanism, or self are each idols. A re-vision of psychology means recognizing that psychology does not take place without religion, because there is always a God in what we are doing. The recognition of the Protestantism of psychology was the first step. Ultimately we shall admit that archetypal psychology is theophanic: personifying, pathologizing, psychologizing, and dehumanizing are the modes of polytheizing, the means of revealing Gods in a pluralistic universe.

JAMES HILLMAN, *Re-Visioning*

The God above the God of theism is present, although hidden, in every divine-human encounter. Biblical religion as well as Protestant theology are aware of the paradoxical character of this encounter. They are aware that if God encounters man God is neither object nor subject and is therefore above the scheme into which theism has forced him. They are aware that personalism with respect to God is balanced by a transpersonal presence of the divine. They are aware that forgiveness can be accepted only if the power of acceptance is effective in man—biblically speaking, if the power of grace is effective in man. They are aware of the paradoxical character of every prayer, of speaking to somebody to whom you cannot speak because he is not "somebody," of asking somebody of whom you cannot ask anything because he gives or gives not before you ask, of saying "thou" to somebody who is nearer to the I than the I is to itself. Each of these paradoxes drives the religious consciousness toward a God above the God of theism.

The courage to be which is rooted in the experience of the God above the God of theism unites and transcends the courage to be as a part and the courage to be as oneself. It avoids both the loss of oneself by participation and the loss of one's world by individualization. The acceptance of the God above the God of theism makes us a part of that which is not also a part but is the ground of the whole. Therefore our self is not lost in a larger whole, which submerges it in the life of a limited group. If the self participates in the power of being-itself it receives itself back. For the power of being acts through the power of the individual selves. It does not swallow them as every limited whole, every collectivism, and every conformism does. This is why the Church, which stands for the power of being-itself or for the God who transcends the God of the religions, claims to be the mediator of the courage to be. A church which is based on the authority of the God of theism cannot make such a claim. It inescapably develops into a collectivist or semicollectivist system itself.

But a church which raises itself in its message and its devotion to the God above the God of theism without sacrificing its concrete symbols can mediate a courage which takes doubt and meaninglessness into itself. It is the Church under the Cross which alone can do this, the Church which preaches the Crucified who cried to God who remained his God after the God of confidence had left him in the darkness of doubt and meaninglessness. To be as a part in such a church is to receive a courage to be in which one cannot lose one's self and in which one receives one's world.

PAUL TILLICH, *The Courage to Be*

The process of the desacralization of the world, of life, and of history, which triumphs today is due above all to our inability to grasp the mystery of the camouflaging of the sacred in the profane.

MIRCEA ELIADE, *Journals*

THERE
where
the House Chief stays, there he IS, the HEART of the earth
whatever he is
perhaps a stone. (*audience member:* yes, a stone)

THAT'S
   WHERE
HE IS.
EVERYTHING
A——LL OVER THE WIDE EARTH
well
EVERYTHING DEPENDED ON HIM AND ON THE
   MIDDLE PLACE FOR FERTILITY.
FOR THEIR PART
the PRIESTS
would sit down to ask for rain.
WHEN IT RAINED AT ZUNI IT WOULD RAIN
   A——LL OVER THE EARTH.

             ZUNI STORY

———————

3 November
At the annual colloquium . . . I spoke of "The Sacred and Reality." I
repeated what I've said over and over again so many times in so many
books: that *homo religiosus* thirsts for the real, that he wants to *be,*
fully and at any cost. I showed how nature, for him, was full of signs
and hierophanies.

             MIRCEA ELIADE, *Journals*

———————

He who is the center of the world, blessed God, is the center of the earth and all spheres and all things which are in the world; he is simultaneously the infinite circumference of all things.

NICHOLAS OF CUSA

But as concerning mine own self, for thy comfort shall I say, daughter, to thee, that mine own conscience in this matter (I damn none other man's) is such as may well stand with mine own salvation. Thereof am I, Megge, so sure, as that is, God is in heaven. And therefore as for all the remnant, goods, lands, and life both (if the chance should so fortune), sith this conscience is sure for me, I verily trust in God, he shall rather strength me to bear the loss, than against this conscience to swear and put my soul in peril, sith all the causes that I perceive move other men to the contrary, seem not such unto me as in my conscience make any change.

THOMAS MORE, *Letter*

If the doors of perception were cleansed every thing would appear to man as it is: infinite.

For man has closed himself up, till he sees all things thro' narrow chinks of his cavern.

WILLIAM BLAKE

9.

RITES AND REVERENCES

Any action that speaks to the soul and to the deep imagination, whether or not it also has practical effects, is a ritual. Some rituals may have more spiritual import than others and therefore assume greater dimensions, but even the smallest rites of everyday existence are important to the soul.

We can give an action a ritual quality by repeating it regularly as remembrance, memorial, celebration, or personal piety and by giving it ceremony, special language, meaningful timing, and placing. If any of our actions lack care and thoughtfulness, they remain largely unconscious and raw. Staying in close touch with religious, cultural, and family traditions may also give our actions an impersonal, eternal quality that is essential to ritual.

We live in a culture that has generally neglected the soul for several centuries, but we could restore a soul sensibility rather easily simply by becoming more adept at ritual.

I read several reviews of *Le Mythe de l'éternel retour*—all excellent. But I have the impression that the most important thesis—the necessity of "repetition," i.e., the periodic recreation of the world—is not understood. The function of repetition (through ritual) is "existential": it is the desire to *continue life*, the hope to prolong it, ad infinitum.

MIRCEA ELIADE, *Journals*

The importance of dance in Crete is intimated by the fact that the *Iliad* still speaks of a dancing place in Knossos which was built by Daedalus for Ariadne. The gold rings often portray dancing figures, mostly women, who are almost certainly to be understood as humans, perhaps as priestesses; the goddess appears among them. The large terracotta figures from the temple at Ayia Irini also betray dance-like movements. But men dance too: a clay model from Kamilari near Phaistos represents four naked men with pointed caps dancing a ring dance between cult horns.

On one of the gold rings from Mycenae, the central figure is that of a dancing woman, while to her right another woman bends low over a kind of altar and to her left a man reaches upwards into the boughs of a sacred tree. Mourning for a vegetation god of the Adonis type has been brought to mind by this image, but no verification is possible. The figure, usually male, who stretches up with both hands towards the inclining tree is a familiar motif on the rings; fruits are never seen being picked, rather it seems that the branches are simply being touched. Occasionally a kneeling figure, apparently embracing or rolling a large boulder, is shown beside the tree. The mysterious scenery admits many interpretations: do the figures here seek contact with the sacred, or do tree and stone participate in the trembling movement of the divine epiphany?

WALTER BURKERT, *Greek Religion*

I was able to convince myself very quickly that I must be on the right track. Almost every shot went off smoothly and unexpectedly, to my way of thinking. Naturally I did not overlook the reverse side of this triumph: the precision work of the right hand demanded my full attention. But I comforted myself with the hope that this technical solution would gradually become so habitual that it would require no further notice from me, and that the day would come when, thanks to it, I would be in a position to loose the shot, self-obliviously and unconsciously, at the moment of highest tension, and that in this case the technical ability would spiritualize itself. Waxing more and more confident in this conviction I silenced the protest that rose up in me, ignored the contrary counsels of my wife, and went away with the satisfying feeling of having taken a decisive step forward.

The very first shot I let off after the recommencement of the lessons was, to my mind, a brilliant success. The loose was smooth, unexpected. The Master looked at me for a while and then said hesitantly, like one who can scarcely believe his eyes: "Once again, please!" My second shot seemed to me even better than the first. The Master stepped up to me without a word, took the bow from my hand, and sat down on a cushion, his back towards me. I knew what that meant, and withdrew.

The next day Mr. Komachiya informed me that the Master declined to instruct me any further because I had tried to cheat him. Horrified beyond measure by this interpretation of my behavior, I explained to Mr. Komachiya why, in order to avoid marking time forever, I had hit upon this method of loosing the shot. On his interceding for me, the Master was finally prepared to give in, but made the continuation of the lessons conditional upon my express promise never to offend again against the spirit of the "Great Doctrine." . . .

By archery in the traditional sense, which he esteems as an art and honors as a national heritage, the Japanese does not understand a sport but, strange as this may sound at first, a religious ritual. And consequently, by the "art" of archery he does not mean the ability of the sportsman, which can be controlled, more or less, by bodily exercises, but an ability whose origin is to be sought in spiritual exercises and whose aim consists in hitting a spiritual goal, so that fundamentally the marksman aims at himself and may even succeed in hitting himself.

EUGEN HERRIGEL, *Zen in the Art of Archery*

Take the dance, for example. All dances were originally sacred; in other words, they had an extrahuman model. The model may in some cases have been a totemic or emblematic animal, whose motions were reproduced to conjure up its concrete presence through magic, to increase its numbers, to obtain incorporation into the animal on the part of man. In other cases the model may have been revealed by a divinity (for example the pyrrhic, the martial dance created by Athena) or by a hero (cf. Theseus' dance in the Labyrinth). The dance may be executed to acquire food, to honor the dead, or to assure good order in the cosmos. It may take place upon the occasion of initiations, of magico-religious ceremonies, of marriages, and so on. But all these details need not be discussed here. What is of interest to us is its presumed extrahuman origin (for every dance was created *in illo tempore,* in the mythical period, by an ancestor, a totemic animal, a god, or a hero). Choreographic rhythms have their model outside of the profane life of man; whether they reproduce the movements of the totemic or emblematic animal, or the motions of the stars; whether they themselves constitute rituals (labyrinthine steps, leaps, gestures performed with ceremonial instruments)—a dance always imitates an archetypal gesture or commemorates a mythical moment. In a word, it is a repetition, and consequently a reactualization, of *illud tempus,* "those days."

MIRCEA ELIADE, *The Myth of Eternal Return*

———

Audacity of Bliss, said Jacob to the Angel "I will not let thee go except I bless thee"—Pugilist and Poet, Jacob was correct—

EMILY DICKINSON, *Letters*

———

We wait expectantly inside the house, dressed in our finest tiered skirts, velveteen blouses, moccasins, and turquoise. Finally, word comes from the sacred hogan, and we rise from our chairs, wrapping our vividly colored Pendleton blankets around us. As we walk across the yard, we talk about how nervous and excited we are; we are both glad to have someone with whom to share the experience.

We can hear the singing as we approach the hogan. Finally, we enter the doorway. The casual atmosphere has given way to an air of greater formality: family and friends now sit with their backs to the walls of the hogan; the tins of sand and other articles used in sand-painting preparation have been removed; the completed sandpainting lies isolated in the center of the floor. The painting appears to have grown in size, power, and beauty while I was gone; its surface is now covered with a light dusting of fine white corn pollen. Pollen balls have been placed in the mouths of Mother Earth and Father Sky and a line of pollen stretches between the two pollen balls, joining the two deities. Some of the plumed prayer sticks stand upright in the sand around the image, while others lie in piles beside Mother Earth and Father Sky; at the western side of the painting stand the four wide boards. The painting is clearly a powerful presence, alive and sacred.

TRUDY GRIFFIN-PIERCE, *Earth Is My Mother*

A quiet night behind my grass hut.
Alone, I play a stringless lute.
Its melody drifts to the wind blown clouds and fades.
Its sound deepens with the running stream,
expanding till it fills a deep ravine,
and echoes through the vast woods.
Who, other than a deaf person,
can hear this faint song.

RYOKAN

The word "ritual" is from Latin *ritus,* from Greek *rheo,* meaning "to flow, run, rush, or stream." A "rite" is a river—*rivus*—"river or stream"; related to "rival," one who uses the same stream as another. One *ar*rives, or, as in this case, *de*rives, by approaching or leading from the river.

To be in ritual, therefore, is to be in the river: Jesus with John the Baptist, the Buddhist on his raft in the river. Using the word from which "ritual" derives, Herakleitos says:

> Everything flows and nothing abides; everything
> gives way and nothing stays fixed.
>
> (Wheelwright, fr. 20)

Everything flows: *panta rhei.* And again Herakleitos, in a familiar phrase: "You cannot step twice into the same river, for other waters are continually flowing on" (*epirrei:* "flowing on").

To be in ritual is to be in the river. One does not find baptism at the river; rather, one finds the river in baptism. It is the river one is searching for.

THOMAS MOORE, *Rituals of the Imagination*

As he went on speaking and Vasudeva listened to him with a serene face, Siddhartha was more keenly aware than ever of Vasudeva's attentiveness. He felt his troubles, his anxieties and his secret hopes flow across to him and then return again. Disclosing his wound to this listener was the same as bathing it in the river, until it became cool and one with the river. As he went on talking and confessing, Siddhartha felt more and more that this was no longer Vasudeva, no longer a man who was listening to him. He felt that this motionless listener was absorbing his confession as a tree absorbs the rain, that this motionless man was the river itself, that he was God Himself, that he was eternity itself. As Siddhartha stopped thinking about himself and his wound, this recognition of the change in Vasudeva possessed him, and the more he realized it, the less strange did he find it; the more did he realize that everything was natural and in order, that Vasudeva had long ago, almost always been like that, only he did not quite recognize it; indeed he himself was hardly different from him.

HERMAN HESSE, *Siddhartha*

———————

At Rome it appears certain that the deity was conceived to be "increased" or "strengthened" (*mactus*) by the wine or other offering. There was a tradition that originally the offering was not animal but grain with salt and wine or milk. Animal sacrifices there almost certainly were on occasion, and in the later period they are familiar; the god received not only the fat (*omentum*) but also the parts concerned in consciousness—heart, lungs, liver and gall—perhaps in connection with *extispicium*. Grain with salt and wine were before the slaughter sprinkled over the victim, and there was a preliminary offering of incense (i.e. the exudations, sap of trees) and wine. Incense had apparently replaced native grain or aromatic leaves, as e.g. of the laurel with their gum and oil, *pinguis verbena,* of which, as we have seen, the "heads of the gods" consisted. "Incense and wine" appear to have been the customary offering in a *supplicatio,* and we hear that they were supplied by the state to private citizens for that purpose at the beginning of the third century B.C. They were also what the dead received, not in vapour as to the gods but directly, as the grease and wine to the bones and the grease to the stones in Homer. Roman deities also received unguent directly. Thus the Arval Brothers "anointed the goddesses"; the Lar was anointed; Terminus (the boundary stone) was anointed; upon Pales milk was poured, etc.

RICHARD ONIANS, *Origins of European Thought*

———————

and Jupiter side by side last night stemmed the sea of clouds and plied their voyage in convoy through the sublime Deep as I walked the old and dusty road. The snow and the enchantment of the moonlight make all landscapes alike, and the road that is so tedious and homely that I never take it by day,—by night is Italy or Palmyra. In these divine pleasures permitted to me of walks in the June night under moon and stars, I can put my life as a fact before me and stand aloof from its honor and shame.

RALPH WALDO EMERSON, *Journals*

The Woodcarver

Khing, the master carver, made a bell stand
Of precious wood. When it was finished,
All who saw it were astounded. They said it must be
The work of spirits.
The Prince of Lu said to the master carver:
"What is your secret?"

Khing replied: "I am only a workman:
I have no secret. There is only this:
When I began to think about the work you commanded
I guarded my spirit, did not expend it
On trifles, that were not to the point.
I fasted in order to set
My heart at rest.
After three days fasting,
I had forgotten gain and success.
After five days
I had forgotten praise or criticism.
After seven days
I had forgotten my body
With all its limbs.

"By this time all thought of your Highness
And of the court had faded away.
All that might distract me from the work
Had vanished.
I was collected in the single thought
Of the bell stand.

"Then I went to the forest
To see the trees in their own natural state.
When the right tree appeared before my eyes,
The bell stand also appeared in it, clearly, beyond doubt.
All I had to do was to put forth my hand
And begin.

"If I had not met this particular tree
There would have been
No bell stand at all.

"What happened?
My own collected thought
Encountered the hidden potential in the wood;
From this live encounter came the work
Which you ascribe to the spirits."

THOMAS MERTON, *The Way of Chuang Tzu*

———————

I myself have proved it to be of no small use, when in bed in the dark, to recall in fancy the external details of forms previously studied, or other noteworthy things conceived by subtle speculation; and this is certainly an admirable exercise, and useful for impressing things on the memory.

LEONARDO DA VINCI, *Notebooks*

———————

Twin loaves of bread have just been born into the world under my auspices—fine children—the image of their *mother*—and *here* my dear friend is the *glory*.

EMILY DICKINSON, Letters

He asked if I knew what a tjuringa was.

"I do," I said.

"What is a tjuringa?"

"A sacred board," I said. "An Aboriginal's 'holy of holies.' Or, if you like, his 'soul.'"

A tjuringa is usually an oval-ended plaque, carved from stone or mulga wood, and covered with patterns which represent the wanderings of its owner's Dreamtime Ancestor. In Aboriginal law, no uninitiated person was *ever* allowed to look on one.

"Have you seen a tjuringa?" Kidder asked.

"I have."

"Where?"

"In the British Museum."

"Did you realise you were acting illegally?"

"I never heard anything so silly."

Kidder folded his arms and squeezed his empty beer can; *clu . . . unk!* His chest was heaving up and down like a pouter pigeon's. "People have been speared for less," he said.

BRUCE CHATWIN, The Songlines

Everywhere in India, Hindu women regularly paint their homes as part of religious ritual. The wall and floor decorations of Indian women are usually ephemeral, remaining hours, days, or weeks before being worn off by the abrasion of activity or weather and replaced by new interpretations of design. In some areas this decoration is very frequent: daily in the far south, as described above, or weekly in eastern India. Elsewhere it is done less often. Women throughout the subcontinent herald important occasions either by repainting their entire houses or by decorating auspicious portions of them. Common occasions are the holy festivals associated with specific gods and goddesses, and rituals involved with seasonal changes—the planting of crops, the first rains, harvest, and special days associated with phases of the sun and moon, or configurations of the planets and stars. Women also repaint their walls or floors to celebrate significant events in their families such as birth, puberty, marriage, pregnancy, and death. Even the arrival of an important guest or the visit of a son or daughter who has moved away may be cause for fresh decoration of the home.

The front door of a house, its threshold, and the walls that face the road are commonly decorated either as an invitation for the goddess's protection or for prevention of evil. In many areas this painting is an unadorned whitewash or a single flat color, which the uninformed might regard as simple household maintenance. In fact, the walls, particularly at the front of a house, are the boundaries that separate the within from without, the familiar from the foreign, the known from the unknown, and must therefore be safeguarded. A farmer's wife in Rajasthan, western India, commented: "How can I know what is outside my house? Anything might be out there! I must protect my family from danger. It is my primary duty in life. So I paint my house inside and out."

STEPHEN HUYLER, *Painted Prayers*

THE ART OF DWELLING

God shield the house, the fire, the kine,
Every one who dwells herein tonight.
Shield myself and my beloved group,
Preserve us from violence and from harm;
Preserve us from foes this night,
For the sake of the Son of the Mary Mother,
In this place, and in every place wherein they dwell tonight,
On this night and on every night,
This night and every night.

Carmina Gadelica

O NE OF THE *symptoms that gives modern life its neurotic flavor is a combination of rootlessness, aimlessness, lack of direction, and deep insecurity. What is missing is a solid and abiding sense of home. This feeling of having a home base may come from many sources, including a secure childhood, a strong feeling of place, a house that is loved and cared for, the comforting presence of family and friends, and a mate or partner with whom we can feel secure and loved.*

Everyone knows that in modern times it isn't always easy to have these sources firmly in place. We move around a great deal, we may have had various kinds of instability in childhood, and there doesn't seem to be much time available for home and family. As a result, we may feel a fundamental insecurity that may not be touched by therapy alone or by superficial changes in lifestyle.

Since these absolute soul needs are not satisfied by the style of modern life, it stands to reason that to care for our souls we may have to step outside this culture, at least momentarily and episodically, and do things that others may not understand or appreciate. At times we may have to put family before career, make an effort to remain an active inhabitant of our neighborhood, community, and indeed our own home.

It's common in modern times to imagine that we can solve our problems by putting our minds to them—figuring them out and coming up with reasonable solutions. But, at least in the area of home, it may be more effective simply to become more intimate with the many things that generate the feeling of home. Whenever I tighten a screw on a door or wash a window, I become more familiar and more intimate with my home. If I neglect these things, the house becomes—allow me to use an unfortunate word from psychology—dysfunctional, demonstrating in its woundedness a failure in our relationship.

The same is true of the natural world that is our home. We can isolate ourselves from it by becoming fully absorbed in the artificial world of modern culture: Air-conditioning can keep us ignorant of the weather, automobiles can seal us off from trees and paths, television and radio can block out environmental sounds, and various deodorants can make us forget the aroma of the world. I'm not recommending abandoning these conveniences, but we might notice how we're becoming alienated from nature and make some simple adjustments.

It isn't enough to arrive at a mental appreciation of nature and feel a fondness for it in the abstract. Intimacy is always developed through daily close contact. It is largely a sensual familiarity and a neighborly acquaintanceship. Home is a body sensation, established by a love of textures, colors, and atmospheres. Often, when we become homesick, we remember concrete events and simple sensations, and poignantly feel the absence of comforting sounds and touches.

Often people can recover a sense of home by drawing on their memories of places, houses, rituals, ornaments, and even food, bringing these memories into present life either directly or simply as a motif. Somehow I have found a way finally to be living down the road from an old and beautiful farm. In my childhood, I found enchantment on a family farm, and although I'm not a farmer now, the mere proximity of a farm in the neighborhood is profoundly satisfying. I've known people who have found a piece of home simply by cooking some old family recipes or holding on to family mementos.

Religious traditions describe the ultimate home as an abiding with divinity. This is a deeply mysterious notion of being at home, and it is one that is relevant to everyone, regardless of belief or religious attachment. In an absolute sense, the longing for home can only be fulfilled by pressing on through the various avatars of home we find or make in this life, arriving at such a profound security that no challenge in life can remove us from that ubiquitous source of stability described by Nicholas of Cusa in the fifteenth century as the circle whose center is everywhere and whose circumference is nowhere. Ultimately home is the "place" where our soul is welcomed, settled, and cared for.

10.

HOMEMAKING

All of life is a rhythm of coming and going from home, to the world, and back. We make our homes and we seek adventure. Out in the world, we long to return home; sitting at home, we dream about wandering the world. Some make wandering the style of their lives, while others stay at home and imagine the world. Both ways are of infinite value, and both make life worth living.

World-wandering and adventure seem to please the spirit most, while homemaking satisfies the soul. The latter, like most things of the soul, is more humble and therefore might be neglected. But home provides the ground, the tether, the foundation, and that elusive quality necessary for psychological peace—security.

We could be better at making our homes. We could give them more attention. We could understand that a society in which people are homeless, in any definition of the word, is one that has dangerously overlooked the one condition that leads to creative tranquillity.

All really inhabited space bears the essence of the notion of home. In the course of this work, we shall see that the imagination functions in this direction whenever the human being has found the slightest shelter: we shall see the imagination build "walls" of impalpable shadows, comfort itself with the illusion of protection—or, just the contrary, tremble behind thick walls, mistrust the staunchest ramparts. In short, in the most interminable of dialectics, the sheltered being gives perceptible limits to his shelter. He experiences the house in its reality and in its virtuality, by means of thought and dreams. It is no longer in its positive aspects that the house is really "lived," nor is it only in the passing hour that we recognize its benefits. An entire past comes to dwell in a new house. The old saying: "We bring our *lares* with us" has many variations. And the daydream deepens to the point where an immemorial domain opens up for the dreamer of a home beyond man's earliest memory. The house, like fire and water, will permit me, later in this work, to recall flashes of daydreams that illuminate the synthesis of immemorial and recollected. In this remote region, memory and imagination remain associated, each one working for their mutual deepening. In the order of values, they both constitute a community of memory and image. Thus the house is not experienced from day to day only, on the thread of a narrative, or in the telling of our own story. Through dreams, the various dwelling-places in our lives co-penetrate and retain the treasures of former days. And after we are in the new house, when memories of other places we have lived in come back to us, we travel to the land of Motionless Childhood, motionless the way all Immemorial things are. We live fixations, fixations of happiness. We comfort our-selves by reliving memories of protection. Something closed must retain our memories, while leaving them their original value as images. Memories of the outside world will never have the same tonality as those of home and, by recalling these memories, we add to our store of dreams; we are never real historians, but always near poets, and our emotion is perhaps nothing but an expression of a poetry that was lost.

Thus, by approaching the house images with care not to break up the solidarity of memory and imagination, we may hope to make others feel all the psychological elasticity of an image that moves us at an unimaginable depth. Through poems, perhaps more than through recollections, we touch the ultimate poetic depth of the space of the house.

This being the case, if I were asked to name the chief benefit of the house, I should say: the house shelters daydreaming, the house protects the dreamer, the house allows one to dream in peace. Thought and experience are not the only things that sanction human values. The values that belong to daydreaming mark humanity in its depths. Daydreaming even has a privilege of autovalorization. It derives direct pleasure from its own being. Therefore, the places in which we have *experienced daydreaming* reconstitute themselves in a new daydream, and it is because our memories of former dwelling-places are relived as daydreams that these dwelling-places of the past remain in us for all time.

Now my aim is clear: I must show that the house is one of the greatest powers of integration for the thoughts, memories and dreams of mankind. The binding principle in this integration is the daydream. Past, present and future give the house different dynamisms, which often interfere, at times opposing, at others, stimulating one another. In the life of a man, the house thrusts aside contingencies, its councils of continuity are unceasing. Without it, man would be a dispersed being. It maintains him through the storms of the heavens and through those of life. It is body and soul. It is the human being's first world. Before he is "cast into the world," as claimed by certain hasty metaphysics, man is laid in the cradle of the house. And always, in our daydreams, the house is a large cradle. A concrete metaphysics cannot neglect this fact, this simple fact, all the more, since this fact is a value, an important value, to which we return in our daydreaming. Being is already a value. Life begins well, it begins enclosed, protected, all warm in the bosom of the house.

GASTON BACHELARD, *Poetics of Space*

". . . what I want and all my days I pine for
is to go back to my house and see my day of homecoming.
And if some god batters me far out on the wine-blue water,
I will endure it, keeping a stubborn spirit inside me,
for already I have suffered much and done much hard work
on the waves and in the fighting. So let this adventure follow."

HOMER, *Odyssey*

oikos, house, not only of built houses, but of any dwelling-place; as
that of Achilles at Troy, of the Cyclops' cave, of a tent, as coming
home. 2. room, chamber, dining hall, room in a temple, a single
house. 3. of public buildings, meeting-house, hall; of treasuries at
Delos, of a funerary monument. 4. a cage for birds. 5. astrological,
domicile of a planet. II. one's household goods, substance, estate,
inheritance. III. a reigning house, also of any family.

LIDDELL-SCOTT, *Greek Lexicon*

People cannot maintain their spiritual roots and their connections to
the past if the physical world they live in does not also sustain these
roots.

Informal experiments in our communities have led us to believe
that people agree, to an astonishing extent, about the sites which do
embody people's relation to the land and to the past. It seems, in
other words, as though "the" sacred sites for an area exist as objective
communal realities.

If this is so, it is then of course essential that these specific sites be
preserved and made important. Destruction of sites which have
become part of the communal consciousness, in an agreed and widespread sense, must inevitably create gaping wounds in the communal body.

Traditional societies have always recognized the importance of
these sites. Mountains are marked as places of special pilgrimage;
rivers and bridges become holy; a building or a tree, or rock or stone,
takes on the power through which people can connect themselves to
their own past.

But modern society often ignores the psychological importance of
these sites. They are bulldozed, developed, changed, for political and
economic reasons, without regard for these simple but fundamental
emotional matters; or they are simply ignored.

We suggest the following two steps.

1. In any geographic area—large or small—ask a large number of people which sites and which places make them feel the most contact with the area; which sites stand most for the important values of the past, and which ones embody their connection to the land. Then insist that these sites be actively preserved.

2. Once the sites are chosen and preserved, embellish them in a way which intensifies their public meaning. We believe that the best way to intensify a site is through a progression of areas which people pass through as they approach the site. This is the principle of "nested precincts," discussed in detail under the pattern HOLY GROUND.

A garden which can be reached only by passing through a series of outer gardens keeps its secrecy. A temple which can be reached only by passing through a sequence of approach courts is able to be a special thing in a man's heart. The magnificence of a mountain peak is increased by the difficulty of reaching the upper valleys from which it can be seen; the beauty of a woman is intensified by the slowness of her unveiling; the great beauty of a river bank—its rushes, water rats, small fish, wild flowers—are violated by a too direct approach; even the ecology cannot stand up to the too direct approach—the thing will simply be devoured.

We must therefore build around a sacred site a series of spaces which gradually intensify and converge on the site. The site itself becomes a kind of inner sanctum, at the core. And if the site is very large—a mountain—the same approach can be taken with special places from which it can be seen—an inner sanctum, reached past many levels, which is not the mountain, but a garden, say, from which the mountain can be seen in special beauty.

Therefore:

Whether the sacred sites are large or small, whether they are at the center of the towns, in neighborhoods, or in the deepest country-side, establish ordinances which will protect them absolutely—so that our roots in the visible surroundings cannot be violated.

CHRISTOPHER ALEXANDER, *A Pattern Language*

There was a time in our past when one could walk down any street and be surrounded by harmonious buildings. Such a street wasn't perfect, it wasn't necessarily even pretty, but it was alive. The old buildings smiled, while our new buildings are faceless. The old buildings sang, while the buildings of our age have no music in them.

JONATHAN HALE, The Old Way of Seeing

The excavation of the Palace at Knossos which first brought Minoan civilization to light was also responsible for establishing the initial picture of Minoan religion. Temples, it seemed, were unknown in this religion; instead there were small cult chambers in the palaces and houses, identified by votive gifts, cult implements, and symbols such as the horns and double axe. Nevertheless, serious uncertainties still remain in regard to both interpretation and reconstruction.

WALTER BURKERT, Greek Religion

Hestia,
you who have received the highest honor,
to have your seat forever
in the enormous houses of all the gods
and all the men who walk on the earth,
it is a beautiful gift you have received,
it is a beautiful honor.
Without you, mankind would have no feasts,
since no one could begin the first and last drink
of honey-like wine without an offering
to Hestia.

And you too, Argeiphontes, son of Zeus and Maia,
messenger of the gods with your gold wand,
giver of good things, be good to me,

protect me along with the venerable and dear
Hestia.
Come, both of you inhabit this beautiful house
with mutual feelings of friendship.
You accompany good work with intelligence
and youth.

Hello, daughter of Cronos,
you too, Hermes, with your gold wand.
As for me, I will remember you in another song.

HOMERIC HYMN

Hestia's value in psychological life is her ability to mediate soul by giving a place to congregate, a gathering point. And through this point the psyche and world merge. Hestia allows *spaciality* to be a form of *psychological reality.* The Greeks never forsook this truth for a purely geometric view of space. Spaciality had a divine aspect. According to Rollo May, "We Americans have very little sense of sacredness of space." May quotes De Tocqueville as saying, "In the United States, a man builds a house in which to spend his old age, and he sells it before the roof is on. . . ."

But the ancients knew that the circularity of the hearth was the expression of sacred space, in accordance with the nature of a specific Goddess. The space echoed the roundness of the earth, but this roundness was domestic and tied to man's cities and homes in a way that nature's circularity was not. It is through the mediumistic presence of Hestia that the abode of man's world is psychological. Imagining, which is the psychological activity *par excellence,* is not severed from the world and retained within an individual body. The imaginal does not equal a literal interior space; and the world, especially the dwelling spaces, reflect back to us an indication of our soul condition. The dwellings we create and in which we abide (interiorly and exteriorly) manifest an aspect of our soul. The "places" of dreams and fantasies, the dwellings—high-rise apartments, old haunted mansions, basements, hallways, and bedrooms—tell us much about where our soul is at the moment.

BARBARA KIRKSEY, "Hestia"

Renaissance artists firmly adhered to the Pythagorean concept "All is Number" and, guided by Plato and the neo-Platonists and supported by a long chain of theologians from Augustine onwards, they were convinced of the mathematical and harmonic structure of the universe and all creation. If the laws of harmonic numbers pervade everything from the celestial spheres to the most humble life on earth, then our very souls must conform to this harmony. It is, according to Alberti, an inborn sense that makes us aware of harmony; he maintains, in other words, that the perception of harmony through the senses is possible by virtue of the affinity of our souls. This implies that if a church has been built in accordance with essential mathematical harmonies, we react instinctively, an inner sense tells us, even without rational analysis, when the building we are in partakes of the vital force which lies behind all matter and binds the universe together. Without such sympathy between the microcosm of man and the macrocosm of God, prayer cannot be effective. A writer like Pacioli goes so far as to say that divine functions are of little value if the church has not been built "with correct proportions" ("con debita proportione"). It follows that perfect proportions must be applied to churches, whether or not the exact relationships are manifest to the "outward" eye.

RUDOLF WITTKOWER, *Architectural Principles*

There is ground for taking the house as a *tool for analysis* of the human soul. With the help of this tool, can we not find within ourselves, while dreaming in our own modest homes, the consolations of the cave? Are the towers of our souls razed for all time? Are we to remain, to quote Gèrard de Nerval's famous line, beings whose "towers have been destroyed"? Not only our memories, but the things we have forgotten are "housed." Our soul is an abode. And by remembering "houses" and "rooms," we learn to "abide" within ourselves. Now everything becomes clear, the house images move in both directions: they are in us as much as we are in them.

GASTON BACHELARD, *Poetics of Space*

11.

Landscapes and City Places

One of the reasons it's difficult to find a place where we can sit down these days is that it's difficult to find a real place. Many of us move so often from region to region that we don't have the time needed really to get to know a place. A place makes friends slowly and shyly. It's also difficult to perceive a place that is wrapped in familiar chain stores and memorized billboard ads and neon signs blocking our views of the homes and the terrain.

We build our homes and cities more for function than for personhood. We seem to have lost the art of making a home in and out of the place. We could move many of our houses and city buildings to entirely different locations, and we would feel no dissonance.

All of this placelessness is profoundly disorienting, and on the positive side hints that to restore a sense of grounding all we would have to do is find ways to honor our place.

The ancients, Varro and Plutarch among others, mention that our ancestors used to set out the walls of their cities according to religious rite and custom. On an auspicious day they would yoke together a bull and cow, to draw a bronze ploughshare and run the first furrow, which would establish the course of the town walls. The fathers of the settlement would follow the plough, the cow on the inside and the bull on the outside, turning any uprooted and scattered clods back onto the furrowed line, and piling them up to prevent their being dispersed. When they reached the point where the gates were to be, they carried the plough by hand, leaving the threshold of the gate untouched. By this means they deemed the whole course and fabric of the walls consecrated, with the exception of the gates, which could not rightly be called sacred.

Dionysius of Halicarnassus says that in the time of Romulus it was customary, when founding a city, for the elders to make a sacrifice and light fires in front of the tents; they would then lead out the people to expiate themselves, by leaping through the flames. Anyone unclean was thought unworthy to partake in the ceremony. This is what they did.

Elsewhere, I find that it was customary to mark out the line of the intended wall with a trail of powdered white earth, known as "pure." When Alexander founded Faro, for want of this type of earth he used flour instead. This gave the soothsayers the opportunity to predict its future: the study of omens of this kind, during the first few days of existence, enabled them, so they thought, to foretell the destiny of a town.

LEON BATTISTA ALBERTI, *On the Art of Building*

What has always struck me about the Tibetan analysis of suffering and its response in the form of compassion—compassion as the basis of a religion—is its emphasis on the wilderness, not merely as metaphor, which was the case in Sinai, I believe, but as a viable proving ground for life. The painting and sculpture suggests this. If you can appreciate the beauty of a glacier at dawn or survive your first winter on the Tibetan plateau, you will find it easier, then, to cherish the company of birds or to sit in an enclosed courtyard, adrift in primrose, painting the surroundings. Paintings abound in the monasteries. Often they are signed, because the whole notion of Tibetan art is that the act of creation is an act of worship, bringing merit to the artist.

If there is room in your heart for a twenty-two-thousand-foot mountain, then there is certainly room for an ant. All creatures are caught out in the gale, according to Buddha. Man, the builder of monasteries, fashioner of mangers, creator of art, must alleviate their suffering. It is his responsibility to do so, lest he suffer intolerable pangs of conscience for having abandoned needier creatures than himself. The wild ass brays, the yaks groan, snow leopards whine, the mastiffs bark mournfully; even the predators, haplessly chattering in the cold, get sick and die. All organisms call to one another in the Himalayas. The Buddhist is attuned to those calls at all times. That is his discipline, his vision.

MICHAEL TOBIAS, *A Vision of Nature*

The position of Tibet atop the world's highest mountains is its single most important characteristic as an imaginal landscape. One has to go *up* just to imagine Tibet. The mountain is traditionally *axis mundi*, the dwelling place of gods or the meeting place between gods and humans. The territory around the mountain is held to be spiritually the highest country. But these high places have been the dwelling place of both benevolent and malevolent supernatural beings, and humanity has long held an ambivalent attitude to such regions. In the eighteenth century, this ambivalence toward mountains began to change, particularly in the British imagination. In earlier times mountains had been referred to as blemishes, warts upon the surface of the globe. But in the romantic view, under the impact of the "discovery" of the Alps by Rousseau, Byron, Wordsworth, Ruskin, and others, mountains came into their own with the new delight in the sublime. If the Alps were the inspiration for mountain mysticism, the Himalayas gradually became its cathedral.

PETER BISHOP, "The Imagination of Place"

Part of the mystery of water baffled humankind for almost all of history; how come it is always falling down out of the sky or down streams and waterfalls and into lakes and the sea? How does it get back up? Savants for millennia have had notions; Plato proposed a seesaw with water running down one way and then up the other. St. Augustine thought the water might climb to the mountain tops, seeking the stars. There are medieval drawings of water out beyond Gibraltar, in the unknown, whirling up into the sky. But none had seen water moving upward, and it was 1723 before Giovanni Poleni described the water cycle that we now learn about in junior high, including the evaporation that lifts water into the sky. The wonder is that with the mystery clarified the poetry got richer: the Trevi Fountain in Rome, the waterworks that set out to give form to the newly discovered water cycle, is surely the greatest, richest, most impressive, and most wondrous fountain yet devised.

Its main glory is the water falling in every manner possible—spouts, wiers, splashes—and finally at the bottom jetting into the air to help suggest the continuousness of the water cycle. The giant statue of Oceanus presides over it all, flanked by Abundance and Fertility and backed by a tablet showing a dancing Virgo, who showed Augustan soldiers the source in the suburbs of Rome of the Aqua Vergine that feeds the Trevi. Below Oceanus and his attendants there are sea horses, one wild and one tame, in the charge of tritons. The figures are of Carrara marble, white and smooth. The rocks and plants are travertine, smooth where the water is flowing, rough where it is not. At the bottom, sunken below the piazza, the water suggests the ocean with tide pools at its edge, from which spouts seek the heavens again. Here is water unabridged.

CHARLES MOORE, *Chambers for a Memory Palace*

Above all, water is seductive. Aphrodite, the goddess of beauty and pleasure, is born from the sea, and Dionysos arrives from the waters. Travel posters of Cancun, even Fort Lauderdale, continue to lure us, just as the mythical nixies and mermaids tempted our ancestors into enchantment. . . . Waters were alive, living beings—and one had to know who it was living in the water: a dragon who could suck you in the maelstrom, a nymph who could drown you in her embrace. These fears of capture by water still echo in our fantasies of pirates, of the great white shark, the giant clam, the enwrapping squid. I wonder what dream figure, what mermaids or dragons, inhabits our Town Lake project? What is its allure? Are we being sucked in? Over our heads? Too deep to get out? Will the taxpayers take a bath? . . .

The dreams in the people of a city are its waters; they make any city an affluent watering place—even Dallas. I suggest to you that Dallas is dry not because it has no big river or bay but because whatever it dreams, it right away places into dry concrete, continually actualizing. Town Lake could make us drier simply by being built, by losing the dream in the project. . . .

If we look closely into the roots of the Greek word for city, *polis,* we find that these roots draw from a pool of meanings related to water. The Sanscrit-Indo-Iranian-Aryan syllable of polis goes back to words meaning pour, flow, fill, fill up, swim. . . . The very word *polis* locates city in the wet regions of the soul. For the true meaning of city is full, pulsating with folk, streaming, subject to waves of emotion, tides of opinion, ripples of gossip, and always feeling too full, too crowded, flooded. The flow must go on. . . .

So I worry about collecting the moisture of Dallas into one literal place, laid out there in another huge development. Dallas needs another kind of development—the moisture that gives pleasure to the soul is that flow of life, of people, of juices, of ourselves crowded with dreams, our streets pleromatic, full of folk. . . . The lake we need to build is a lake in the soul of the city, following this path of water, ever downward, ever spreading out to moisten the lowest reaches of the polis, the body politic. . . .

JAMES HILLMAN, "Soul Takes Pleasure in Moisture"

A lake is the landscape's most beautiful and expressive feature. It is earth's eye; looking into which the beholder measures the depth of his own nature. The fluviatile trees next the shore are the slender eyelashes which fringe it, and the wooded hills and cliffs around are its overhanging brows.

HENRY DAVID THOREAU, *Walden*

In Thomas of Britain's version the rotting, reeking hero begged his friends to place him in a coracle, equipped only with his harp, and in this floated wonderfully to Ireland; so that the same marvelous child who had been carried by storm to Cornwall, now, as a youth, was again borne by the tides. . . .

Tristan, resting trustfully on the bosom of those cosmic powers by which the movements of the heavens and all things on earth are controlled, has been carried on the concord of his Orphic-Irish harp, resounding to the music of the sea and spheres, to that very Dublin Bay where Joyce's hero Dedalus was to go walking centuries later, questioning his heart as to whether he would ever have the courage to entrust himself to life.

JOSEPH CAMPBELL, *Masks of God*

This course of evolution exhibits a certain analogy with the phases of development of the erotic reality sense in the individual, as we attempted to describe these in an earlier place. For the at first merely groping effort of the male animal to introduce a part of its body as well as its sexual secretion into the uterus reminds us of the attempts of the child, awkward and clumsy as they are in the beginning but pursued with ever increasing energy, to obtain by force, with the help of his erotic instinctual organization, a return to the maternal womb, and to reexperience, at least in a partial and symbolic sense, and at the same time to nullify, the process of being born. This view corresponds also with Freud's conception, in accordance with which we may perceive in the curious behavior which characterizes procreation in the animal kingdom the biological antecedents both of the various ways in which infantile sexuality manifests itself and of the behavior of perverts.

At this point, however, we shall once again have to allow our fantasies free rein if we are to arrive at even a merely provisional answer to the hitherto unsolved problem of the motive which could have actuated the amphibians and the reptiles to provide themselves with a penis—for according to our Lamarckian conception, no evolution or development occurs without some motive, nor any variation which is not an adaptation to an external disturbance. This motive may well be the striving to restore the lost mode of life in a moist *milieu* which at the same time provides a supply of nourishment; in other words, to bring about *the reestablishment of the aquatic mode of life in the form of an existence within the moist and nourishing interior of the mother's body.* In accordance with the "reversed symbolism" already met with several times, the mother would, properly, be the symbol of and partial substitute for the sea, and not the other way about. We believe, indeed, that just as the sex cells of the higher animals perish in the absence of provision for their protection, as for that matter do the offspring brought into the world without maternal protection, so every species of animal, as was actually the case with many, would have been destroyed on the occasion of the retreat of the oceans, had not accidental circumstances of a favorable nature and the regressive striving towards an ecto- and endoparasitic existence provided for their maintenance during the period of adaptation to a land existence. It was then eventually given to the higher vertebrates to effect, in the device of internal impregnation and of growth within the uterus, a happy combination of this parasitic mode of life and the thalassal regressive trend.

SANDOR FERENCZI, *Thalassa*

The analysis and interpretation of dreams confront the conscious standpoint with the statements of the unconscious, thus widening its narrow horizon. This loosening up of cramped and rigid attitudes corresponds to the solution and separation of the elements by the *aqua permanens,* which was already present in the "body" and is lured out by the art. The water is a soul or spirit, that is, a psychic "substance," which now in its turn is applied to the initial material. This corresponds to using the dream's meaning to clarify existing problems. "Solutio" is defined in this sense by Dorn.

The situation is now gradually illuminated as is a dark night by the rising moon. The illumination comes to a certain extent from the unconscious, since it is mainly dreams that put us on the track of enlightenment. This dawning light corresponds to the *albedo,* the moonlight which in the opinion of some alchemists heralds the rising sun. The growing redness (*rubedo*) which now follows denotes an increase of warmth and light.

C. G. JUNG, *Mysterium Coniunctionis*

First of all is the question of the place, still only partly our own and which, in some strange way, we tend to feel is threatened by us. We do not trust ourselves in relation to it. Twenty years ago we began to become aware that our modern architecture and urbanism were ruining it with enormous rapidity. Redevelopment followed, with what came to be one social and urbanistic horror piled on another, slashing cruel wounds in our cities and our people that have not yet been healed. In most of our cities, that is, especially in those of our own Northeast. But elsewhere, as in the famous Sunbelt, a clear new pattern has emerged out of the turmoil of the past twenty years. Dallas shows it; Houston even more so. Their shining curtain-wall towers and rings of freeways are of course direct legacies from the International Style of modern architecture and planning, which was obsessed with the free passage of the automobile. But the result has been a peculiarly American structure, growing out of longstanding

American attitudes and conditions. Only in America, for example, do the towers rise with no one in the streets. The cars circle endlessly on the freeways around the blank and glittering slabs. The suburbs stretch out without end; new battalions of towers suddenly shoot up among them. Is it a city or several cities? The energy is enormous, the power overwhelming; everything of any age that stands in its way is swallowed up by it. The old, along with the poor, are helpless before it. There is no center. The point of it all is hard to grasp, because the relationships all seem to be by car, plane, and computer with other towers far off, in other cities out of sight and awareness. With the landscape, there seems to be no relationship at all. And here we become most uneasy. North of Dallas, a gentle, dry, parklike country rolls out, ideal for horses, studded with thin groves of live oak, beautiful in scale. What does the city have to do with that Arcadian landscape? Nothing, though it would like to build a racetrack there. . . .

Here New Haven is indeed ideal: a perfect square, made up of nine smaller squares of which the central one is common land. It is wholly abstract and imported but not wholly unrelated to the place. Colonial drawings show the grid canted off a perfect north-south orientation, in order, apparently, both to fit between two small rivers running into the harbor and to afford straight views down its streets toward the spectacular red plugs of the two small mountains, East Rock and West Rock, that bound the site on its inland side.

The ritual life of the town did not, however, focus outward upon those natural forms. It turned inward, toward the center of the central square. There the original meeting house stood, itself a square, like the one that still exists at Hingham, Massachusetts. There the congregation, too, all faced inward toward each other and toward the preacher, who was unemphatically positioned to one side. A later schematic plan of New Haven, drawn up in the late nineteenth century from the records of the original settlement of 1641, shows that the lots of the town were assigned to individuals, alone or as the head of households. When the beautiful plan of 1748 was made (by James Wadsworth, an undergraduate at Yale), each family could be seen as ensconced in its single-family house, each on its own lot and set well back from its boundaries on what would, at some point, become its own lawn. Eventually there might be a picket fence and a sidewalk, beyond which would stretch another thin grass plot, planted with trees and bordering the street.

VINCENT SCULLY, *Household Gods*

In front of the Palace of Nestor in Pylos there stands a stone which always glistens with oil and on which the king takes his seat. Stones glistening with oil stand at crossroads; whoever it was that had made libation there, the superstitious man at least is careful to demonstrate his veneration for these stones. In this case it is obviously simply a matter of demarcation, of fixing a centre or point of orientation. Whoever pours out oil here assures himself of the spatial order of things; any stranger who passes by recognizes from the glistening that other men have established their order here. Similarly, the traces of offerings at the grave of Agamemnon announce the presence of Orestes, and this is also the sense given by the stains of blood left on the white-chalked altar. The centre of the world is, as mythology knows, the Omphalos stone at Delphi; this too is a place of libations.

WALTER BURKERT, *Greek Religion*

Dionysos generally prefers modest dwellings to sumptuous temples. The one god in the pantheon who is clearly an architect is Dionysos' brother Apollo, a veritable beaver, who at the tender age of four was already building altars, erecting walls, constructing his own temples. In Delphi as well as Delos, Apollo planned his estates and assiduously improved his property. He was the founding god of two great cities and a bold promoter of colonial expeditions. His hymns are filled with the rumor of his activities: great and beautiful founda-

tions, splendid walls, broad temple entries, impressive frames, impos-
ing, heavy roofs. At the beginning of the *Iliad* his priest Chryses,
offended by the Greeks, reminds him that among other generosities
of his priesthood he built a roof over the abode of Smintheus, the rat
god of the Troad. Compared to Apollo, Dionysos seems a rather
humble suburban god, not to say a cave-dweller. He travels from furnished room to furnished room, from simple house to modest sanctuary. He is particularly delighted to find makeshift shelter, such as
the lair provided for him in the sanctuary of Apollo during the
Pythian Games. To be sure, in the fourth century B.C. Dionysos was
also honored with great temples, but his preferred dwelling place was
of the sort he was offered somewhat later by a physician from
Thasos: "A temple in the open air, an open-air *naos* with an altar and
a cradle of vine branches; a fine lair, always green; and for the initi-
ates a room in which to sing the evoe." It is hard to take this deliberately nomadic god seriously as an architect.

MARCEL DETIENNE, *Dionysos at Large*

What attracts people most in a city are other people. It is amazing how
many pedestrian malls are designed on the assumption that what
people want to do is get away from other people. We see this in the
design of sitting areas where the backs of people are turned to the
main flow of people. A brief study will convince you of the deep
desire of people to be in the center and at the crossroads. We became
aware of this in our early research on street corner behavior. When
people meet on a street corner, do they move out of the pedestrian
stream or do they stay in the middle of it? My hypothesis was that
people would gravitate to the little-used strip along the side of the
buildings. But, we found, people did not move out of the traffic
stream. Quite the contrary, they moved into it, and the longer the
conversation, the more likely that it would take place smack in the
very middle of the traffic stream.

Learn to look at steps. If people are sitting on steps and actually blocking passage, it is a good thing. It means they are very comfortable there.

Probably the greatest public space in the city—the most unifying of all—is the street corner. Street corners are the place where so much of the congress of the city goes on, and it has a very functional reason. Take "smoozing" in the garment district of New York. If you go along Seventh Avenue, any time from 10 o'clock in the morning until dark, you will see these knots of men standing on the sidewalks talking, sometimes not talking. Smoozing is a Yiddish term which means "nothing talk." Of course, there is a lot of business talk, a lot of gossip, but then you begin to notice they resemble men standing around a county courthouse. It is a very ancient city position that fulfills some deep human impulse. Smoozing is not necessarily talking. Right after lunch, usually three or four men will line up—three abreast. They are not necessarily saying anything but seem to be engaged in a contented amiable silence. Watch their feet. The feet reflect a communication. If a girl goes by, the feet reveal what they are thinking. Or some crazy person goes by and one guy stops his foot pattern and then another will take it up. Larger groups reveal similar foot motions, and you will also notice the tendency to reciprocal gestures.

I have never broken the code about the meaning of these foot motions, but I feel that there is in these non-verbal patterns a human congress that is terribly important, and that if we do not see them in a city there is something very wrong with the city. There are a number of places where you do not see this kind of activity: something about the collection of buildings and streets which prohibits this kind of thing. Now, I could give you other ways to buttress this point, but instead will repeat my former statement: *what attracts people most to the city are other people.*

WILLIAM H. WHYTE, "The City as Dwelling"

It was at this time that Gertrude Stein conceived the idea of writing a history of the United States consisting of chapters wherein Iowa differs from Kansas, and wherein Kansas differs from Nebraska etcetera. She did do a little of it which also was printed in the book, Useful Knowledge.

GERTRUDE STEIN, *The Autobiography of Alice B. Toklas*

————

That human beings were born from the Earth is a belief of universal distribution: one need only look at the few books written on this subject, such as the *Mutter Erde* of Dieterich, or Nyberg's *Kind und Erde*. In many languages man is named "the Earth-born." The belief is that babies "come" from the depths of the Earth, from caves, grottoes, fissures, but also from swamps and streams. In the form of legends, superstitions or simply of metaphors, similar beliefs still survive in Europe. Every region, and almost every town and village, knows a rock or a spring which "brings" children, by some such name as *Kinderbrunnen, Kinderteiche* or *Bubenquellen.*

We should be wary of supposing that these superstitions or metaphors are no more than explanations for the children: the reality is not so simple. Even among Europeans of today there lingers an obscure feeling of mystical unity with the native Earth; and this is not just a secular sentiment of love for one's country or province, nor admiration for the familiar landscape or veneration for the ancestors buried for generations around the village churches. There is also something quite different; the mystical experience of autochthony, the profound feeling of having come from the soil, of having been born of the Earth in the same way that the Earth, with her inexhaustible fecundity, gives birth to the rocks, rivers, trees and flowers. It is in this sense that autochthony should be understood: men feel that they are *people of the place.*

MIRCEA ELIADE, *Myths, Dreams, and Mysteries*

————

The physician must give heed to the region in which the patient lives, that is to say, to its type and peculiarities. For one country is different from another; its earth is different, as are its stones, wines, bread, meat, and everything that grows and thrives in a specific region. This means that each country, in addition to the general properties common to the whole world, also has its own specific properties. The physician should take this into account and know it, and accordingly he should also be a cosmographer and geographer, well versed in these disciplines.

PARACELSUS

The dragon, being what he was, the living embodiment of underground waters, a creature of dread and wonderful shapes and powers, was seen in the whole system of springs, their underground channels, the issuing streams, and the sea into which they flowed. At every spring one of his eyes looked forth.

But the particular spring may very well be a wife or daughter of the dragon, as the earth from which he rises is his mother. Every spring, we know, had its nymph, who might be beneficent or evil. The good nymph might become distinguished from the bad nymph, and yet both be housed in the same spring: such is the inconsistency that meets us at every turn on this level of thought. So on the scenes of the combat myth the nymph becomes identified with the dragoness: Delphyne, Telphusa, Sybaris, Dirke, Sphinx. In the spring, in the underground waters, dragon and dragoness live together.

Springs rise from the lower depths, the realm of death, and are therefore chthonian powers. It was early in mankind's history that prophecy and divination were associated with underworld powers and the dead. So the spring, a living deity that rises from the lower world, must have prophetic powers. There one can call forth spirits, dream visions, from the deep. So oracular shrines grow up around springs, where men receive visions and responses from the dragon-lord and the dragoness-nymph. The ancient *mantis* of the Corycian oracle could later be called Python, Poseidon, Earth, Night.

JOSEPH FONTENROSE, *Python*

———————

All Greek sacred architecture explores and praises the character of a god or a group of gods in a specific place. That place is itself holy and, before the temple was built upon it, embodied the whole of the deity as a recognized natural force. With the coming of the temple, housing its image within it and itself developed as a sculptural embodiment of the god's presence and character, the meaning becomes double, both of the deity as in nature and the god as imagined by men. Therefore, the formal elements of any Greek sanctuary are, first, the specifically sacred landscape in which it is set and, second, the buildings that are placed within it.

The landscape and the temples together form the architectural whole, were intended by the Greeks to do so, and must therefore be seen in relation to each other. Edith Hamilton echoed Choisy and put the problem in simplest visual terms when she wrote:

> to the Greek architect the setting of his temple was all-important. He planned it seeing it in clear outline against sea or sky, determining its size by its situation on plain or hilltop or the wide plateau of an acropolis. . . . He did not think of it in and for itself, as just the building he was making; he conceived of it in relation to the hills and the seas and the arch of the sky. . . . So the Greek temple, conceived as a part of its setting, was simplified, the simplest of all the great buildings of the world . . .

VINCENT SCULLY, *The Earth, the Temple, and the Gods*

———————

Daily encounters with the city of the world are imaginative moments to the child's mind. To the imagination, events are stories, people are figures, things and words are images. To the imagination, the world itself is a mother, a great mother. We are nestled in its language, held by its institutions, nourished by its things. The great mother-complex that so afflicts our Western psyche—its dread and fascination with matter, its denial of dependency that we call Free Will, the oral craving of consumer economics as cure for depression—cannot be resolved by personal therapy alone. Personal therapy as cure, and that notion of cure itself, is an apotropaic defense against her—banning the city from the consulting room. The little mother of the consulting room can take care of us for a while, but outside lies the great wide world, and only the great wide world can cure us—not *of* the Great Mother, but by means of her, for the word *cure* comes from *cura,* 'care.' Like cures like because likes care for each other. The city itself mothers us once we recover the child of imagination.

We need but remember that the city, the *metro-polis,* means at root a streaming, flowing, thronging Mother. We are her children, and she can nourish our imaginations if we nourish hers. So, the *magna mater* is not the *magna culpa.* The actual blame for it all—the whole caboodle of downtown and the budget, of illiteracy and rearmament, ethical decay and ecological poison, the cause of the withering of our institutions: government, schools, family, trades and services, publishing and language—is the neglect of the city. And the city can be restored as mother by the child of imagination. Without that child we cannot imagine further our civilization or further our civilization's imagination, so that civilization itself becomes a bad mother, offering no ground or drink to the soul. Of course the individual mother feels a failure. The experience of bad mothering is given with the civilization itself when the education of imagination is neglected.

JAMES HILLMAN, *The Bad Mother*

I will not tell you what New York is like *from the outside,* because New York, like Moscow (two antagonistic cities), is the subject of countless descriptive books. Nor will I narrate a voyage. What I will give is my lyrical reaction, with sincerity and simplicity: two qualities that come with difficulty to intellectuals, but easily to the poet. To come here, I have had to overcome my poetic modesty.

The two elements the traveler first captures in the big city are extrahuman architecture and furious rhythm. Geometry and anguish. At first glance, the rhythm may be confused with gaiety, but when you look more closely at the mechanism of social life and the painful slavery of both men and machines, you see that it is nothing but a kind of typical, empty anguish that makes even crime and gangs forgivable means of escape.

The sharp-edged buildings rise to the sky with no desire for either clouds or glory. The angles and edges of Gothic architecture surge from the hearts of the dead and buried, but these climb coldly skyward with a beauty that has no roots and reveals no longing, stupidly complacent and utterly unable to transcend or conquer, as does spiritual architecture, the perpetually inferior intentions of the architect. There is nothing more poetic and terrible than the skyscrapers' battle with the heavens that cover them. Snow, rain, and mist highlight, drench, or conceal the vast towers, but those towers, hostile to mystery and blind to any sort of play, shear off the rain's tresses and shine their three thousand swords through the soft swan of the fog.

FEDERICO GARCÍA LORCA

―――――――

While we easily imagine or project an ideal (or merely a better) place-to-be and remember a number of good places we have been, we find that the very idea, even the bare image, of no-place-at-all occasions the deepest anxiety.

The prospect of no-place is dismaying not only when pulling up stakes or in wartime (part of the horror of nuclear war is its annihilation of places as well as persons) but at many other times: indeed, every time we are out of place, whether we are lost in a snowstorm, or our house has burned down, or we are simply without lodging for the night. In such situations we find ourselves entering into a special form of panic: place-panic.

EDWARD CASEY, *Getting Back into Place*

_____

You set the stone back in place or chopped up the tree to clear the breach and strung more wire. And you looked around you in the October woods at the extended private exhibition, low pale Autumn sunlight striking through the diminishing leafy air to catch on reds and yellows of the great woods. After hauling rocks it was good to catch your breath; it was good to look, and look, and look.

And everyone looked and still *looks*. Even people who have lived their whole lives here never become bored with this looking—the old farmers I remember; my cousins now. When I was young I thought maybe the old didn't see, didn't relish the beauty they lived in. Then I learned: For more than a hundred years, anybody willing to leave this countryside has been rewarded for leaving it by more money, leisure, and creature comforts. A few may have stayed from fecklessness or lack of gumption; more have stayed from family feeling or homesickness; but most stay from love. I live among a population, extraordinary in our culture, that lives where it lives because it loves its place. We are self-selected place-lovers. There's no reason to live here except for love.

DONALD HALL, *Seasons at Eagle Pond*

_____

12.

NATURE'S HEART AND SOUL

Daily we build a world that treats nature as a commodity and exploits it without conscience, wisdom, or reverence. It's odd that religious leaders, so vocally concerned about sexual morality and faithfulness to a creed, have not been tireless in speaking on behalf of the earth and its creatures. Nature suffers when our precious conscience is caught up in our own complexes and anxieties and becomes neglectful of the world around us.

We have forgotten that nature is us and that we are a manifestation of nature. When we treat nature as inanimate, without a soul, then we are dooming ourselves to all the suffering that stems from neglect of soul.

I can imagine a "natural spirituality," a religious sensibility rooted in nature. Nature's mysteries, vastness, and beauty offer an important grounding for spiritual vision and sensitivity. Without this grounding, evident in religious literature from around the world, our very spiritual lives become mostly mental and dangerously narcissistic. Nature is the beginning of spiritual wisdom and the irreplaceable matrix of the soul.

The valley spirit never dies;
It is the woman, primal mother.
Her gateway is the root of heaven and earth.
It is like a veil barely seen.
Use it; it will never fail.

LAO TZU, *Tao Te Ching*

Don't you ever,
You up in the sky,
Don't you ever get tired
Of having the clouds between you and us?

NOOTKA PRAYER

Cleave a (piece of) wood, I
am there; lift up the stone and you will
find Me there.

GOSPEL OF THOMAS

O most powerful path
that has entered into everything
the heights, the earth,
and the depths,
you fashion and gather everything
around you:
clouds float, air streams,
stones become wet,
waters create rivers
and the earth perspires greenness.

HILDEGARD OF BINGEN

You have noticed that everything an Indian does is in a circle, and
that is because the Power of the World always works in circles, and
everything tries to be round. In the old days when we were a strong
and happy people, all our power came to us from the sacred hoop of
the nation, and so long as the hoop was unbroken, the people flourished. The flowering tree was the living center of the hoop, and the

circle of the four quarters nourished it. The east gave peace and light, the south gave warmth, the west gave rain, and the north with its cold and mighty wind gave strength and endurance. This knowledge came to us from the outer world with our religion. Everything the Power of the World does is done in a circle. The sky is round, and I have heard that the earth is round like a ball, and so are all the stars. The wind, in its greatest power, whirls. Birds make their nests in circles, for theirs is the same religion as ours.

JOHN G. NEIHARDT, *Black Elk Speaks*

Yellow Afternoon

It was in the earth only
That he was at the bottom of things
And of himself. There he could say
Of this I am, this is the patriarch,
This it is that answers when I ask,
This is the mute, the final sculpture
Around which silence lies on silence.
This reposes alike in springtime
And, arbored and bronzed, in autumn.

He said I had this that I could love,
As one loves visible and responsive peace,
As one loves one's own being,
As one loves that which is the end
And must be loved, as one loves that
Of which one is a part as in a unity,
A unity that is the life one loves,
So that one lives all the lives that comprise it
As the life of the fatal unity of war.
Everything comes to him
From the middle of his field. The odor

Of earth penetrates more deeply than any word.
There he touches his being. There as he is
He is. The thought that he had found all this
Among men, in a woman—she caught his breath—
But he came back as one comes back from the sun
To lie on one's bed in the dark, close to a face
Without eyes or mouth, that looks at one and speaks.

WALLACE STEVENS, *Collected Poems*

Freeing the definition of nature from the narrow limits of natural things and disentangling the need for beauty from the need for nature—have consequences for our daily environment.

First, we would no longer have to split the natural from the urban. If God-given and man-made are an unnecessary, even false, opposition, then the city made by human hands is also natural in its own right. Surely, it is as "natural" to human beings to make burial grounds, market places, political and social communities, and to erect structures for worship, education, protection, and celebration as it is for them to gather nuts and berries, trap animals, or hoe the soil. Cities belong to human nature; nature does not begin outside the city walls. Therefore, the city does not have to copy the green world in order to be beautiful, a habit which puts a premium on suburbia, each citizen with his private tree, turf, and Toro. Urban beauty would not draw its standards from approximation to wild nature, requiring potted trees and vine interiors, noisy artificial waterwalls that impede the natural flow of running conversation, and plastics that fake the look of leather and stone. Again, pop-art in sculptural forms has revealed the simple, genuine givenness of plastic masses that do not imitate anything prior to themselves.

Second, if we can take back the experience of God-givenness from its location only in nature, then we might be able to find this experience elsewhere. The great cathedrals of Europe, for instance, were God-given and man-made both—and these were built at a time when the large outdoors was usually felt to be haunted by evil. The soul's need for beauty was met mainly by urban events such as pageants, music, contests, and feasts centered around the huge cathedrals and their stalls. What we now turn to nature for—inspiration in the face of might and majesty, wonder over intricacy, rhythms, and detail—could as well appear in our constructions. Skyscrapers, power stations, airports, market halls, and hotels can be re-imagined as structures for the soul to find beauty, rather than conceived merely as secular and cost-efficient service functions.

Third, the imitation of nature changes. We would imitate the process of nature rather than what the process has made, the way of nature rather than the things of nature, *naturans* rather than *naturata* as the philosophers say. It would be less a matter of building a false river through a mall than of building a mall so it reminds of a draw, reflecting the actual way nature works this specific Texan geography. It would be less a matter of planting trees in a row along a sidewalk than of making the sidewalk itself meander organically as if it were itself growing along with irregular ramifications. We would remember nature in the way we construct so that nature echoes in the constructed object.

The majestic, descending torrent of the Fort Worth Water Garden hasn't a single leaf, a single loose pebble; it is utterly "unnatural"—stone, cement, hidden piping plunked down into the usual downtown wasteland. Yet that construction completely overwhelms with the experience we expect from natural beauty—its wild adventure, its encompassing grandeur. The Henry Moore sculpture in the City Hall plaza of Dallas is more "natural" than the trees around it, even though they are organic. The Moore piece remembers nature's contours, skin, and volumes. The trees, however, are engineered according to a designer's plans, enlarged plantings from an architectural-scale model. (Perhaps that is why they haven't been able to grow since having been stuck down there five years ago.) The Moore sculpture does not imitate a great beast, a mother and brood, a group of hills—yet those echoes resonate within it. Children touch it, play around it. They ignore the unnatural trees.

JAMES HILLMAN, "Natural Beauty"

Autumn

Again the wind
flakes gold-leaf from the trees
and the painting darkens—
as if a thousand penitents
kissed an icon
till it thinned
back to bare wood,
without diminishment.

JANE HIRSHFIELD, *The October Palace*

Through the frequent use of plants and things that are alive you can take a great deal from the spirit of the world, and especially if you nourish and strengthen yourself either with living things or with things only recently rooted in mother earth. Also, as much as possible you should be among plants that smell sweet or at least not bad. All herbs, flowers, trees, and fruits are aromatic, even though we may not always notice it. By means of this fragrance, as though it were the breath and spirit of the world's vitality, they nourish you and refresh you. Indeed, I would say that your own spirit is very much like these fragrances, and through this spirit, the link between your body and soul, these fragrances refresh your body and wonderfully restore your soul.

MARSILIO FICINO, *Book of Life*

The word *vegetable* comes from a root that means the very opposite of immobile, passive, dull, or uneventful. *Vegere* means to animate, enliven, invigorate, arouse. *Vegete* means to grow, to be refreshing, to vivify, animate. From these roots come words such as vigil, vigilant, and vigor, with all their connotations of being wide-awake, alert, of keeping watch. "The understanding . . . was vegete, quick, and lively," observed one critic in 1662. In 1609 Ben Johnstone described what he saw as desirable characteristics in a woman: "faire, yong, and vegetous." Such respect for the vegetable soul was not confined merely to a robust sensual life, but extended into the religious dimension. "Man is righteous in his Vegetated Spectre," proclaimed Blake when commenting about the beliefs of the ancient Druids. Elsewhere it was insisted that "A vegetous faith is able to say unto a mountain, Be removed into the sea."

The downward pull of vegetables, of the vegetable soul, has also provided exemplary images of being placed, of being grounded, and of having roots. For example, Jung said, "I am fully committed to the idea that human existence should be rooted in the earth." He bemoaned modern culture's lack of earth-based ancestral connections. As Henry Corbin put it, the past is not behind us, but beneath our feet. What better way to touch the ground than through cabbages, which the poet Robert Bly says "love the earth." The word *root* comes from the Indo-European root *ra,* meaning to derive, to grow out of. To be "radical" is to get back to the roots. *Radish* stems from the same etymological roots.

PETER BISHOP, *The Greening of Psychology*

I went to Yosemite National Park, and I saw some huge waterfalls. The highest one there is 1,340 feet high, and from it the water comes down like a curtain thrown from the top of the mountain. It does not seem to come down swiftly, as you might expect; it seems to come down very slowly because of the distance. And the water does not come down as one stream, but is separated into many tiny streams. From a distance it looks like a curtain. And I thought it must be a very difficult experience for each drop of water to come down from the top of such a high mountain. It takes time, you know, a long time, for the water finally to reach the bottom of the waterfall. And it seems to me that our human life may be like this. We have many difficult experiences in our life. But at the same time, I thought, the water was not originally separated, but was one whole river. Only when it is separated does it have some difficulty in falling. It is as if the water does not have any feeling when it is one whole river. Only when separated into many drops can it begin to have or to express some feeling: When we see one whole river we do not feel the living activity of the water, but when we dip a part of the water into a dipper, we experience some feeling of the water, and we also feel the value of the person who uses the water. Feeling ourselves and the water in this way, we cannot use it in just a material way. It is a living thing.

SHUNRYU SUSUKI, *Zen Mind*

———————

Music is being played to the cows in the milking barn. Rules have been made and confirmed: only sacred music is to be played to the cows, not "classical" music. The music is to make the cows give more milk. The sacred music is to keep the brothers who work in the cow barn recollected. For sometime now sacred music has been played to the cows in the milking barn. They have not given more milk. The brothers have not been any more recollected than usual. I believe the cows will soon be hearing Beethoven. Then we shall have classical, perhaps worldly milk and the monastery will prosper. (Later: It was true. The hills resounded with Beethoven. The monastery has prospered. The brother mainly concerned with the music, however, departed.)

THOMAS MERTON, *Conjectures*

———————

One day (for instance) when he was come to the fortress of Alviano to set forth the word of God, he went up on an eminence where all could see him, and asked for silence. But though all the company held their peace and stood reverently by, a great number of swallows who were building their nests in that same place were chirping and chattering loudly. And as Francis could not be heard by the men for their chirping, he spoke to the birds and said: "My sisters, the swallows, it is now time for me to speak too, because you have been saying enough all this time. Listen to the word of God and be in silence, and quiet, until the sermon is finished!" And those little birds (to the amazement and wonder of all the bystanders) kept silence forthwith, and did not move from that place till the preaching was ended. So those men, when they had seen that sign, were filled with the greatest admiration, and said: "Truly this man is a Saint, and a friend of the Most High." And with the utmost devotion they hastened at least to touch his clothes, praising and blessing God.

TALE ABOUT ST. FRANCIS

God, as Eriugena defines him, is, indeed, "he who runs through." He "proceeds into all things and is made in everything . . . contains all things . . . and is the creative Cause of everything, and is created and made in everything which he creates, and contains everything in which he is created and made."

At the exposition of these ideas in the *Periphyseon,* the student in the dialogue is amazed and paralyzed in thought. But the teacher chides him, disturbed that he would seek "reason in which lacks all reason, or understanding in what surpasses understanding." Then he concludes:

How and according to what principle God's Word is made in everything made in him eludes our mental insight. Nor is that strange, since in sensible things no one can say how the incorporeal force of the seed, bursting out into visible species and forms, into various colors and fragrant odors, becomes manifest to the senses and is made in things, although it does not stop being hidden while it becomes manifest. And whether manifest or hidden, it is never deserted by its natural powers. Wholly present in all things, whole in itself, it neither increases when it seems to be multiplied, nor is diminished when it is thought to be contracted into a small number; but it remains unchangeably the same in its nature. For example, *it is no smaller in a single grain of wheat than in abundant harvests of the same grain; and, what is more remarkable, it is no larger in a single whole grain than in part of the same grain.*

CHRISTOPHER BAMFORD, *The Voice of the Eagle*

The physician comes from nature, from nature he is born; only he who receives his experience from nature is a physician, and not he who writes, speaks, and acts with his head and with ratiocinations aimed against nature and her ways.

The physician is only the servant of nature, not her master. Therefore it behooves medicine to follow the will of nature.

He who would be a good physician must find his faith in the rational light of nature, he must work with it, and not undertake anything without it. . . . For Christ would have you draw your faith from knowledge and not to live without knowledge. . . . If you desire to apply an art, let it be only in the light of nature, and not in superficial action.

It must not surprise the physician that nature is more than his art. For what can equal the forces of nature? He who has no expert knowledge of them has not mastered the art of medicine. In one herb there is more virtue and force than in all the folios that are read in the high colleges and that are not fated to live long.

God has given to each man the light that was his due; so that he need not go astray.

Who possesses a truth unless he has received it of a master? No one! We have the truth of the soul from God, otherwise we would not have it. Similarly we have the truths of philosophy from nature; she has taught us these without idle talk. . . . Just as Christ offered his person to our eyes, so we have personal teachers in nature. . . . They are born through seeing and touching, and not through nonseeing. For seeing and touching beget the truth.

No disease comes from the physician, nor any medicine. But he can aggravate the course of the disease, and he can also improve it. What teacher can be better in this respect than nature herself? Nature possesses the knowledge and makes the meaning of all things visible; it is nature that teaches the physician. Since nature alone possesses this knowledge, it must also be nature that compounds the recipe. . . . The art of healing comes from nature, not from the physician. Therefore the physician must start from nature, with an open mind.

PARACELSUS

Last night I spent an hour in the dark transept of St. Patrick's Cathedral where I go now and then in my more lonely moods. An old argument with me is that the true religious force in the world is not the church but the world itself: the mysterious callings of Nature and our responses. What incessant murmurs fill that ever-laboring, tireless church! But to-day in my walk I thought that after all there is no conflict of forces but rather a contrast. In the cathedral I felt one presence; on the highway I felt another. Two different deities presented themselves; and, though I have only cloudy visions of either, yet I now feel the distinction between them. The priest in me worshipped one God at one shrine; the poet another God at another shrine. The priest worshipped Mercy and Love; the poet, Beauty and Might. In the shadows of the church I could hear the prayers of men and women; in the shadows of the trees nothing human mingled with Divinity. As I sat dreaming with the Congregation I felt how the glittering altar worked on my senses stimulating and consoling them; and as I went tramping through the fields and woods I beheld every leaf and blade of grass revealing or rather betokening the Invisible.

WALLACE STEVENS, *Journal*

———————

The clitter of granite boulders, bare on the windswept moors, here provides a tumbling and chaotic floor of moss-covered mounds and humps, which add both to the impression of frozen movement and to that of an astounding internal fertility, since they seem to stain the upward air with their vivid green. This floor like a tilted emerald sea, the contorted trunks, the interlacing branches with their luxuriant secondary aerial gardens . . . there is only one true epithet to convey the first sight of Wistman's Wood, even today. It is fairy-like. It corresponds uncannily with the kind of setting artists like Richard Dadd imagined for that world in Victorian times and have now indelibly given it: teeming, jewel-like, self-involved, rich in secrets just below the threshold of our adult human senses.

We enter. The place has an intense stillness, as if here the plant side of creation rules and even birds are banned; below, through the intricate green gladelets and branch-gardens, comes the rush of water in a moorland stream, one day to join the sea far to the south. This water-noise, like the snore of the raven again, the breeding-trill of a distant curlew, seems to come from another world, once one is inside the wood. There are birds, of course . . . an invisible hedge-sparrow, its song not lost here, as it usually is, among all the sounds of other common garden birds, nor lost in its own ubiquity in Britain; but piercing and peremptory, individual, irretrievable; even though, a minute later, we hear its *prestissimo* bulbul shrill burst out again. My wood, my wood, it never shall be yours.

Parts of all the older trees are dead and decayed, crumbling into humus, which is why, together with the high annual humidity, they carry their huge sleeves of ferns and other plants. Some are like loose brassards and can be lifted free and replaced. The only colour not green or bronze or russet, not grey trunk or rich brown of the decaying wood, are tiny rose-pink stem-beads, future apples where some gall-wasp has laid its eggs on a new shoot. But it is the silence, the waitingness of the place, that is so haunting; a quality all woods will have on occasion, but which is overwhelming here—a drama, but of a time-span humanity cannot conceive. A pastness, a presentness, a skill with tenses the writer in me knows he will never know; partly out of his own inadequacies, partly because there are tenses human language has yet to invent.

JOHN FOWLES, *The Tree*

INTIMACIES

Loves mysteries in soules doe grow,
But yet the body is his booke.

JOHN DONNE

ONE OF THE *challenges one encounters when speaking about the soul in modern times is a profound inversion of values. To the soul it makes sense to fall apart, fail, be passive rather than active, and be affected rather than be creative and productive. In the same vein, while the spirit of the times champions action at a distance— quantitative studies, machinery, digital sound and video, polls—the soul cherishes action up close. In all things it prefers intimacy over distance.*

This intimacy is not only the emotional closeness between persons but also a preference for an immediate and primary encounter with the things of nature and culture. A scientist may value objectivity in his or her studies of nature, but the person interested in nature's soul will appreciate many unmeasurable aspects, such as the history of a mountain, its stories and mythologies, and its meaning to local inhabitants.

In our modern context, these intimacy values may be completely neglected or considered irrelevant or even absurd. A person driving his bulldozer over a mound of earth or a patch of bushes may not care about the meaning of that mound or foliage to the people who live near them, but may simply assume that all things fall before progress. With our eyes to the future, which we often consider inevitable, we can easily overlook the precious value of the things close at hand.

Care of the soul asks for the cultivation of intimate ways of being in the world, for a set of standards and customs that give the heart the emotional affinity it requires and the skin the brush with real things it craves. To know things in this friendly way we have to hold them close, visit them in their flesh, become familiar with their past, and hear about them from those who have known them over time. This heart kind of knowing would lead to a mutual exchange—an imparting of their gifts in return for our protecting and tending.

If you move into a new neighborhood, you can get to know it by walking its streets and lanes, becoming acquainted with the shopkeepers and tradespeople, and being visible and available to your new neighbors.

When you travel, again you can walk the streets, take side roads, eat and shop locally. When you go to school or take a class, you can study your subject firsthand in all its particulars and mindful of its history.

Musicians have the advantage of playing notes written by the hand of their forebears, and artists can paint studies of classic works. There is no reason why, with a little imagination, we could not do the same in all kinds of learning—enter into the very being of what we're studying. Our fathers and mothers learned their trades in many cases by apprenticeship, which provided skill and hands-on knowledge not available in books and training courses.

The intimate style has its place, of course, in one's personal life, but here, too, we can become forgetful of the often simple means that are at hand for addressing the heart. Conflict between people is not a desirable thing, but it does provide the occasion for conversation—a precious activity for the soul. In some cultures and among some individuals it is of prime importance to provide ubiquitous opportunities for conversation. It's a modern habit instead to prefer conflict resolution, debate, self-expression, and therapeutic discourse—means that lack the intimacy of "mere" conversation.

Letters, postcards, diaries, homespun poetry, sketches, and notebooks all maintain the dialogue between our daily awareness and our deep inner figures, our dreams, our past, our friends and family, and our hopes and fears. This dialogue, a major work of intimacy, precludes the modern, painful condition of alienation, solitariness, and desperate quest for romance and community.

If we were to cultivate a general sense of intimacy in all that we do, we might automatically take good care of our friendships, family connections, and various loves. Sex is difficult in a world always seeking to avoid intimate contact. Marriage is folly, unless we appreciate the essential value of closeness and mutuality. Everything in our daily lives, without exception, could be carried out in a friendlier, more heartfelt manner.

Living in a world of telescopes, televisions, and telephones—"tele" means "distance"—we might turn our attention toward the heart as often as possible to give it the closeness it needs to sustain a life of beauty, relatedness, and mutual regard.

13.

MARRIAGE, FAMILY, AND FRIENDSHIP

When philosophers and writers sit down to write about the soul, they often focus on certain common themes that are different from those of the more technical and spirited writers. They write about friendship, family, neighborhood, marriage, conversation, letter-writing, the arts, home, pleasure, and beauty. Most modern books on marriage and family have a therapeutic or analytical tone, which may miss the soul altogether as they present relationships as a problem.

Our task as we move beyond modernism might be to perceive the poetry, the spirituality, and the mystery in all forms of relationship, understanding that both the joys and the trials constitute an education in the soul. We might also stand against current values and realize deeply and seriously that a good friend is perhaps more valuable than a good job, that a genuine marriage of hearts means more than success, and that the endings, failures, arguments, divorces, and ruptures that are so painful in the pursuit of intimacy have their mysterious necessity.

For the Children

The rising hills, the slopes,
of statistics
lie before us.
the steep climb
of everything, going up,

up, as we all
go down.

In the next century
or the one beyond that,
they say,
are valleys, pastures,
we can meet there in peace
if we make it.

To climb these coming crests
one word to you, to
you and your children:

stay together
learn the flowers
go light

GARY SNYDER

You ask, what is human love? What is its purpose? It is the longing to procreate with a beautiful thing to bring eternal life to mortal things.

MARSILIO FICINO, *Commentary on Plato's Symposium*

A teacher can expect success in the classroom if he displays the qualities of gentleness and kindness and also possesses the skill and ingenuity to devise various means of making the studies pleasant and keeping the child from feeling any strain. Nothing is more harmful than an instructor whose conduct causes his students to take an intense dislike to their studies before they are sufficiently mature to appreciate them for their own sake. A prerequisite for learning is that the teacher must be liked. Gradually, after first enjoying learning because of their instructor, children will come to like their teacher for the sake of learning. Just as we cherish many gifts because they were given to us by those whom we consider our dearest friends, so also children who are still too young for any intellectual appreciation take pleasure in school because of their fondness for their teacher. There is a good deal of truth in Isocrates' saying we learn best when we have the desire to learn; and it is from those whom we like and respect that we learn most eagerly.

ERASMUS, "On Education for Children"

You have noticed that the truth comes into this world with two faces. One is sad with suffering, and the other laughs; but it is the same face, laughing or weeping.

JOHN G. NEIHARDT, *Black Elk Speaks*

Someday there will be girls and women whose name will no longer mean the mere opposite of the male, but something in itself, something that makes one think not of any complement and limit, but only of life and reality: the female human being.

This advance (at first very much against the will of the outdistanced men) will transform the love experience, which is now filled with error, will change it from the ground up, and reshape it into a relationship that is meant to be between one human being and another, no longer one that flows from man to woman. And this more human love (which will fulfill itself with infinite consideration and gentleness, and kindness and clarity in binding and releasing) will resemble what we are now preparing painfully and with great struggle: the love that consists in this: that two solitudes protect and border and greet each other.

And one more thing: Don't think that the great love which was once granted to you, when you were a boy, has been lost; how can you know whether vast and generous wishes didn't ripen in you at that time, and purposes by which you are still living today? I believe that *that* love remains so strong and intense in your memory because it was your first deep aloneness and the first inner work that you did on your life.

RAINER MARIA RILKE, *Letters to a Young Poet*

So far as reason or calculation or the so-called loving care of the parents does not arrange the marriage, and the pristine instincts of the children are not vitiated either by false education or by the hidden influence of accumulated and neglected parental complexes, the marriage choice will normally follow the unconscious motivations of instinct. Unconsciousness results in non-differentiation, or unconscious identity. The practical consequence of this is that one person presupposes in the other a psychological structure similar to his own. Normal sex life, as a shared experience with apparently similar aims, further strengthens the feeling of unity and identity. This state is described as one of complete harmony, and is extolled as a great happiness ("one heart and one soul")—not without good reason, since the return to that original condition of unconscious oneness is like a return to childhood. Hence the childish gestures of all lovers. Even more is it a return to the mother's womb, into the teeming depths of an as yet unconscious creativity. It is, in truth, a genuine and incontestable experience of the Divine, whose transcendent force obliterates and consumes everything individual; a real communion with life and the impersonal power of fate. The individual will for self-possession is broken: the woman becomes the mother, the man the father, and thus both are robbed of their freedom and made instruments of the life urge.

C. G. JUNG, *The Development of Personality*

A man and a woman
Are one.
A man and a woman and a blackbird
Are one.

WALLACE STEVENS, "Thirteen Ways of Looking at a Blackbird"

The factors which come together in the coniunctio are conceived as opposites, either confronting one another in enmity or attracting one another in love. To begin with they form a dualism; for instance the opposites are *humidum* (moist) / *siccum* (dry), *frigidum* (cold) / *calidum* (warm), *superiora* (upper, higher) / *inferiora* (lower), *spiritus-anima* (spirit-soul) / *corpus* (body), *coelum* (heaven) / *terra* (earth), *ignis* (fire) / *aqua* (water), bright / dark, *agens* (active) / *patiens* (passive), *volatile* (volatile, gaseous) / *fixum* (solid), *pretiosum* (precious, costly; also *carum,* dear) / *vile* (cheap, common), *bonum* (good) / *malum* (evil), *manifestum* (open) / *occultum* (occult; also *celatum,* hidden), *oriens* (East) / *occidens* (West), *vivum* (living) / *mortuum* (dead, inert), *masculus* (masculine) / *foemina* (feminine), Sol / Luna.

C. G. JUNG, *Mysterium Coniunctionis*

---

1 November 1951

Dear Herr N.,

I am sorry to be late with my answer. I was away on holiday and your letter was lying around for some time.

You have experienced in your marriage what is an almost universal fact—that individuals are different from one another. Basically, each remains for the other an unfathomable enigma. There is never complete concord. If you have committed a mistake at all, it consisted in your having striven too hard to understand your wife completely and not reckoning with the fact that in the end people don't want to know what secrets are slumbering in their souls. If you struggle too

...uch to penetrate into another person, you find that you have thrust him into a defensive position, and resistances develop because, through your efforts to penetrate and understand, he feels forced to examine those things in himself which he doesn't want to examine. Everybody has his dark side which—so long as all goes well—he had better not know about. That is no fault of yours. It is a universal human truth which is nevertheless true, even though there are plenty of people who will assure you that they'd be only too glad to know everything about themselves. It is as good as certain that your wife had many thoughts and feelings which made her uneasy and which she wanted to hide even from herself. That is simply human. It is also the reason why so many elderly people withdraw into their own solitude where they won't be disturbed. And it is always about things they would rather not be too clearly conscious of. Certainly *you* are not responsible for the existence of these psychic contents. If nevertheless you are still tormented by guilt feelings, then consider for once what sins you have not committed which you would have liked to commit. This might perhaps cure you of your guilt feelings towards your wife. With kind regards,

Yours sincerely, *C. G. Jung*

C. G. JUNG, *Letters*

The Daimon comes not as like to like
but seeking its own opposite, for man and Daimon
feed the hunger in one another's hearts.

W. B. YEATS, "Anima Hominis"

Lou entered upon a love relationship with Zemek which was to continue for many years, and this was presumably part of what she meant by having to grow into her youth. Intent on explaining to Rilke the truth of how she was changing towards him, she made no bones about letting him know how unimportant he had become to her: she called him a tiny speck in a vast landscape, and was ecstatic about that landscape:

> Without knowing it I was obeying the great plan of life, which—beyond all comprehension and expectation—already smilingly held a gift ready for me. With deep humility I accept it.

One has to admire the rather rare ability to seize the happiness that came along, and to feel not merely glad but wholly right to do so; one is struck both by her ruthless honesty and by her recognition of her own ruthlessness. Later, she was to quote back to herself a sentence she had jotted down at that time in relation to her treatment of Rilke, recognising it as a nakedly honest sentence: "I am faithful to memories for ever; to people I shall never be faithful." She was also being a consistent individualist: each person had his *own* way and must find it, and so she advised Rilke:

> go the same way towards your dark God! He can do what I can no longer do with you—and have been for such a long time now unable to do with full devotion: he can bless you to sunshine and ripeness.

ANGELA LIVINGSTONE, *Salomé*

INTERIOR: Bus.
Most of the passengers are sleeping. MRS. WATTS *has her eyes closed and is humming "Softly and Tenderly."* THELMA *is eating a sandwich.*
THELMA: That's a pretty hymn. What's the name of that?
MRS. WATTS: "Softly and Tenderly, Jesus Is Calling." Do you like hymns?
THELMA: Yes, I do.
MRS. WATTS: So do I. Jessie Mae says they're going out of style, but I don't agree. What's your favorite hymn?
THELMA: I don't know.

MRS. WATTS: The one I was just singing is mine. I bet I sing that a hundred times a day. When Jessie Mae isn't home. Hymns make Jessie Mae nervous. (THELMA *laughs*.) Jessie Mae hates me. I don't know why, she just hates me. (*A pause*.) I gotta get back and smell that salt air and work that dirt. Callie said I could always come back and visit her. And she meant it, too. That's who I'm going to see now. Callie Davis. The whole first month of my visit I am going to work in Callie's garden. I haven't had my hands in dirt in twenty years. My hands just feel the need of dirt. Do you like to work the ground?

THELMA: I never have.

MRS. WATTS: Try it sometimes. It'll do wonders for you. I bet I live to be . . . I bet I live to be a hundred if I can just get outdoors again.

HORTON FOOTE, *Trip to Bountiful*

A friend is called a guardian of love or, as some would have it, a guardian of the spirit itself. Since it is fitting that my friend be a guardian of our mutual love or the guardian of my own spirit so as to preserve all its secrets in faithful silence, let him, as far as he can, cure and endure such defects as he may observe in it; let him rejoice with his friend in his joys, and weep with him in his sorrows, and feel as his own all that his friend experiences.

AELRED OF RIEVAULX, *Spiritual Friendship*

Quod amicus est in amico

That a friend is within a friend

Marsilio Ficino to the magnanimous Giuliano de' Medici: greetings.

Tell me, now I beg you, Giuliano, if someone should watch carefully over your affairs while you slept, would you be angry with him

because he was not rude enough to wake you? Would you not
be in his debt? Certainly you would, and in no small measure.
so you are in mine. While you were resting, I was here considering
and protecting important interests of yours.

But why, you say, did you not summon me, since you could have
done so? Even if I had thought you absent, I would not have sum-
moned you, lest I should cause you trouble. But in truth my great
love for you has long impressed your image on my soul. And just as
I sometimes see myself outside myself in a mirror, so very often I see
you within me in my heart. Besides, your brother, Lorenzo, your
other self, both in nature and will, was then here. And so since I
clearly saw this Giuliano of mine both within and outside me, I
could not think him absent. It was therefore not from negligence,
but an excess of love that I neither called you then to attend to your
affairs, nor afterwards rendered an account of what had been done.

Another time would you like to be called, dearest Giuliano? Then
you must take care to be loved less. That would indeed be hard, perhaps impossible, for you would first have to take care you were not
Giuliano. You will only reject love when you reject yourself. So what
shall I do in future? Shall I call you another time? By no means, I
think. For long enough has Love called both of us to each other, and
to himself.

Farewell.

MARSILIO FICINO, *Letters*

In a monogamous culture, by definition, only one marriage at a time
is allowed; if I desire to have an intimate relationship with another
woman the coupling instinct soon enters and my marriage is immediately threatened. The soul-splitting tension this rather common
situation creates can become unbearable and destructive. It results in
a holding back in both relationships even if the tension is resolved in
the traditional manner by maintaining a dayworld legitimate marriage and going underground with the other person. Even with this
resolution the pressure to choose one or the other is always present.

For a man this tension is experienced as a terrible pull between two women (internally between two polarized aspects of the feminine), and the fact that the split is *within the marriage archetype itself* gets lost. Instead of dealing with the soul's need to be free and unattached, the split is experienced as being between Wife-Mother and Adventurous, Exciting, Mysterious Other Woman. This tricks each woman into deeper identification with her role, which becomes increasingly oppressive to all parties involved. The phenomenon is similar when it is a woman who takes a lover: Husband becomes identified with Husband-Father, the lover with Adventurous, Exciting, Other Man. This soap-opera pattern has accompanied the marriage commitment for a long time. Because of this, I believe the split within the marriage archetype has been largely overlooked. . . .

What is missed in the Western love affair as well as in polygamous systems is the soul's need to be both married and unmarried. If we can now begin to view the need for extramarital intimacy as arising from this polarization within the marriage archetype, perhaps something new may emerge. While the need to feel free and unattached within my marriage may lead me to seek an intimate involvement with another woman, won't I experience this polarity with the other woman? If so, won't it be more to the point if I focus on the split within my soul which has led me toward the other woman in the first place? I resist being coupled to the other woman as much as I resist being coupled to my wife, yet experience the desire to be coupled to both. If I can resolve this conflict in either relationship, it may lead me to a resolution in the other. If I can experience being bound and coupled, free and uncoupled with the other woman, perhaps I can achieve that state with the woman to whom I am literally married. Here is a clue to a possible resolution, a deliteralization of the marriage bond as well as a deliteralization of the soul's need to be free and unattached.

ROBERT STEIN, "Coupling / Uncoupling"

"What man
has put my bed in another place? But it would be difficult
for even a very expert one, unless a god, coming
to help in person, were easily to change its position.
But there is no mortal man alive, no strong man, who lightly
could move the weight elsewhere. There is one particular feature
in the bed's construction. I myself, no other man, made it.
There was the bole of an olive tree with long leaves growing
strongly in the courtyard, and it was thick, like a column.
I laid down my chamber around this, and built it, until I
finished it, with close-set stones, and roofed it well over,
and added the compacted doors, fitting closely together.
Then I cut away the foliage of the long-leaved olive,
and trimmed the trunk from the roots up, planing it with a brazen
adze, well and expertly, and trued it straight to a chalkline,
making a bed post of it, and bored all holes with an auger.
I began with this and built my bed, until it was finished,
and decorated it with gold and silver and ivory.
Then I lashed it with thongs of oxhide, dyed bright with purple.
There is its character, as I tell you; but I do not know now,
dear lady, whether my bed is still in place, or if some man
has cut underneath the stump of the olive, and moved it elsewhere."

"But now, since you have given me accurate proof describing
our bed, which no other mortal man beside has ever seen,
but only you and I, and there is one serving woman,
Aktor's daughter, whom my father gave me when I came here,
who used to guard the doors for us in our well-built chamber;
so you persuade my heart, though it has been very stubborn."

She spoke, and still more roused in him the passion for weeping.
He wept as he held his lovely wife, whose thoughts were virtuous.
And as when the land appears welcome to men who are swimming,
after Poseidon has smashed their strong-built ship on the open
water, pounding it with the weight of wind and the heavy
seas, and only a few escape the gray water landward

by swimming, with a thick scurf of salt coated upon them,
and gladly they set foot on the shore, escaping the evil;
so welcome was her husband to her as she looked upon him,
and she could not let him go from the embrace of her white arms.
Now Dawn of the rosy fingers would have dawned on their
    weeping,
had not the gray-eyed goddess Athene planned it otherwise.
She held the long night back at the outward edge, she detained
Dawn of the golden throne by the Ocean, and would not let her
harness her fast-footed horses who bring the daylight to people:
Lampos and Phaethon, the Dawn's horses, who carry her.

HOMER, *Odyssey*

But if I lose you, what is left for me to hope for? What reason for continuing on life's pilgrimage, for which I have no support but you, and none in you save the knowledge that you are alive, now that I am forbidden all other pleasures in you and denied even the joy of your presence which from time to time could restore me to myself? O God—if I dare say it—cruel to me in everything! O merciless mercy! O Fortune who is only ill-fortune, who has already spent on me so many of the shafts she uses in her battle against mankind that she has none left with which to vent her anger on others. She has emptied a full quiver on me, so that henceforth no one else need fear her onslaughts, and if she still had a single arrow she could find no place in me to take a wound. Her only dread is that through my many wounds death may end my sufferings; and though she does not cease to destroy me, she still fears the destruction which she hurries on.

LETTER FROM HELOISE TO ABELARD

We must have a new way of grasping what goes on in our lives our practices, another view of the women who leave their children for a lover; the women who fall in love with youth, as the men do with beauty; the insupportable triangles and jealousies we suffer; the repetitive erotic entanglements which, because they are soulless and without psychological reflection, lead only to more despair; the divorces that become the necessary path for psychic development when there is no possibility for eros in a marriage; the marriages that need to be held together if only for the sake of the psychic suffering, which then may constellate eros in a new way; the analyses that are haunted by images of former loves, going back sometimes fifty years, and how these become the redeemed and redeeming figures; or the fact that failed love often means failure as a person and leads to suicide, and why the worst of all betrayals are those of love. These situations, and the intense emotions flowing from them, feel central to a person's being and may mean more to working out his fate than the family problem and his conscious development as a heroic course. These events create consciousness in men and women, initiating us into life as a personal-impersonal mystery beyond problems that can be analyzed.

When these events are told through this tale, portraying "an Odyssey of the human soul"—a tale of union, separation, and suffering and an eventual reunion of love and soul blessed by the archetypal powers—they can be handled in another spirit: one of confirmation and encouragement. *For whatever the disguise, what is taking place is the creative eros connecting with an awakening psyche.* All the turns and torments are part of—shall we say Bhakti yoga?—a psychological discipline of eros development, or an erotic discipline of psychological development, aiming toward psychic integration and erotic identity. Without this devotional discipline we have the easy playboy's pairings of Alcibiades, anima and sex, ending in power, not love. Thus we can understand why we meet so much "impossible love": the dead lover or bride, unrequited and humiliating love, the love choice of the "wrong" person (who is married, or cannot divorce, or is the analyst, or is homosexual, or is in a distant land or ill). The arrow falls where it will; we can only follow.

Of all forms of impossibility, the arrow strikes us into triangles to such an extraordinary extent that this phenomenon must be examined for its creative role in soul-making. The sudden dynamic effect on the psyche of jealousy and other triangular fears and fantasies hint that this constellation of "impossibility" bears as much significance as does the conjunction. To explain it Oedipally or through the anima/animus, to see it morally and negatively, does not allow it objective necessity. So necessary is the triangular pattern that, even where two exist only for each other, a third will be imagined. In the fantasies of analysis, when there is no third, the two collude for one; or the analyst is the third in the patient's life, while the patient is the third in the analyst's; or the previous patient is the third. The constructive-destructive aspect of eros creativity intervenes like a daimon to prevent the *hieros gamos* by insisting upon "the other," who becomes the catalyst of impossibility. We witness the same Eros which joins two now breaking the reciprocity of the couple by striking his arrow into a third. The stage is set for tragedy and for every extreme sort of psychic and erotic aberration. Perhaps this is its necessity: the triangles of eros educate the psyche out of its girlish goodness, showing it the extent of its fantasies and testing its capacity. The triangle presents eros as the transcendent function creating out of two a third, which, like all impossible love, cannot be lived fully in actuality, so that the third comes as imaginal reality. But it comes not as imagery in meditation but through violence and pain and in the shape of actual persons, teaching the psyche by means of the triangle that the imaginal is most actual and the actual symbolic. We say, at one and the same time: "It's nonsense, a projection, all in my imagination" and "I can't go on without the actual you."

All impossible love forces upon us a discipline of interiorizing. Anima becomes psyche as the image of the impossibly loved person who tends to represent the daimon that, by inhibiting compulsion, fosters new dimensions of psychic awareness. These experiences show most transparently eros actually making soul. They also show the countereffects of the soul upon eros. The psyche acts as a *formalis,* making qualitative changes possible in eros. This maturing process provides the basic pattern described in so many fictional "love stories." The effect of psyche upon eros is primarily one of a process character, a change in timing, yielding qualities of subtlety, awareness, and indirection within involvement. These qualitative changes come about when one accepts as *necessary for the soul* all the desires, impulses, attachments, and needs of eros; these form the primary material for the transformation. Similarly, the effect of eros on psyche is characterized by what we have already described as an awakening and engendering. And this too has a prerequisite: bringing eros to *all psychic contents whatsoever*—symptoms, moods, images, habits—and finding them fundamentally lovable and desirable.

JAMES HILLMAN, *Myth of Analysis*

———————

The church's formula in the wedding liturgy does not marry two people. Rather, it speaks of "one man, one woman, and God." The third of this constellation, like that of the Holy Trinity itself, is a nonsubstantialistic factor, differing from the other two in kind, yet one with them in the wedding. And so it goes throughout the marriage, as if marriage were ineluctably a triangle. There is one man, one woman, and love. If this fails, then perhaps there will be one man, one woman, and a pet animal or a mutual hobby. Or there may come a time when she notes, not without appropriate jealousy, that he seems wed to his work, which is now a third in the marriage. And, of course, there are a seemingly infinite number of triangles when children come along. But the children grow up and leave home. So the wife seeks another third: gardening, jogging, country club, service club, an education she never finished, or a new life in business. In midlife there may come therapy as a third, or a lover for the man or woman or both. We enact the triangle dramatically and eternally. Nor does it ever end, for at the end there comes the angel of death, a crucial and ultimate third bringing to a focus the concerns and the cares, the anxieties and griefs, the unity and the differentiations of the love of one man and one woman, two who have dwelled together (*oikonomia*) as one.

It is an "affair" from beginning to end, a *ménage à trois,* a divine menagerie of love. The formula of the Christian doctrine of the Trinity, together with its residual fantasy, brings to expression what we all know all-too-well from life.

DAVID MILLER, Three Faces of God

He, who is our Grandfather and Father, has established a relationship with my people the Sioux; it is our duty to make a rite which should extend this relationship to the different people of different nations.

"O Grandfather, *Wakan-Tanka,* behold us! Here we shall make relatives and peace; it is Your will that this be done. With this sweet grass which is Yours, I am now making smoke, which will rise to You. In everything that we do, You are first, and this our sacred Mother Earth is second, and next to Her are the four quarters. By making this rite we shall carry out Thy will upon this earth, and we shall make a peace that will last to the end of time. The smoke from this sweet grass will be upon everything in the universe. It is good!"

JOHN G. NEIHARDT, Black Elk Speaks

Erasmus of Rotterdam
to the Honourable Ulrich von Hutten, Knight, Greeting
The affection—one might almost say, the passion—that you feel for that gifted man Thomas More, fired as of course you are by reading his books, which you rightly call as brilliant as they are scholarly—all this, believe me my dear Hutten, you share with many of us, and between you and More it works both ways: he in his turn is so delighted with the originality of your own work that I am

almost jealous of you. Surely this is an example of that wisdom which Plato calls the most desirable of all things, which rouses far more passionate desire in mortal hearts than the most splendid physical beauty. The eyes of the body cannot perceive it, but the mind has its own eyes, so that here too we find the truth of the old Greek saying that the eye is the gateway to the heart. They are the means through which the most cordial affection sometimes unites men who have never exchanged a word or set bodily eyes on one another. It is a common experience that for some obscure reason one man is captivated by this form of beauty and another by something different; and in the same way between one man's spirit and another's there seems to be a kind of unspoken kinship, which makes us take great delight in certain special people, and less in others.

Be that as it may, you ask me to draw a picture of More for you. . . .

Friendship he seems born and designed for; no one is more openhearted in making friends or more tenacious in keeping them, nor has he any fear of that plethora of friendships against which Hesiod warns us. The road to a secure place in his affections is open to anyone. In the choice of friends he is never difficult to please, in keeping up with them the most compliant of men, and in retaining them the most unfailing. If by any chance he has picked on someone whose faults he cannot mend, he waits for an opportunity to be quit of him, loosening the knot of friendship and not breaking it off. When he finds open-hearted people naturally suited to him, he enjoys their company and conversation so much that one would think he reckoned such things the chief pleasure in life. For ball games, games of chance, and cards he hates, and all the other pastimes with which the common run of grandees normally beguile their tedious hours. Besides which, though somewhat negligent in his own affairs, no one could take more trouble in furthering the business of his friends. In a word, whoever desires a perfect example of true friendship, will seek it nowhere to better purpose than in More.

ERASMUS, *Letters*

There is a male fantasy in developmental psychology that goes this way: the mother's maternal preoccupation makes her baby's desires her own. This taking on of the child's agenda is imagined as an effortless process, aided by maternal hormones and female proclivities toward caretaking. It is not always like this in our culture. Though raised to be nurturant, women are also taught to retreat to their own subjectivities, to take care of themselves in solitude, to identify themselves as individuals, and to experience their own desire over against the other's.

Coming to be with one's first child bulldozes these notions, as psychic survival requires finding joy in the other's satisfaction, in finding a way to surrender what cannot be accomplished during the child's early years, in wiping away large portions of one's identity that require separateness and solitude to maintain. None of this comes "naturally," easily. Each refigures our understanding of desire away from a personalistic, individualistic, privatistic model: my desire, internal, private; my desire to have and to do; my desire experienced as need, as right. In its stead, the arising of desire comes to be experienced as grace, its satisfaction seeming not as important as its advent. The mother's psychic reality becomes gradually restructured so that satisfying the child's desire is often experienced as sweeter than satisfying any of her own. Thus the child's desire has really become the mother's in this baffling psychic melange called mother and child. But this has not occurred naturally, suddenly, always, or for all time.

MARY WATKINS, "Some Teachings of Desire"

14.

SEX AND ROMANCE

Sex brings living beings into the world, but it also invites the vitality and exuberance of sheer life. Sex is infinitely more than the biological, because it is one of the most potent and creative manifestations of the soul. Sex has an abundance of soul, and perhaps that is why it is both immensely attractive and fervently contained. It creates friendships, families, and cultures, and at the same time it threatens these very accomplishments. Full of contradictions, easily distanced by religious moralism and scientific explanation, sex challenges us to the very limits of imagination.

Fortunately, we have widespread and ancient traditions in literature, art, and ritual that help us glimpse the sublime implications of sex and the deeper workings of romance. Sex is implicated in all movement toward union, the reconciliation of opposites, and the fulfillment and completion of all our activities. Our relations with nature and culture all have a sexual dimension to the extent that they involve our bodies and senses, our desires and pleasures, our creativity and procreativity.

The Ring of

it was the west wind caught her up, as
she rose
from the genital
wave, and bore her from the delicate
foam, home
to her isle

and those lovers
of the difficult, the hours
of the golden day welcomed her, clad her, were
as though they had made her, were wild
to bring this new thing born
of the ring of the sea pink
& naked, this girl, brought her
to the face of the gods, violets
in her hair

Beauty, and she
said no to zeus & them all, all were not or
was it she chose the ugliest
to bed with, or was it straight
and to expiate the nature of beauty, was it?

knowing hours, anyway,
she did not stay long, or the lame
was only one part. & the handsome
mars had her   And the child
had that name, the arrow of
as the flight of, the move of
his mother who adorneth

with myrtle the dolphin and words
they rise, they do who
are born of like
elements

                    CHARLES OLSON

                    ————————

        The Cytherean
            born at Cyprus
                is who I shall sing,
        she who presents

humans
with such nice presents.
That seductive face of hers
is always smiling, always
carrying its seductive flower.
Hello, goddess,
sovereign of Salamis
with its good buildings,
and of the sea place, Cyprus.
Give me the kind of song
that seduces, please,
and I will remember you
in another one.

HOMERIC HYMN TO APHRODITE

We have the word of Diodorus that Priapos Ithyphallos played a role in nearly all the mysteries, though it was "with laughter and in a playful mood" that he was introduced, and this was hardly the core of the mystery. Processions with a huge phallus were the most public form of Dionysus festivals, the great Dionysia themselves. In puberty initiations, of course, the encounter with sexuality is normal and necessary. The change from childhood through puberty to maturity and marriage is the natural, archetypal model for change of status, and elements of this sequence may well be preserved in mysteries, especially in Dionysiac mysteries.

WALTER BURKERT, *Ancient Mystery Cults*

Subsect. V.—The last and best Cure of Love-Melancholy is, to let them have their Desire

The last refuge and surest remedy, to be put in practice in the utmost

place, when no other means will take effect, is to let them go together, and enjoy one another: *Potissima cura est ut heros amasia sua*
potiatur [the most effective cure is to let the lover enjoy his sweet-
heart], saith Guianerius. Æsculapius himself, to this malady, cannot
invent a better remedy, *quam ut amanti cedat amatum* (Jason Pra-
tensis), than that a lover have his desire.

> *Et pariter torulo bini jungantur in uno,*
> *Et pulchro detur Æneæ Lavinia conjux.*

> And let them both be joined in a bed,
> And let Æneas fair Lavinia wed.

'Tis the special cure, to let them bleed in *vena hymenæia,* for love is a
pleurisy, and if it be possible, so let it be, *optataque gaudia carpant*
[and let them enjoy their longed-for bliss]. Arculanus holds it the
speediest and the best cure, 'tis Savonarola's last precept, a principal
infallible remedy, the last, sole, and safest refuge.

> *Julia, sola potes nostras extinguere flammas,*
> *Non nive, non glacie, sed potes igne pari.*

> Julia alone can quench my desire,
> With neither ice nor snow, but with like fire.

When you have all done, saith Avicenna, "there is no speedier or
safer course than to join the parties together according to their
desires and wishes, the custom and form of law; and so we have seen
him quickly restored to his former health, that was languished away
to skin and bones; after his desire was satisfied, his discontent ceased,
and we thought it strange; our opinion is therefore that in such cases
nature is to be obeyed." Aretæus, an old author, hath an instance of
a young man, when no other means could prevail, was so speedily
relieved. What remains then but to join them in marriage?

> *Tunc et basia morsiunculasque*
> *Surreptim dare, mutuos fovere*
> *Amplexus licet, et licet jocari;*
> [Then to snatch kisses and bite playfully,
> to cuddle and play;]

they may then kiss and coll, lie and look babies in one another's
as their sires before them did; they may then satiate themselves with
love's pleasures, which they have so long wished and expected;

> *Atque uno simul in toro quiescant,*
> *Conjuncto simul ore suavientur,*
> *Et somnos agitent quiete in una.*
> [And they may rest together on one couch, their lips
> joined in a kiss, and so sleep peacefully together.]

ROBERT BURTON, *Anatomy of Melancholy*

The Greek word *eros* denotes "want," "lack," "desire for that which is
missing." The lover wants what he does not have. It is by definition
impossible for him to have what he wants if, as soon as it is had, it is
no longer wanting. This is more than wordplay. There is a dilemma
within eros that has been thought crucial by thinkers from Sappho
to the present day. Plato turns and returns to it. Four of his dialogues
explore what it means to say that desire can only be for what is lacking, not at hand, not present, not in one's possession nor in one's
being: *eros* entails *endeia*. As Diotima puts it in the *Symposium,* Eros
is a bastard got by Wealth on Poverty and ever at home in a life of
want. . . .

All human desire is poised on an axis of paradox, absence and
presence its poles, love and hate its motive energies.

ANNE CARSON, *Eros the Bittersweet*

"Resource was drunk (on nectar, since wine hadn't been invented),
so he went into Zeus' garden, and was overcome by sleep. Poverty,
seeing here the solution to her own lack of resources, decided to have
a child by him. So she lay with him, and conceived Eros. That's why
Eros is a follower & servant of Aphrodite, because he was conceived
at her birthday party—and also because he is naturally attracted to
what is beautiful, and Aphrodite is beautiful.

"So Eros' attributes are what you would expect of a child of Resource and Poverty. For a start, he's always poor, and so far from being soft and beautiful (which is most people's view of him), he is hard, unkempt, barefoot, homeless. He sleeps on the ground, without a bed, lying in doorways or in the open street. He has his mother's nature, and need is his constant companion. On the other hand, from his father he has inherited an eye for beauty and the good. He is brave, enterprising and determined—a marvellous huntsman, always intriguing. He is intellectual, resourceful, a lover of wisdom his whole life through, a subtle magician, sorcerer and thinker.

"His nature is neither that of an immortal nor that of a mortal. In one and the same day he can be alive and flourishing (when things go well), then at death's door, later still reviving as his father's character asserts itself again. But his resources are always running out, so that Eros is never either totally destitute or affluent. Similarly he is midway between wisdom and folly, as I will show you. None of the gods searches for wisdom, or tries to become wise—they are wise already. Nor does anyone else wise search for wisdom. On the other hand, the foolish do not search for wisdom or try to become wise either, since folly is precisely the failing which consists in not being fine and good, or intelligent—and yet being quite satisfied with the way one is. You cannot desire what you do not realise you lack."

PLATO, *Symposium*

Vigils

It is repose in the light, neither fever nor languor, on a bed or on a meadow.

It is the friend neither violent nor weak. The friend.

It is the beloved neither tormenting nor tormented. The beloved.

Air and the world not sought. Life.

—Was it really this?

—And the dream grew cold.

ARTHUR RIMBAUD, *Illuminations*

The Kama Sutra of Kindness: Position No. 2

should I greet you
as if
we had merely eaten
together one night
when the white birches
dripped wet
and lightning etched
black trees on your walls?

it is not love
I am asking

love comes from years
of breathing
skin to skin
tangled in each other's dreams
until each night
weaves another thread
in the same web
of blood and sleep

      and I have only
      passed through you quickly
      like light

      and you have only
      surrounded me suddenly
      like flame

the lake is cold
the snows are sudden
the wild cherry bends
and winter's a burden

      in your hand I feel
      spring burn in the bud.

MARY MACKEY

Ed

Ed was in love with a cocktail waitress,
but Ed's family, and his friends,
didn't approve. So he broke it off.

He married a respectable woman
who played the piano. She played well enough
to have been a professional.

Ed's wife left him . . .
Years later, at a family gathering
Ed got drunk and made a fool of himself.

He said, "I should have married Doreen."
"Well," they said, "why didn't you?"

LOUIS SIMPSON

Axiom

Axiom: you are a sea.
Your eye -
lids curve over chaos

My hands
where they touch you, create
small inhabited islands

Soon you will be
all earth: a known
land, a country.

MARGARET ATWOOD

To go looking for pleasure is far from cowardice, it's life's remotest edge, a raving courage. It's a ploy used by a horror in us of ever being satisfied.

Lovers discover each other only in mutual laceration. Each of the two craves suffering. Desire desires in them what's impossible. Otherwise desire would be quenched, desire would die.

GEORGES BATAILLE

Several years ago, when a group of friends gathered for dinner, we began to tell each the stories of our first sexual encounters. The psychologist Rollo May recalled himself as a gravely serious young man, shy and completely inexperienced in such matters. An older woman, sophisticated and "European," as he told us, invited him to her room. He was stiff and uncertain of himself, she the pursuer. At the door she moved to embrace him, holding him close to her and then moving away, close and apart, close and apart until an irresistible force field existed between them. This was, he said, among the most erotic movements he had known.

Time, if one pays attention, is filled with such meetings. Not only between lovers, or parent and child, but also friends, community, and the common air. Waking, my hand meets the cotton sheets on my bed, my mouth meets the water I drink as I arise, my eyes meet the morning light, shadows of clouds, the pine tree newly planted in our backyard, my ears meet the sounds of a car two blocks east. Everything I encounter permeates me, washes in and out, leaving a tracery, placing me in that beautiful paradox of being by which I am both a solitary creature and everyone, everything.

SUSAN GRIFFIN, *The Eros of Everyday Life*

15.

LETTERS AND CONVERSATIONS

Unconsciously, we generally assume that it's important to have goals and objectives, to be heading somewhere, our eyes fixed on the accomplishments we hope for. In this context, our written and verbal expressions often take the form of debate, explanation, analysis, persuasion, and many forms of manipulation. The soul has different needs. It seeks out rumination, contemplation, the slow unfolding of an idea or a reflection. It isn't satisfied with a goal, but appreciates the process. Its revelations come forward briefly and unexpectedly, not as conclusions but as insights and perceptions.

Letters, diaries, conversations, moments of reflection, poetry, sketches— these more reflective and intimate forms of expression are especially suited to the needs of the soul. In modern life they may not be valued as highly as more spirited, active forms of communication, but without them we become too absorbed in life, excessively external in our point of view. Even if they have a clear purpose, they can be carried out with relaxed attention to detail and with an eye toward their poetry. The shift from debate to conversation opens a door to the soul, resolves issues that we may not have realized were so deep-seated, and ushers in a form of creativity far deeper in its sources than ego and intention. There are extraordinary muses of the letter and the conversation whose task is to grace life with all the blessings of intimacy and beauty.

May 1886

To Louise and Frances Norcross

Little Cousins,
    Called back.
        Emily.

Manuscript: destroyed.
Publication: L (1894) 438; LL 381; L (1931) 430.

It was in a letter written to the Norcrosses in January 1885 (no. 962) that ED spoke of having read Hugh Conway's *Called Back.* During the second week in May she probably came to know that she had but a short time to live. This letter was evidently her last. On the thirteenth she went into a coma. Vinnie sent for Austin and for Dr. Bigelow, who remained with her much of the day. She never regained consciousness, and died about six in the evening, Saturday, 15 May 1886.

EMILY DICKINSON, *Letters*

Kafka:

The easy possibility of letter-writing must—seen merely theoretically—have brought into the world a terrible dislocation [*Zerruttung*] of souls. It is, in fact, an intercourse with ghosts, and not only with the ghost of the recipient but also with one's own ghost which develops between the lines of the letter one is writing and even more so in a series of letters where one letter corroborates the other and can refer to it as a witness. How on earth did anyone get the idea that people can communicate with one another by letter! Of a distant person one can think, and of a person who is near one can catch hold—all else goes beyond human strength. Writing letters, however, means to denude oneself before the ghosts, something for which they greedily wait. Written kisses don't reach their destination, rather they are drunk on the way by the ghosts. It is on this ample nourishment that they multiply so enormously. . . . The ghosts won't starve, but we will perish.

Thinking and holding are here opposed to writing. The former belongs to "the real world" of persons, bodies, and minds, of distance and proximity. If a person is near, one can touch him, hold him, kiss him (or her). If a person is distant one can think of that person. Such thinking relates one real "soul" to another. It is as genuine a "means of communication" as touch. The souls or selves preexist the thinking that joins them, as much as two bodies pre-exist their kiss. Writing is another matter. Nothing is easier than writing—a letter, for example. The writing of a poem, a story, a novel, is no more than an extension of the terrible power of dislocation involved in the simplest "gesture" of writing a note to a friend. The dislocation is precisely a "dislocation of souls." Writing is a dislocation in the sense that it moves the soul itself of the writer, as well as of the recipient, beyond or outside of itself, over there, somewhere else. Far from being a form of communication, the writing of a letter dispossesses both the writer and the receiver of themselves. Writing creates a new phantom written self and a phantom receiver of that writing. There is correspondence all right, but it is between two entirely phantasmagorical or fantastic persons, ghosts raised by the hand that writes. Writing calls phantoms into being, just as the ghosts of the dead appear to Odysseus, to Aeneas, or to Hardy in his poem "In Front of the Landscape." In this case, however, the ghosts are also of the witnesses of those ghosts. The writer raises his own phantom and that of his correspondent. Kafka's ghosts, in his "commerce with phantoms," drink not blood but written kisses. They flourish and multiply on such food, while the one who writes the kisses and the correspondent they do not reach die of hunger, eaten up by the very act through which they attempt to nourish one another at a distance.

J. HILLIS MILLER, "Thomas Hardy"

To Margaret Roper.

Tower of London

5 July 1535

Sir Thomas More was beheaded at the Tower hill in London on Tuesday the sixth day of July in the year of our Lord 1535, and in the twenty-seventh year of the reign of King Henry the Eighth. And on the day next before, being Monday and the fifth day of July, he wrote with a coal a letter to his daughter Mistress Roper, and sent it to her (which was the last thing that ever he wrote). The copy whereof here followeth.

Our Lord bless you good daughter and your good husband and your little boy and all yours and all my children and all my god-children and all our friends. Recommend me when you may to my good daughter Cecilye, whom I beseech our Lord to comfort, and I send her my blessing and to all her children and pray her to pray for me. I send her an handekercher and God comfort my good son her husband. My good daughter Daunce hath the picture in parchment that you delivered me from my Lady Coniers; her name is on the back side. Show her that I heartily pray her that you may send it in my name again for a token from me to pray for me.

I like special well Dorothy Coly, I pray you be good unto her. I would wit whether this be she that you wrote me of. If not I pray you be good to the other as you may in her affliction and to my good daughter Joan Aleyn to give her I pray you some kind answer, for she sued hither to me this day to pray you be good to her.

I cumber you good Margaret much, but I would be sorry, if it should be any longer than tomorrow, for it is Saint Thomas even, and the utas of Saint Peter and therefore tomorrow long I to go to God, it were a day very meet and convenient for me. I never liked your manner toward me better than when you kissed me last for I love when daughterly love and dear charity hath no leisure to look to worldly courtesy.

Fare well my dear child and pray for me, and I shall for you and all your friends that we may merrily meet in heaven. I thank you for your great cost.

I send now unto my good daughter Clement her algorism stone and I send her and my good son and all hers God's blessing and mine.

I pray you at time convenient recommend me to my good son John More. I liked well his natural fashion. Our Lord bless him and his good wife my loving daughter, to whom I pray him be good, as he hath great cause, and that if the land of mine come to his hand, he break not my will concerning his sister Daunce. And our Lord bless Thomas and Austen and all that they shall have.

THOMAS MORE, *Letter*

3299: To Vanessa Bell

Monks House [Rodmell, Sussex]

Monday [23 August 1937]

I half sent a message through Angelica to ask if we could dine with you tomorrow, that is Tuesday? May we? We shall be coming back from London, and I'll bring some more Roger letters; and it would be a great treat to see you. But if you've had too many humans, you can prevent us by sending a tactfully phrased wire to Tavistock Sqre.

Oh I'm so furious! Just as we'd cleared off our weekend visits, the telephone rings, and there comes to lunch, late, hungry yet eating with the deliberation and mastication of a Toad, Mr Gillies of the Labour Party. It's 5:30. He's still there, masticating. Half a plum cake has gone down crumb by crumb. Mercifully he was ceased [*sic*] with such a choking fit that I made off to my Lodge to write this. You cant conceive what the mind of a Labour party leader is like—George [Duckworth] is advanced, Saxon [Sydney-Turner] rash, and Barbara [Bagenal] wildly imaginative in comparison. And they scrape their knives on their plates. Never let Angelica marry a Labour leader: on the other hand dont tell Leonard this, for he lives in the delusion that they are good men.

Do you like Helen Anrep better than me? The green goddess, Jealousy alit on my pillow this very dawn and shot this bitter shaft through my heart. I believe you do. Its not so much the private wound I mind—its the deficiency of taste on your part. All the same I admit she has her moss rose charm: and in her breast instead of dew is a heart, I admit. I fell in love—this is to make you jealous—(but it wont) with Marie [Mrs Charles Mauron], whom I kissed as we exchanged roses under the mistletoe. She is a gypsy I'm sure. Once the paint cracks out comes the juice of the grape. Lord how I love writing to you. But I know you never read what I write. Heres Gillies: he's stopped choking alas: he's talking about the Labour Party Conference at Bournemouth. You see, theyre old maids wiping their china, gossiping about Sally and the policeman in the scullery. I liked Eddy [Playfair] too. I see I'm a snob. I really prefer Eton and King's to the elementary school at Glasgow, where Gillies took a prize.

here's L. so I'll discuss Eddie tomorrow if you'll have us

B

G[illies]. is going!!!

Berg

VIRGINIA WOOLF, *Letters*

September 27 was a fine day, and Hawthorne and I set forth on a walk. We went first to the Factory where Mr. Damon makes Domett cloths, but his mills were standing still, his houses empty. Nothing so small but comes to honor and has its shining moment somewhere; and so was it here with our little Assabet or North Branch; it was falling over the rocks into silver, and above was expanded into this tranquil lake. After looking about us a few moments, we took the road to Stow. The day was full of sunshine, and it was a luxury to walk in the midst of all this warm and colored light. The days of September are so rich that it seems natural to walk to the end of one's strength, and then fall prostrate, saturated with the fine floods, and cry, *Nunc dimittis me*. Fringed gentians, a thornbush with red fruit, wild apple trees whose fruit hung like berries, and grapevines were the decorations of the path. We scarcely encountered man or boy in our road nor saw any in the fields. This depopulation lasted all day. But the outlines of the landscape were so gentle that it seemed as if we were in a very cultivated country, and elegant persons must be living just over yonder hills. Three or four times, or oftener, we saw the entrance to their lordly park. But nothing in the farms or in the houses made this good. And it is to be considered that when any large brain is born in these towns, it is sent, at sixteen or twenty years, to Boston or New York, and the country is tilled only by the inferior class of the people, by the second crop or *rowan* of the Men. Hence all these shiftless poverty-struck pig-farms. In Europe, where society has an aristocratic structure, the land is full of men of the best stock, and the best culture, whose interest and pride it is to remain half of the year at least on their estates and to fill these with every convenience and ornament. Of course these make model-farms and model-architecture, and are a constant education to the eye and hand of the surrounding population.

Our walk had no incidents. It needed none, for we were in excellent spirits, had much conversation, for we were both old collectors who had never had opportunity before to show each other our cabinets, so that we could have filled with matter much longer days. We agreed that it needed a little dash of humor or extravagance in the traveller to give occasion to incident in his journey. Here we sober men, easily pleased, kept on the outside of the land and did not by so much as a request for a cup of milk creep into any farmhouse. If want of pence in our pocket or some vagary in our brain drove us into these "huts where poor men lie," to crave dinner or night's lodging, it would be so easy to break into some mesh of domestic romance, learn so much pathetic private history, perchance see the first blush mantle on the cheeks of the young girl when the mail stage came or did not come, or even get entangled ourselves in some thread of gold or grey. Then again the opportunities which the taverns once offered the traveller, of witnessing and even sharing in the joke and the politics of the teamster and farmers on the road, are now no more. The Temperance Society emptied the bar-room. It is a cold place. Hawthorne tried to smoke a cigar, but I observed he was soon out on the piazza. After noon we reached Stow, and dined, and then continued our journey towards Harvard, making our day's walk, according to our best computation, about twenty miles. The last miles, however, we rode in a wagon, having been challenged by a friendly, fatherly gentleman, who knew my name, and my father's name and history, and who insisted on doing the honors of his town to us, and of us to his townsmen; for he fairly installed us at the tavern, introduced us to the Doctor, and to General———, and bespoke the landlord's best attention to our wants. We get the view of the Nashua River Valley from the top of Oak Hill, as we enter Harvard village. Next morning we began our walk at 6.30 o'clock for the Shaker Village, distant three and a half miles. Whilst the good Sisters were getting ready our breakfast, we had a conversation with Seth Blanchard and Cloutman of the Brethren, who gave an honest account, by yea and by nay, of their faith and practice. They were not stupid, like some whom I have seen of their Society, and not worldly like others. The conversation on both parts was frank enough; with the downright I will be downright, thought I, and Seth showed some humor.

RALPH WALDO EMERSON, *Journals*

———————

The Picture of Dorian Gray was his [Oscar Wilde's] longest prose narrative, and gave him much trouble. "I am afraid it is rather like my own life—all conversation and no action," he wrote early in 1890 to a writer friend, Beatrice Allhusen.

RICHARD ELLMAN

———————

As I was saying Fernande, who was then living with Picasso and had been with him a long time that is to say they were all twenty-four years old at that time but they had been together a long time, Fernande was the first wife of a genius I sat with and she was not the least amusing. We talked hats. Fernande had two subjects hats and perfumes. This first day we talked hats. She liked hats, she had the true french feeling about a hat, if a hat did not provoke some witticism from a man on the street the hat was not a success. Later on once in Montmartre she and I were walking together. She had on a large yellow hat and I had on a much smaller blue one. As we were walking along a workman stopped and called out, there go the sun and the moon shining together. Ah, said Fernande to me with a radiant smile, you see our hats are a success.

Miss Stein called me and said she wanted to have me meet Matisse. She was talking to a medium sized man with a reddish beard and glasses. He had a very alert although slightly heavy presence and Miss Stein and he seemed to be full of hidden meanings. As I came up I heard her say, Oh yes but it would be more difficult now. We were talking, she said, of a lunch party we had in here last year. We had just hung all the pictures and we asked all the painters. You know how painters are, I wanted to make them happy so I placed each one opposite his own picture, and they were happy so happy that we had to send out twice for more bread, when you know France you will know that that means that they were happy, because they cannot eat and drink without bread and we had to send out twice for bread so they were happy. Nobody noticed my little arrangement except Matisse and he did not until just as he left, and now he says it is a proof that I am very wicked, Matisse laughed and said, yes I know Mademoiselle Gertrude, the world is a theatre for you, but there are theatres and theatres, and when you listen so carefully to me and so attentively and do not hear a word I say then I do say that you are very wicked. Then they both began talking about the vernissage of the independent as every one else was doing and of course I did not know what it was all about. But gradually I knew and later on I will tell the story of the pictures, their painters and their followers and what this conversation meant.

GERTRUDE STEIN, *Autobiography*

———————

March 13, 1839

Conversation.—The office of conversation is to give me self-possession. I lie torpid as a clod. Virtue, wisdom, sound to me fabulous,—
all cant. I am an unbeliever. Then comes by a safe and gentle spirit
who spreads out in order before me his own life and aims, not as
experience, but as the good and desirable. Straightway I feel the presence of a new and yet old, a genial, a native element. I am like a
Southerner, who, having spent the winter in a polar climate, feels at
last the south wind blow, the rigid fibres relax, and his whole frame
expands to the welcome heats. In this bland, flowing atmosphere, I
regain, one by one, my faculties, my organs; life returns to a finger, a
hand, a foot. A new nimbleness,—almost wings, unfold at my
side,—and I see my right to the heaven as well as to the farthest
fields of the earth. The effect of the conversation resembles the effect
of a beautiful voice in a church choir as I have noted it above, which
insinuates itself as water into all chinks and cracks and presently
floats the whole discordant choir and holds it in solution in its
melody. Well, I too am a ship aground, and the bard directs a river to
my shoals, relieves me of these perilous rubs and strains, and at last
fairly uplifts me on the waters, and I put forth my sails, and turn my
head to the sea. Alcott is the only majestic converser I now meet.

He gives me leave to be, more than all others.

Alcott is so apprehensive that he does not need to be learned.

RALPH WALDO EMERSON, *Journals*

———————

It is easier for a naturally introverted person to engage in the process
of being "sunk in thought." But the pull of inertia or fate in an outgoing person can sometimes be as great as the pull of an introverted
nature. Jung writes that "when the libido leaves the bright upper
world, whether from choice, or from inertia, or from fate, it sinks
back into its own depths, into the source from which it originally

flowed, and returns to the point of cleavage, the navel, where it first entered the body. This point of cleavage is called the Mother, because from her the current of life reached us." And it is here that Jung says a person goes when there is a great work to be accomplished, an effort from which one recoils; when you doubt your strength or creativity or force of imagination, you move back to the source. (You may dive deep into the water in a dream or find yourself in the arms of your mother or sit sybil-like on a mound, the earth's navel, that leaks psychic messages from the underground.)

This is another potentially dangerous psychic moment: being back at the breast of the Mother, the (creative) matrix. It is possible to get stuck there and die. Or you can struggle loose again by pulling away from the inner world to forge or fabricate a way up, back to life. For the visitor to Delphi this meant directing the next step according to the interpretation of the oracle. For an artist this would mean starting the next work, bringing your creativity to bear on a piece of material, taking up the tool again. For the followers of Brahma, the Creator God, the rising to the surface meant the coming of wisdom represented by the books of the Vedas. It is said that Vishnu, the Everywhere-Active-One, sank into a profound trance. The outgoing godhead was drawn in a direction opposite to the world. In his slumber he brought forth a flower-enthroned, book-bearing god from his navel. This god was Brahma, who brought with him the Vedas, which he diligently read even as he was being born.

NOR HALL, *The Moon and the Virgin*

Amicitia vera externis non eget officiis

True friendship needs no outer formalities

Marsilio Ficino to Giovanni Cavalcanti, his unique friend: greetings.

"Are letters never to be passed back and forth between us? Let it not be that from such brimming abundance of the inmost spring nothing should ever flow forth, nothing overflow to outside. God forbid that what burns within should never cast its radiance beyond. Indeed, the reason we have often written and shall continue to write to each other is so that others may understand through our letters those matters which our minds, or rather our mind, considers, and in considering speaks to itself.

"If you wish me to fare well, which you certainly wish before all else, fare well yourself."

MARSILIO FICINO, *Letters*

———————

The
Common
Life

What is the prince but a physician to the state?

Erasmus

ERHAPS IT IS *a reflection of the individualism in current phi-losophies that the phrase "care of the soul" is sometimes taken to mean work on one's individual psyche or personality. Older philoso-phies recognize that the soul has individual, social, and cosmic dimen-sions, and so we can speak of a person's soul, a nation's soul, and the soul of the world. To care for the soul, we can't stop at the borders of our own lives, but must engage somehow with the people around us and the nat-ural world that is neither inanimate nor without personality.*

It's incorrect to speak of the human being as a "social animal"; we are social souls and can find our individuality only in community, and com-munity only where we have the opportunity to be full individuals. Even the person who by fate and taste lives a rather secluded life may be engaged with nature, like Dickinson in her garden, or with the political world, like Ficino in his many letters to political leaders.

In his letters to Bernardo Bembo and Lorenzo il Magnifico, Ficino spells out the requirements for a convivial life, a life quickened by the pleasure of living with common will and purpose. It is easy to forget that ultimately we find our personal goals fulfilled when the common good is kept in mind. Political parties can thrive only when they preserve the dialectic between their own precious values and the welfare of the com-munity at large. Religious people sometimes forget that community is not the same as homogeneity of belief. They may not realize that religion is served only when they pursue their vision and conviction in a setting where they not only tolerate but support and appreciate alternative points of view. As individuals, too, we may become so absorbed in our own efforts that we fail to give equal attention to the various communi-ties in which we live. The soul is most present on the border between the individual and the communal.

In this context, economics ideally addresses the needs of the commu-nity and the individual. We have to keep both in mind: expansive oppor-

tunities for private enterprise and responsiveness to all individuals within the community, a community that more and more must be defined globally. To live convivially means not merely distributing resources and opportunities, but more than that, taking pleasure in the other's success and well-being. Ficino's words may sound out of step with the pragmatism and cynicism of our time, but he presents a tough challenge: to give up the narcissistic pursuit of personal success and take up a vision that is essentially communal, based on a profound appreciation of the other as a piece in the creation of a soul-filled life.

History has demonstrated how difficult it is to tend both one's own agendas and the other's well-being. The stories of our past show only fleeting moments of "the sweet communion of life." The work is so difficult that it is tempting to find enemies everywhere we look, especially outside our own community. We often approach our goals with a false innocence, pretending that our national interest or religious convictions offer exclusive criteria for the morality of our behavior. An important element in the nurturing of the common life is an honest and courageous confrontation with our own evil inclinations and behavior.

Often we fail in the attempt to serve the common life, and so the emotions and attendant rituals of remorse and atonement are essential for sustaining the soul in our daily life. To confess our failures and offer compensation even for our collective injustices transforms misdeed into a soul initiation where we find our sensitivities deepened. Moral pollution weakens a society, but a people can restore itself through visible, tangible, honest reflection and repentance. The religions of the world unite in teaching us the importance of such rituals, and only a society that has forgotten the religious and spiritual roots of community could pollute itself without remorse.

We can also come to terms with our own capacity for evil by deepening our innocence. True innocence is an achievement that comes through a thorough acknowledgment of our own moral shadow, by taking neither the moral high ground nor the low ground, but struggling with the lifelong attempt to ever deepen our ethical vision and responses.

In our lifetime individualism has been so strong in our philosophy that we may not yet have had the occasion to consider radically the notion of a truly common life. It wouldn't take much to conceive business as an enterprise in service of families and communities. It wouldn't take much imagination to connect work with individual calling and orient it toward the real needs of a community. Then we might discover to our surprise that money, business, commerce, and industry can all be part of our work of the soul.

16.

POLITICS AND COMMUNITY

The self-absorption characteristic of modern life has become so pervasive and common that it isn't easy to perceive, until perhaps an accident or an illness teaches us how much we depend on one another. Our technological advances, too, tend to make us self-reliant and hidden away in our homes and workplaces so that community becomes barely visible. Yet we are indeed dependent on each other for our survival and for the spirit of community that excites the soul and gives it security.

In the best of worlds, politics is the work of nurturing community and caring for the commons—that broad spectrum of public life that we all own and use. Somehow we have allowed politics to lose its soul. Where wisdom is called for, we provide studies, theories, and agendas of control and ideology. In place of genuine community service, too often we find mere exercise of power.

If an average citizen acted the way our political entities do—reaching for weapons to resolve dispute, destroying the reputations of colleagues for political advantage, and using language to conceal rather than to reveal, we would consider that person emotionally immature or neurotic, at best. Politics needs a soul to make its work humane and to give it its appropriate communal context.

De sufficientia, fine, forma, materia, modo,
condimento, auctoritate conuiuij

*Concerning the satisfaction, end, form, provision,
regulation, seasoning and authority of the convivium*

Marsilio Ficino, the Florentine, to Bernardo Bembo, the distinguished Venetian nobleman and doctor of law: greetings.

The end of the convivium is the sweet communion of life

Now, to show more clearly what a lawful convivium is, let us look at its end, its form and its substance. Its end appears to be what its name indicates: not an eating or drinking together, as it is among the Greeks, but a sweet communion of life, in that just as we partake of one physical food, so too do we enjoy the same good of mind and life and a common will.

The form of the convivium is the proper number and quality of participants, conversation and music

The number and the quality of the participants are of the greatest importance in determining the form of the convivium. In this we entirely agree with Varro that there should be neither fewer than the three Graces nor more than the nine Muses. Moreover, from this fellowship of the Graces and the Muses, it is quite clear what kind of people the participants should be: they should be graced by the Graces, gifted by the Muses, and men of letters. Therefore, be wary of readily admitting anyone aggressive or easily heated unless such a person may be calmed by the first draught or by one short word. Bitter and deeply melancholic men should also be excluded unless they be similar to Zeno, the Stoic, or Xenocrates, the Platonist who, it appears, like coarse beans moistened with water, became sweet when moistened with wine.

If divine matters are to be discussed, they should be discussed by those who are temperate; if the participants are to discuss subjects relating to nature, it should be after the table has been removed. During the meal discourse should be varied, agreeable and brief, and a story briefer still; a fable, however, may be a little longer. Let the speakers imitate Nature, the master artist of creation and mistress of life, so that as she brings forth fruits bearing the sweetest tastes so should their discourses convey sweetness. Certainly they should mix sweetness with sharpness, humour with gravity, profit with pleasure;

let their wit be fine, both pointed and salty, but not offensive or bitter. The convivium can certainly tolerate vinegar but not worm-
wood.

We do not admit a jester, except he observe good measure. The
filthy and obscene we detest, for dirt in soul, mouth and counte-
nance offends men of discernment much more than dirt on clothes
and personal belongings.

The necessary victuals for the convivium are the fruits of Bacchus and
of Ceres
As to the victuals for the convivium, in our view misery is the poison
of life, and gloom is poison at the table. Now, the antidote to misery
and gloom is a smooth clear wine, whose potency Aesculapius
equalled to that of the gods. According to our Plato, natural capacity
and vigour are marvellously enlivened by the tempering warmth of
wine. But now, lest like Homer I be criticised for my praise of wine,
away with Bacchus! I shall take refuge with Ceres, the protectress of
gardens. Certainly we have no desire for the over-fat and oily ban-
quets of Sardanapalus. But we do not want by any means to lack the
Pythagorean fruits, cabbages and apples, for there is no easier nor
healthier table than that which bountiful nature provides for us.

The regulation and seasoning of the convivium
There is little to praise about an austere convivium, but we abhor an
extravagant one; for this is to die together rather than to live together.
We do not look for great ostentation and splendour lest in that we
discover servile poverty where we seek prosperous freedom. We desire
a well ordered and pure table and loathe a disordered and dirty one.
Finally, lest anything be tasteless or unseasoned, dirty or gloomy in
our presence, everything should be seasoned with the salt of genius
and illumined by the rays of mind and manners, so that, as was said
about the dinner of Plato and Xenocrates, the fragrance of our convivium may spread further and be sweeter the next day.

The authority of the convivium is from philosophy, heaven, and God
Should anyone wonder why we make so much of the convivium, he

should remember that convivia were similarly celebrated by Plato, Xenophon and Varro; and also by Julian, Apuleius and the Platonist Macrobius. And did not Themistocles, Socrates, Empedocles and very many other philosophers also frequent convivia? According to the men of old, do not the heroes and the heavenly beings take their ease at table? Heaven itself holds the Milky Way; the wine bowl of Father Liber, the Pitcher and the Crab, the Fish and the Birds, the young Ram, the Goat and the Bull; not to mention that Mohammed promised such convivia to the blessed. And who does not know that Christ, the Master of Life, frequently attended convivia, and performed his first public miracle at one, when he is said to have converted water into wine. Moreover, at that gathering on the mountain he satisfied many thousands with a few loaves of bread and some fishes. What more could a comb of honey want for itself? What more could broiled fish, or the breaking of bread, desire? And was it not at supper that he made the supreme mysteries of the divine world known to his disciples in melodious sounds? Here, too, he extends the marvellous sacrament of the Eucharist. And there also are read often whatever is written of divine food and drink in the sacred writings of the Hebrews and Christians.

To what end is all this written about the convivium? Simply, that we who live separated lives, though not without vexation, may live together in happiness as one. And let us remember that the true food of man is not so much plant and animal, as man; and that the perfect food of man is not so much man, as God, with whose nectar and ambrosia human hunger and thirst are continuously aroused and increased till, at length, they are wonderfully and abundantly satisfied. Thus in Him alone does the highest pleasure coexist forever with the highest satisfaction.

Good fortune go with you, most distinguished Bernardo; and with your most fortunate Senate. The whole Academy commends itself to you a thousand times; for your part, keep on commending our dim moon to the shining Phoebus.

MARSILIO FICINO, *Letters*

Those who wear out their intelligence to try to make things one without knowing that they are really the same may be called "three in the morning." What is meant by "three in the morning"? A monkey keeper once was giving out nuts and said, "Three in the morning and four in the evening." All the monkeys became angry. He said, "If that is the case, there will be four in the morning and three in the evening." All the monkeys were glad. Neither the name nor the actuality has been reduced but the monkeys reacted in joy and anger [differently]. The keeper also let things take their own course. Therefore the sage harmonizes the right and wrong and rests in natural equalization. This is called following two courses at the same time.

CHUANG TZU

In her essay "Place and Fiction," Eudora Welty speaks of place as one of the "lesser angels that watch over the racing hand of fiction" and indicates that this guardian spirit has been neglected of late and perhaps could do with a little petitioning. . . . "It is only too easy," she continues,

> to conceive that a bomb that could destroy all traces of places as we know them, in life and through books, could also destroy all feelings as we know them. . . . From the dawn of man's imagination, place has enshrined the spirit; as soon as man has stopped wandering and stood still and looked about him, he found a god in that place, and from then on, that was where the god abided and spoke, if he ever spoke.

> . . . This is the overt mark of what we might call the sacred—the conviction that some places are intimately bound up with divine presences, that gods abide in places of their own choosing—in shrines—and that human beings should rightly build their cities around those shrines and hold them sacred.

Our attitude toward place is at the very heart of our dilemma today; too much emphasis on it seems idolatry; too little, impiety.

And yet, as we know, human building stands under the curse placed upon the Tower of Babel and further indicated by the invisible God of the ark of the covenant, when He would not allow a temple to be built for Him in David's newly won city. How do we resolve this conflict in our soul and in our cities? . . .

Martin Buber, the twentieth-century Jewish theologian, has written: "We expect a theophany of which we know nothing but the *place,* and the place is called community."

Place is indeed, then, sacred to us; but our real place is community. Place is not nature, or man-made objects, but community—a group or groups of people united by a common endeavor and by love and trust. Wherever community appears, spirit descends. But, since man is in motion, community may have to take on new forms. Family may never again in our time be a real source of community; only with vast trouble and some sentimentalizing do we renew neighborhoods in a modern city such that they become true communities; institutions may not now as they did in the past provide the vitality of community that we not only desire but desperately need. Buildings that we love may have to be removed to make room for new growth. We may have to make our own communities, wherever we can find them; we cannot always choose our place. But we can from time to time return to our roots, the sacred things in our lives—and "know the place for the first time."

Memory, imagination, and spirit must redeem the "exasperated soul," caught in a desire for order and stability. We must learn to live in cities that are constantly being built and constantly passing away. The city the poet builds, according to Allen Tate, is Memoria. And when memory catches up the past, imagination gives it a new form, and spirit illumines it, what is achieved is community, that one perpetual truth which, as Tate has said, must be constantly rediscovered. Jerusalem—people—and not Babylon—buildings—must be the image we hold of our city.

LOUISE COWAN, "Poetic Form and Place"

Love is an ontological need because it personifies and gives life to the world. Not by chance, Ficino recalls all the parts of the Socratic legend and presents them to the reader with evident satisfaction. Socrates was "thin, arid and squalid," very poor and without fixed abode, but also prudent, a full-time philosopher, daring and fierce, an enchanter, a sophist. And worthy to be compared with Eros. His enemies, who will lead him to the tribunal and the fatal sentence, did not attack him for being a devotee of Eros. Though, in fact, Socrates initiated a whole culture of love. What does it mean? It means, Marsilio Ficino seems to say, to "play" one's life with beauty and eros is not only a game. Normally when I play, nothing forbids me retiring from the game, but when I play "myself," I can not do this. There is a risk, because if I "play myself," I cannot calculate or make accurate evaluations; rather I must face the unexpected! In playing myself there is—as an ingredient—some irresponsibility. I have to go beyond all guarantees. A bit of madness, a taste for adventure, imagination and images.

Without Eros, in fact, social life becomes simply endurance, the solidarity of egoism, the kindness of hypocrisy. We could not understand, in other words, the debacle of civil society, held in the vice of individualism, without considering the absence of Eros—in the sense Marsilio Ficino gives to this word—as a medicine against human harshness. The failure of the democratic project also results from modern man's inability—the frailty of his "erotic" dimension—to have a relationship with others.

CARMELO MEZZASALMA, "Marsilio Ficino's *De Amore*"

Individuals need tools to move and to dwell. They need remedies for their diseases and means to communicate with one another. People cannot make all these things for themselves. They depend on being supplied with objects and services which vary from culture to culture. Some people depend on the supply of food and others on the supply of ball bearings.

People need not only to obtain things, they need above all the freedom to make things among which they can live, to give shape to them according to their own tastes, and to put them to use in caring for and about others. Prisoners in rich countries often have access to more things and services than members of their families, but they have no say in how things are to be made and cannot decide what to do with them. Their punishment consists in being deprived of what I shall call "conviviality." They are degraded to the status of mere consumers.

I choose the term "conviviality" to designate the opposite of industrial productivity. I intend it to mean autonomous and creative intercourse among persons, and the intercourse of persons with their environment; and this in contrast with the conditioned response of persons to the demands made upon them by others, and by a man-made environment. I consider conviviality to be individual freedom realized in personal interdependence and, as such, an intrinsic ethical value. I believe that, in any society, as conviviality is reduced below a certain level, no amount of industrial productivity can effectively satisfy the needs it creates among society's members.

Present institutional purposes, which hallow industrial productivity at the expense of convivial effectiveness, are a major factor in the amorphousness and meaninglessness that plague contemporary society.

IVAN ILLICH, *Tools for Conviviality*

———————

We have considered the depth of the world and the depth of our souls. But we are only in a world through a community of men. And we can discover our souls only through the mirror of those who look at us. There is no depth of life without the depth of the common life.

PAUL TILLICH, "Shaking the Foundations"

———————

The true remedy for mistakes is to keep from making them. It is not in the piecemeal technological solutions that our society now offers, but in a change of cultural (and economic) values that will encourage in the whole population the necessary respect, restraint, and care. Even more important, it is in the possibility of settled families and local communities, in which the knowledge of proper means and methods, proper moderations and restraints, can be handed down, and so accumulate in place and stay alive; the experience of one generation is not adequate to inform and control its actions. Such possibilities are not now in sight in this country.

WENDELL BERRY, Recollected Essays

When I stand upon O'Connell Bridge in the half-light and notice that discordant architecture, all those electric signs, where modern heterogeneity has taken physical form, a vague hatred comes up out of my own dark and I am certain that wherever in Europe there are minds strong enough to lead others the same vague hatred rises; in four or five or in less generations this hatred will have issued in violence and imposed some kind of rule of kindred.

W. B. YEATS, Essays and Interviews

17.

MONEY AND WORK

In all the work we do—the job and career, daily chores, creative activity, hobbies, and housework—impenetrable mysteries are involved. In our work we find deep pleasure, meaning, fulfillment, and a way to make a living. Fate has a strong presence in our work—accounting for talent, aptitude, and opportunity—and at the same time it gives our work its depth and individuality. When the unique character of our soul blends with the character and quality of our work, we find a sweet blend of nature and effort that heals many wounds.

Money, too, is full of soul, even though it is surrounded by shadow. It may appear to be a mere inconsequential materialistic commodity, but it, too, is a totem of soul, working its magic, good and bad, in the lives of us all. Money can be full of illusions, as when it substitutes for the intrinsic value of an object or an activity, but it is also a material to be used, like clay in the hands of a sculptor, to make a world and to sustain a community.

Both money and work are valuable sources for the soulful life, but they are each deceptive as well, and so they call for every effort of reflection and imagination, lest in our unconsciousness about them we lose our souls.

The very act of putting my work on paper, of, as we say, kneading the dough, is for me inseparable from the pleasure of creation. So far as I am concerned, I cannot separate the spiritual effort from the psychological and physical effort; they confront me on the same level and do not present a hierarchy.

The word *artist* which, as it is most generally understood today, bestows on its bearer the highest intellectual prestige, the privilege of being accepted as a pure mind—this pretentious term is in my view entirely incompatible with the role of the *homo faber*.

At this point it should be remembered that, whatever field of endeavor has fallen to our lot, if it is true that we are *intellectuals*, we are called upon not to cogitate, but to perform.

The philosopher Jacques Maritain reminds us that in the mighty structure of medieval civilization, the artist held only the rank of an artisan. "And his individualism was forbidden any sort of anarchic development, because a natural social discipline imposed certain limitative conditions upon him from without." It was the Renaissance that invented the artist, distinguished him from the artisan and began to exalt the former at the expense of the latter.

The idea of work to be done is for me so closely bound up with the idea of the arranging of materials and of the pleasure that the actual doing of the work affords us that, should the impossible happen and my work suddenly be given to me in a perfectly completed form, I should be embarrassed and nonplused by it, as by a hoax.

Invention presupposes imagination but should not be confused with it. For the act of invention implies the necessity of a lucky find and of achieving full realization of this find. What we imagine does not necessarily take on a concrete form and may remain in a state of virtuality, whereas invention is not conceivable apart from actual working-out.

Thus, what concerns us here is not imagination in itself, but rather creative imagination: the faculty that helps us to pass from the level of conception to the level of realization.

IGOR STRAVINSKY, *Poetics*

This equation—"money = psyche"—is what we Jungians have been trying to say when we translate money images in dreams into "psychic energy." "Energy," however, is heroic Promethean language. It transforms the equation into "money = ego," that is, energy available to ego-consciousness. Then, Hermes/Mercurius, Guide of Souls, has to appear as the thief, and in our sense of loss (of money, of energy, of identity) in order for the equation "money = psyche" to return again. (Poverty is simply a way out of ego, but not a hermetic way.) For Hermes the Thief is also Hermes Psychopompos, implying that from the hermetic perspective exactly there, where money is no longer available to ego-consciousness, is also where Hermes has stolen it for the sake of soul. In soul work, losing and gaining take on different meanings, a sensibility that Promethean language about "energy" is too active and goal-directed to apprehend.

If money has this archetypal soul value, again like the ancient coins bearing images of Gods and their animals and backed by these powers, money will not, cannot, accept the Christian depreciation, and so Christianity time and again in its history has had to come to terms with the return of the repressed—from the wealth of the churches and the luxury of its priests, the selling of indulgences, the rise of capitalism with protestantism, usury and projections on the Jews, the Christian roots of marxism, and so on. . . .

Where exactly is the money complex hidden? Most often it hides in the guises of love, where so much soul is anyways hidden. As Tawney showed, Protestantism and Capitalism enter the world together. And, after all these centuries, they still hold hands in mutual affection in so many protestant families where giving, receiving, saving, participating, supporting, spending, willing (inheritance) are the ways one learns about loving. "Spending" for a long time in English had both a genital and a monetary meaning, while the words bond, yield, safe, credit, duty, interest, share and debt (as *schuld* or guilt) all bear double meanings of love and money. The double meanings double-bind: to protestant-capitalist consciousness renunciating the family's psychological attitudes often becomes refusing money from home which is felt at home as a rebuff of love. The money = psyche equation is a powerful variant of the Eros and Psyche myth where money stands in for love.

But finally, what does money do for the soul: what is its specific function in possibilizing the imagination? It makes the imagination possible in the world. Soul needs money to be kept from flying off into the Bardo realm of 'only-psychic' reality. Money holds soul in the vale of the world, in the poetry of the concrete, in touch with the sea as *facts,* those hard and slippery facts, so perduring, annoying, and limiting, and ceaselessly involving one in economic necessity. For economy means originally "householding," making soul in the vale of the world, charging and being overcharged, crimping and splurging, exchanging, bargaining, evaluating, paying off, going in debt, speculating. . . .

JAMES HILLMAN, "Soul and Money"

Gold and shit are not, in any case, such unlikely metaphors. The former offers immortality; the latter offers the fantasy of self-generation. The connection between dung and the creation of life is as old as ancient Egypt. The sacred scarab beetle was venerated because it seemed to reproduce itself by rolling up within a ball of dung. A single rolled-up beetle would in a short time, through the magic of shit, become several beetles. Perhaps this is the first bankroll. It shows the ultimate heroic fantasy: self-generation without reliance on the mother.

The child psychologist Jean Piaget finds that children do experience excrement as alive. One child says: "You know the noise my tummy makes? Well, it's all my plops squeaking. They squeak if they're hungry." When Piaget asked the child if they were alive, the child responded, "Oh, yes. They're alive because they're inside me. But they die as soon as they come out. That's why they like to stay inside."

Gold and shit both carry the fantasies of life-generating funds. The former recognizes money in its connection with a divine element. That archetypal character of money, never completely lost, gives to the human world lofty, regal inspiration; it motivates the making of the city. The latter supports the fantasy that creation relies upon the control of the human will, just as toilet training concerns the body's will learning the discipline of holding on and letting go, of saving and spending—the fantasy of man making something of himself. No wonder money evokes such ambivalence. It is divine and filthy; it promises immortality and death; it is priceless and worthless. What we seem unable to do is to hold together both images of money at the same time. Sitting on the throne is an apt metaphor bringing into cohesion the image of money as gold with the image of money as shit. We have to be able to imagine money as golden excrement. . . .

Money is a specialized type of ritual that makes visible the needs and desires of the individual and the gifts of the community. Money mediates transactions between them, places the relation into a context of worth, and thus supports the making of a culture. From this point of view, wealth does not depend on the amount of cash accumulated—that in itself can never be the measure of well-being. The sense of worth depends on a sensitive, aesthetic awareness of the qualities of the ritual transaction. A quarter for an apple can be worth a great deal or worth very little. It all depends on the comprehensiveness of feeling. Money shows us the breadth and depth of our love of the world. Realizing that money transactions are gift exchanges places monetary matters into a context of communal worth. When the exchange carries the complex of emotional relationships and reaches back in gratitude to our ancestors, outward in many directions to embrace a network of communal ties, inward to the needs of the soul, then we are living in a city of taste.

Money is a kind of magic talisman through which transformations of the city take place. The medium is the message. When we think of this medium as a quantity, we are in an economics of fear and power. Those with the greatest quantities protect their interests, the city develops in lop-sided ways, like a body with a tumor. When the mass begins to show its ugliness, beauticians are brought in to do a facial. When we imagine this medium in its qualitative actions, we are in an economics of delight. We may think that the things we want to buy will give us pleasure. What is so easily forgotten is that the pleasure is not to be found in things acquired for the city, but in the gathering of relationships into the flow of the medium. And money is a perfect medium; not a literal quantity, but a flexible metaphor, able to act in a variety of ways. A dollar bill can be many different things—a pack of cigarettes, a short long-distance phone call, a half-gallon of gasoline, a hamburger. Economics tries to place money outside of things, to be completely forgetful of its metaphorical quality, to establish a simplistic cause-effect relationship. The ritual sense of money recognizes no such separations.

ROBERT SARDELLO, *Money and the Soul of the World*

"Every man willing to work should be ensured: First, Honourable and fitting work; Second, A healthy and beautiful house; Third, Full leisure for rest of mind and body."

WILLIAM MORRIS, "Art and Socialism"

People usually fail when they are on the verge of success.
So give as much care to the end as to the beginning;
Then there will be no failure.

LAO TZU, *Tao Te Ching*

The growth of culture consists, as we know, in a progressive subjugation of the animal in man. It is a process of domestication which cannot be accomplished without rebellion on the part of the animal nature that thirsts for freedom. From time to time there passes as it were a wave of frenzy through the ranks of men too long constrained within the limitations of their culture. Antiquity experienced it in the Dionysian orgies that surged over from the East and became an essential and characteristic ingredient of classical culture. The spirit of these orgies contributed not a little towards the development of the stoic ideal of asceticism in the innumerable sects and philosophical schools of the last century before Christ, which produced from the polytheistic chaos of that epoch the twin ascetic religions of Mithraism and Christianity. A second wave of Dionysian licentiousness swept over the West at the Renaissance. It is difficult to gauge the spirit of one's own time; but, if we observe the trend of art, of style, and of public taste, and see what people read and write, what sort of societies they found, what "questions" are the order of the day, what the Philistines fight against, we shall find that in the long catalogue of our present social questions by no means the last is the so-called "sexual question." This is discussed by men and women who challenge the existing sexual morality and who seek to throw off the burden of moral guilt which past centuries have heaped upon Eros. One cannot simply deny the existence of these endeavours nor condemn them as indefensible; they exist, and probably have adequate grounds for their existence. It is more interesting and more useful to examine carefully the underlying causes of these contemporary movements than to join in the lamentations of the professional mourners of morality who [with hysterical unction] prophesy the moral downfall of humanity. It is the way of moralists not to put the slightest trust in God, as if they thought that the good tree of humanity flourished only by dint of being pruned, tied back, and trained on a trellis; whereas in fact Father Sun and Mother Earth have allowed it to grow for their delight in accordance with deep, wise laws.

Serious-minded people know that there is something of a sexual problem today. They know that the rapid development of the towns, with the specialization of work brought about by the extraordinary division of labour, the increasing industrialization of the countryside, and the growing sense of insecurity, deprive men of many opportunities for giving vent to their affective energies. The peasant's alternating rhythm of work secures him unconscious satisfactions through its symbolical content—satisfactions which the factory workers and office employees do not know and can never enjoy.

What do these know of his life with nature, of those grand moments when, as lord and fructifier of the earth, he drives his plough through the soil, and with a kingly gesture scatters the seed for the future harvest; of his rightful fear of the destructive power of the elements, of his joy in the fruitfulness of his wife who bears him the daughters and sons who mean increased working-power and prosperity? [Alas!] From all this we city-dwellers, we modern machine-minders, are far removed. Is not the fairest and most natural of all satisfactions beginning to fail us, when we can no longer regard with unmixed joy the harvest of our own sowing, the "blessing" of children? [Marriages where no artifices are resorted to are rare. Is not this an all-important departure from the joys which Mother Nature gave her first-born son?] Can such a state of affairs bring satisfaction? See how men slink to work, only observe the faces in trains at 7:30 in the morning! One man makes his little wheels go round, another writes things that interest him not at all. What wonder that nearly every man belongs to as many clubs as there are days in the week, or that there are flourishing little societies for women where they can pour out, on the hero of the latest cult, those inarticulate longings which the man drowns at the pub in big talk and small beer? To these sources of discontent there is added a further and graver difficulty. Nature has armed defenceless and weaponless man with a vast store of energy, to enable him not only passively to endure the rigours of existence but also to overcome them. She has equipped her son for tremendous hardships [and has placed a costly premium on the over-coming of them, as Schopenhauer well understood when he said that happiness is merely the cessation of unhappiness]. As a rule we are protected from the most pressing necessities, and for that reason we are daily tempted to excess; for the animal in man always becomes rampant unless hard necessity presses. But if we are high-spirited, in what orgiastic feasts and revels can we let off our surplus of energy? Our moral views forbid this outlet.

C. G. JUNG, *Two Essays*

We have to find our way backward, go in some sense through the romantic heart to recover again the heart of things. It requires seeing that the anima always appears amidst the particularity of things, as if she is the maker of soul things. Lacking recognition of the depth of things, depth psychology perpetuates the cult of subjectivity and abandons imagination in the world.

How do we know when we are being perceived by the thing? Its revelation does not take place in the form of general categories, classes, or meanings but with all the alluring charm of particularity, the nearness of intimacy, the glow of beauty. That is not to say that it shows itself as pretty. It may show forth terror—but insofar as it is absolutely particular, unable to be subsumed under some class of what we already know, it is beautiful. This penetration by the particular constitutes the difference between a physical object and a thing. The ego knows objects. Only the heart knows things. The relation of the heart to things is one of breathing in, gasping, inspiring the presentation of thing-as-image.

Direct intimacy with the particular rarely occurs. It requires a concentration of the heart. A clue to how this happens comes from Matisse. While working on a series of drawings in Nice, working in a very concentrated manner, six hours a day drawing female models, he wrote: "When I take a new model, I intuit the pose that will best suit her from her unselfconscious attitude of repose, and then I become the slave of that repose." Things, too, reveal themselves in moments catching them at repose. Nature, which lives a more relaxed life, displays itself more readily than the things of the built world. Nature may not be more beautiful than the things of urban life. Lewis Mumford said: "The city is a fact of nature." So, it is not that nature is beautiful and built things ugly. It is a matter of repose, of allowing ourselves to be caught off guard, of being aware of the fantasy of consumption that directs the modern relation to things so that this fantasy does not eat up the object before it has an opportunity to speak as thing.

ROBERT SARDELLO, "Taking the Side of Things"

———————

That vast insensate edifice—the doctrine of a soulless world—now streaked with acid rain and stained by graffiti has in our fantasies already exploded into dust. Yet, that cataclysm, that pathologized image of the world destroyed, is awakening again a recognition of the soul in the world. The *anima mundi* stirs our hearts to respond: we are at last, *in extremis,* concerned about the world; love for it arising, material things again lovable. For where there is pathology there is psyche, and where psyche, eros. The things of the world again become precious, desirable, even pitiable in their millennial suffering from Western humanity's hubristic insult to material things.

JAMES HILLMAN, "Anima Mundi"

———————

Things Men Have Made

Things men have made with wakened hands, and put soft life into
are awake through years with transferred touch, and go on glowing
for long years.
And for this reason, some old things are lovely
warm still with the life of forgotten men who made them.

D. H. LAWRENCE

———————

18.

SHADOW AND POWER

As we walk in the sunlight, we are generally unaware of the shadow that walks with us, our dark double without a face. It is a similar forgetfulness of the psychological shadow that often gets us into trouble, as we identify with certain values and understandings and sever ourselves from their opposites and tandems. To become aware of the shadow is sometimes like seeing ourselves and our world for the first time.

Simply discovering and then acknowledging in simple, direct ways the fullness of who we are, the good and bad sides of our intentions and wishes, the light and dark nature of our deepest emotions, can give us a presence in the world and to others that is uncommonly creative. We may discover that the shadow, so objectionable and repugnant, is the very gold in our personalities and at times the rarely appreciated elixir by which we find life and vitality.

Yet the shadow is full of complexity and contradiction. Only when we become capable of thoroughly appreciating the ultimate paradoxes that rule a life can we embrace the shadow, allowing its unrecognized divinity to grace our thoughts and actions with vitality and effect.

Those whom he saved from their sins are saved simply for beautiful moments in their lives. Mary Magdalen, when she sees Christ, breaks the rich vase of alabaster that one of her seven lovers had given her, and spills the odorous spices over his tired dusty feet, and for that one moment's sake sits for ever with Ruth and Beatrice in the tresses of the snow-white rose of Paradise. All that Christ says to us by the way of a little warning is that every moment should be beautiful, that the soul should always be ready for the coming of the bridegroom, always waiting for the voice of the lover, Philistinism being simply that side of man's nature that is not illumined by the imagination. He sees all the lovely influences of life as modes of light: the imagination itself is the world of light. The world is made by it, and yet the world cannot understand it: that is because the imagination is simply a manifestation of love, and it is love and the capacity for it that distinguishes one human being from another.

But it is when he deals with a sinner that Christ is most romantic, in the sense of most real. The world had always loved the saint as being the nearest possible approach to the perfection of God. Christ, through some divine instinct in him, seems to have always loved the sinner as being the nearest possible approach to the perfection of man. His primary desire was not to reform people, any more than his primary desire was to relieve suffering. To turn an interesting thief into a tedious honest man was not his aim. He would have thought little of the Prisoners' Aid Society and other modern movements of the kind. The conversion of a publican into a Pharisee would not have seemed to him a great achievement. But in a manner not yet understood of the world he regarded sin and suffering as being in themselves beautiful holy things and modes of perfection.

OSCAR WILDE, *De Profundis*

This archetypal shadow naturally continues to be a factor in all people, even after they have reached adulthood. The average healthy individual repeatedly falls victim to his own self-destructive and aggressive tendencies, destroying what he has built, sabotaging relationships which are important to him, tormenting his own family and friends—or shifting his destructiveness to his environment. But the psychotherapist is in a particularly unfortunate situation vis-a-vis this archetypal shadow. Earlier I mentioned the psychological "law" which states that the more we strive for something bright, the more its dark counterpart is constellated. I indicated that as a psychotherapist tries to become more conscious and to help his patients do the same, his unconscious side is constellated more powerfully than that of the average person. This might be expressed in paradoxical terms as follows: The more conscious a psychotherapist becomes, the more unconscious he becomes; the more light is cast upon a dark corner of a room, the more the other corners appear to be in darkness.

The most difficult thing for everyone, however, is to become conscious of the workings of the archetypal shadow, of one's own destructive and self-destructive tendencies, and to experience them in oneself rather than only in projections. Thus the psychotherapist, who in a certain respect is a particularly unconscious individual, is subject even more than others to the archetypal shadow. The therapist's conscious efforts are directed at helping people by freeing them from their own destructiveness. For eight hours each day, he encounters people whom he wishes to lead away from destructiveness and back to health and joy in life. But this endeavor places excessive demands on him. So much conscious good will must constellate a roughly equal amount of unconscious evil intent and destructivity.

ADOLF GUGGENBÜHL-CRAIG, *Power in the Helping Professions*

Tyranny ultimately rests on a carrying myth, an inner conviction given by an archetypal force. For instance, the myth of the hero who can overcome all obstacles; the myth of the divinely inspired and protected child who can run unlimited risks and who skateboards through life without any afterthoughts; the myth of romantic sexual passion that inspires beyond the human even to its destruction. But myths don't get much credit in our profit-and-loss accounting of life. We believe only in those myths that are presented as facts and truths, like neo-Darwinian competition. Since myths go unrecognized we

live them, or they live us, blindly. In this blindness we are each, as
Freud said, enacting Oedipus, the tyrant, who could not see what
myth he was living on, and dying from.

JAMES HILLMAN, *Kinds of Power*

After walking about all afternoon
barefoot, in my shack,
I have grown long and transparent . . .
like the sea slug
who has lived along doing nothing
for eighteen thousand years.

ROBERT BLY, *Jumping Out of Bed*

The individual loses his guilt and exchanges it for infantile innocence; once more he can blame the wicked father for this and the un-
loving mother for that, and all the time he is caught in this inescap-
able causal nexus like a fly in a spider's web, without noticing that he
has lost his moral freedom. But no matter how much parents and
grandparents may have sinned against the child, the man who is
really adult will accept these sins as his own condition which has to
be reckoned with. Only a fool is interested in other people's guilt,
since he cannot alter it. The wise man learns only from his own guilt.
He will ask himself: Who am I that all this should happen to me? To
find the answer to this fateful question he will look into his own
heart.

C. G. JUNG, *Psychology and Alchemy*

One of the current shadows cast by our Western notions of individuality and independence is called "codependence." It stands to rea-

son that if our developmental theories placed inordinately high values on independence and individuality, it would logically lead to viewing too much relatedness as a disease. I'm not arguing that unhealthy codependency does not exist, any more than I intend to argue that multiple personality disorder does not exist or that there are not legitimate self-affirmation issues. It's just that how we see these issues, that is, what we make of them, is based on a perspective that in large part is established by the developmental theories with which we are aligned. Those theories make up the light source that determines the shape and size of the shadow.

Let me go back for a moment and borrow from my experiences in Switzerland. In Zürich, I saw myself as an ugly American because I had momentarily stepped into the light of the European perspective—or at least what I imagined to be the European perspective. From this vantage point I could see myself as an ugly American. But that particular shadow was a product not only of my culturally assimilated American values, which up to then had remained fairly invisible to me, but also of the position of the light offered by the European perspective.

It is the same with our developmental theories: as Westerners, our light is individuality and autonomy. Merging, fusion, and joining are interpreted as the shadows cast by that light. We take the position that children should outgrow fused relationships and become independent. If they don't, we define them as codependent, and that's bad. That's the shadow.

But we can shift the light and get a slightly different shadow. If I stand in Zürich and view my European neighbors from my American perspective, I see them as stilted, overstructured, inefficient, nonproductive (or, at least, not as productive as they could be). The children, though quiet and well-behaved, aren't as emotionally free and creative as we believe our American children to be.

Let's try shifting the light again, seeing the shadow take on still another form. Let's imagine that in this case we are placing a high value on fusing, merging, and dependence, or mutual interdependence. Autonomy would begin to be viewed as the shadow—let us call it "the Lone Wolf Syndrome." In this light, the clear-eyed, young, visionary pioneer, wandering unfettered off across the plains—Davy Crockett, Daniel Boone, Jim Bowie, the Lone Ranger—all begin to look like psychopaths. What were heroes in the light of the independence-autonomy model suddenly become shadow. Can you imagine how the Japanese might view these characters? As terrifying and "insane" as the kamikaze pilot might be to us, these heroes of autonomy must seem quite berserk, though perhaps fascinating, to them!

So we begin to learn about our shadow and the assumptions we make about the world when we momentarily take the position of another vantage point, another perspective.

PATRICIA BERRY, "Light and Shadow"

———————

We enter the church; the doors are closed; a lamp is lit near the confessional. Dom Severino bids me assume my place, he sits down and requests me to tell him everything with complete confidence.

I was perfectly at ease with a man who seemed so mild-mannered, so full of gentle sympathy. I disguised nothing from him: I confessed all my sins; I related all my miseries; I even uncovered the shameful mark wherewith the barbaric Rodin had branded me. Severino listened to everything with keenest attention, he even had me repeat several details, wearing always a look of pity and of interest.

MARQUIS DE SADE, *Justine*

———————

What we see on the streets of our cities are two dramas, both of which cut to the troubled heart of the culture and demand from us a response we may not be able to make. There is the drama of those struggling to survive by regaining their place in the social order. And there is the drama of those struggling to survive outside of it.

The resolution of both struggles depends on a third drama\
ring at the heart of the culture: the tension and contention be\
the magnanimity we owe to life and the darker tendings of the
human psyche: our fear of strangeness, our hatred of deviance, our
love of order and control. How we mediate by default or design
between those contrary forces will determine not only the destinies
of the homeless but also something crucial about the nation, and
perhaps—let me say it—about our own souls.

PETER MARIN, *Freedom and Its Discontents*

———————

Deeply ingrained in the infantile psyche is the conscious or unconscious assumption that the cure for depression is to replace it with
pleasant, happy feelings, whereas the only valid cure for any kind of
depression lies in the acceptance of real suffering. To climb out of it
any other way is simply a palliative, laying the foundations for the
next depression. Nothing whatever has happened to the soul. The
roots of all our neuroses lie here, in the conflict between the longing
for growth and freedom and our incapacity or refusal to pay the
price in suffering of the kind which challenges the supremacy of the
ego's demands. This is the crux of the matter (and we may pause here
to recognize the exact meaning of the word "crux"). The ego will
endure the worst agonies of neurotic misery rather than one moment
of consent to the death of even a small part of its demand or its sense
of importance.

We can do something towards tracking down some of the continual evasions of the ego by uncovering our fear of humiliation. From
this fear of degradation in our own eyes or in the eyes of others, real
or imagined, comes a dead weight of moods and depression. For the
truly humble person no humiliation exists. It is impossible to humil-
iate him or for him to feel humiliation, for "grades" and prestige,
questions of his own merit or demerit, have no more meaning for
him. But the way to humility lies through the pain of accepted

humiliation. In the moment of picking it up and carrying it without any movement towards self-justification, we cease to be humiliated and begin to suffer.

HELEN LUKE, The Way of Woman

Love and war have traditionally been coupled in the figures of Venus and Mars, Aphrodite and Ares. This usual allegory is expressed in usual slogans—make love not war, all's fair in love and war—and in usual oscillating behaviors—rest, recreation and rehabilitation in the whorehouse behind the lines, then return to the all-male barracks. Instead of these couplings which actually separate Mars and Venus into alternatives, there is a Venusian experience within Mars itself. It occurs in the sensate love of life in the midst of battle, in the care for concrete details built into all martial regulations, in the sprucing, prancing and dandying of the cavaliers (now called "boys") on leave. Are they sons of Mars or of Venus?

In fact, we need to look again at the aesthetic aspect of Mars. Also there a love lies hidden. From the civilian sidelines, military rites and rhetoric seem kitsch and pomposity. But look instead at this language, these procedures as the sensitization by ritual of the physical imagination. Consider how many different kinds of blades, edges, points, metals and temperings are fashioned on the variety of knives, swords, spears, sabers, battle-axes, rapiers, daggers, lances, pikes, halberds that have been lovingly honed with the idea for killing. Look at the rewards for killing: Iron Cross, Victoria Cross, Medal of Honor, Croix de Guerre; the accoutrements: bamboo baton, swagger stick, epaulets, decorated sleeves, ivory-handled pistols. The music: reveille and taps, drums and pipes, fifes and drums, trumpets, bugles, the marching songs and marching bands, brass, braid, stripes. The military tailors: Wellington boots, Eisenhower jackets, Sam Brown belts, green berets, red coats, "whites." Forms, ranks, promotions. Flags, banners, trooping to the colors. The military mess—its postures, toasts. The manners: salutes, drills, commands. Martial rituals of the feet—turns, steps, paces, warriors' dances. Of the eyes—eyes front! Of the hands, the neck, the voice, ramrod backbone, abdomen—"Suck in that gut, soldier." The names: Hussars, Dragoons, Rangers, Lancers, Coldstream Guards, and nicknames: bluejacket, leatherneck, doughboy. The great walls and bastions of severe beauty built by Brunelleschi, da Vinci, Michelangelo, Buontalenti. The decorated horse, notches in the rifle stock, the painted emblems on metal equipment, letters from the front, poems. Spit and polish and pent emotion. Neatsfoot oil, gunsmith, swordsmith; the Shield of Achilles on which is engraved the whole world.

Gun control is a further case in point. It raises profound perplexities in a civilian society. The right to bear arms is constitutional, and our nation and its territorial history (for better or for worse) have depended on a citizen-militia's familiarity with weapons. But that was when the rifle and the Bible (together with wife and dog) went alone into the wilderness. The gun was backed by a God; when it stood in the corner of the household, pointing upward like the Roman spear that *was* Mars, the remembrance of the God was there, and the awe and even some ceremony. With the neglect of Mars, we are left only the ego and the guns that we try to control with civilian secular laws.

JAMES HILLMAN, "Wars, Arms, Rams, Mars"

A man is born gentle and weak.
At his death he is hard and stiff.
Green plants are tender and filled with sap.
At their death they are withered and dry.

Therefore the stiff and unbending is the disciple of death.
The gentle and yielding is the disciple of life.

Thus an army without flexibility never wins a battle.
A tree that is unbending is easily broken.

The hard and strong will fall.
The soft and weak will overcome.

LAO TZU, *Tao Te Ching*

This non-violence is not the non-violence of the weak. It does not give one the joy of jail-going. One can have that joy and also cover thereby the ill-will one harbours in his breast against the Government. One can also non-co-operate with the Government. But where swords, knives, lathis and stones are freely used, what is a man to do single-handed? Is it possible for one to receive these deadly blows without ill-will in one's heart? It is clear that it is impossible to do so, unless one is saturated with charity. It is only he who feels one with his opponent that can receive his blows as though they were so many flowers. Even one such man, if God favours him, can do the work of a thousand. It requires soul force—moral courage—of the highest type.

The man or woman who can display this non-violence of the brave can easily stand against external invasion. This is the third field for the exercise of non-violence. The Congress Working Committee were of opinion that, while it might be possible for us to exercise ahimsa in internal disturbances, India has not the strength to exercise ahimsa against the invasion of a foreign foe. This their want of faith has distressed me. I do not believe that the unarmed millions of India cannot exercise ahimsa with success in this wide field. It is for Congressmen to reassure the Sardar, whose faith in ahimsa of the strong has for the moment been shaken, that ahimsa is the only weapon that can suit India in the fields mentioned. Let no one ask, "But what about the martial races in India?" For me that is all the more reason why Congressmen should train themselves to defend their country with a non-violent army. This is an entirely new experiment. But who, save the Congress, is to try it—the Congress which has tried it successfully in one field? It is my unshakable faith that, if we have a sufficient number of non-violent soldiers, we are sure to succeed even in this new field, apart from the saving of the needless waste of crores of rupees.

I am therefore hoping that every Gujarati Congressite—man and woman—will declare their adherence to ahimsa and reassure the Sardar that they will never resort to violence. Even if there is sure hope of success in the exercise of violence, they will not prefer it to the exercise of non-violence. We are sure to learn by our mistakes. "We fall to rise, are baffled to fight better, sleep to wake."

On the Train to Wardha, July 7, 1940

MOHANDAS GANDHI, *Gandhi in India*

Forgive
    not sevenfold
    but seventyfold sevenfold

JOHN DOMINIC CROSSAN, *The Essential Jesus*

Zazen on the Mountain

The birds have vanished down the sky.
Now the last cloud drains away.

We sit together, the mountain and me,
until only the mountain remains.

LI PO

PASSAGES

The world is my origin, but soul have I drawn from the stars.

PROPHECY OF THE GREAT SYBIL

T HE GREATEST OF *all mysteries is the role of suffering, igno-rance, failure, illness, and death in human life. In our day, we do everything we can to overcome these painful experiences, but since* our methods are primarily mechanical and physical, we have made con-siderable progress only with gross problems of the body. We are still plagued with what we call mental illness and social conflict. Alternative approaches to illness are available in our past and in cultures that retain ancient wisdom about plant medicines and spiritual aspects of illness, but defensively we generally restrict our medicine and psychotherapy to methods we're comfortable with and that fit snugly into our worldview.

To begin really to heal ourselves we might first take note of the suffer-ing that is due to the way of life we have created: the fast pace, alienation from nature, neglect of tradition, the poisoning of the natural world, noise, loss of social intimacy, belligerent politics—the list is long. Then we might broaden our minds and take heed of the wisdom of cultures other than our own, learning from those we misguidedly consider our inferiors. We can also step outside the paradigm of modernism and reimagine the very nature of our illnesses and suffering.

What fantasies lie behind our notions of health, adjustment, nor-malcy, balance, and even creativity? Sometimes it appears that in the name of these ideals we're trying to escape from our humanity. In rela-tion to illness, we use the language of battles, wars, conquering, and overcoming. In psychotherapy, we talk about resolutions, solutions, solv-ing problems, and understanding. And yet, as Jung asks pointedly, have we ever seen a fully adjusted person? Would we even want to know such a perfect individual?

One alternative point of view is to see illness and emotional conflict as opportunities for deepening our humanity: not merely as learning expe-riences, but as occasions for substantive personal transformation. Ancient authors claimed that it is the soul that makes us human. I'd want to extend that notion and suggest that it is the soul-wrenching trials that evoke our humanity. If there is anything crucial lacking in the modern world, it is a profound appreciation for the common effort of making a beautiful life out of daily struggles.

A collective narcissism lies at the base of our heroic efforts to rid our lives of conflict and disease. We take pride in our few successes, while we seem to lack the pious humility of those cultures that see a divine presence at the core of our daily challenges. We would rather invent a new machine than look at the way we live for signs of our own self-destruction. We'd rather distill a new drug than find the issues of soul deep in our distress.

In some cultures, illness and emotional turmoil are seen as visitations of a divinity, and rather than fall into the hubris of thinking they can conquer these illnesses, people pray and practice rituals. The ancient Greeks visited the temple of the healing God Asklepios, made their sacrifices, and waited for a curative dream. In many other cultures as well, people address the spiritual dimensions of illness and recognize that a society's and an individual's way of life and behavior are implicated in suffering. Lacking an attitude of natural religion, when we do consider lifestyle and action, we tend to blame the individual instead of examining our cultural development.

We could respond to illness and other kinds of suffering by shaping a philosophy of life that recognizes the role of loss and pain in the process of humanization that cultures and individuals go through. In this sense, soul is made; it is not a mere given. We could also find an intelligent and yet pious, humble, and spiritual perspective on suffering, allowing us to both seek relief and appreciate its necessity.

19.

SUFFERING AND LOSS

No mysteries are more profound and confounding than loss, suffering, ending, illness, and death. The death of someone close reminds us of what is important and may give us back our soul, but still the cruelties of life seem senseless. They tarnish our optimism and challenge our faith, and yet, oddly, they retain the power to make us ever more human. They do so only when we give them attention and speak for, ritualize, and keep in memory events that hurt, confuse, and keep us in the dark.

Modern psychology has manufactured a philosophy of light, with goals of adjustment, normalcy, mental hygiene, and correctness. But actual life demands a more inclusive worldview that honors the gaps and failures that bring both pain and humanity. We need to respect the mysteries of death without understanding them and to express our confusion and pain so as to create a communal and honest humanity.

There is, to begin with, the first and most terrible revelation, that of the sacred as the *tremendum*. The adolescent begins by being terrorised by a supernatural reality of which he experiences, for the first time, the power, the autonomy, the incommensurability; and, following upon this encounter with the divine terror, the neophyte dies: he dies to childhood—that is, to ignorance and irresponsibility. That is why his family lament and weep for him: when he comes back from the forest he will be another; he will no longer be the child he was. As we have just seen, he will have undergone a series of initiatory ordeals which compel him to confront fear, suffering and torture, but which compel him above all to assume a new mode of being, that which is proper to an adult—namely, that which is conditioned by the almost simultaneous revelation of the sacred, of death and of sexuality.

MIRCEA ELIADE, *Myths, Dreams*

To live in this world

you must be able
to do three things:
to love what is mortal;
to hold it

against your bones knowing
your own life depends on it;
and, when the time comes to let it go,
to let it go.

MARY OLIVER, "In Blackwater Woods"

God isn't humanity's limit-point, though humanity's limit-point is divine. Or put it this way—humanity is divine when experiencing limits.

GEORGES BATAILLE

Jennie Hitchcock's mother was buried yesterday, so there is one orphan more, and her father is very sick besides. My father and mother went to the service, and mother said while the minister prayed, a hen with her chickens came up, and tried to fly into the window. I suppose the dead lady used to feed them, and they wanted to bid her good-by.

Life is death we're lengthy at, death the hinge to life.

Love from all,

Emily.

EMILY DICKINSON, *Letters*

"My Father, if it is possible, let this cup pass by me. Yet not as I please but as you do!"

JESUS

There's an old joke. Two elderly women are at a Catskills mountain resort, and one of them says, "Boy, the food at this place is really terrible." The other one says, "Yeah, and such small portions." Well, that's essentially how I feel about life. Full of loneliness and misery and suffering and unhappiness, and it's all over much too quickly.

WOODY ALLEN

Let us come back once more to the primitive mysteries of initiation. Everywhere we have found the symbolism of death as the ground of all spiritual birth—that is, of regeneration. In all these contexts death signifies the surpassing of the profane, non sanctified condition, the condition of the "natural man," ignorant of religion and blind to the spiritual. The mystery of initiation discloses to the neophyte, little by little, the true dimensions of existence; by introducing him to the sacred, the mystery obliges him to assume the responsibilities of a man. Let us remember this fact, for it is important—that access to the spiritual is expressed, in archaic societies, by a symbolism of Death.

MIRCEA ELIADE, *Myths, Dreams*

Grace strikes us when we are in great pain and restlessness. It strikes us when we walk through the dark valley of a meaningless and empty life. It strikes us when we feel that our separation is deeper than usual, because we have violated another life, a life which we loved, or from which we were estranged. It strikes us when our disgust for our own being, our indifference, our weakness, our hostility, and our lack of direction and composure have become intolerable to us. It strikes us when, year after year, the longed-for perfection of life does not appear, when the old compulsions reign within us as they have for decades, when despair destroys all joy and courage. Sometimes at that moment a wave of light breaks into our darkness, and it is as though a voice were saying: "You are accepted. *You are accepted,* accepted by that which is greater than you, and the name of which you do not know. Do not ask for the name now; perhaps you will find it later. Do not try to do anything now; perhaps later you will do much. Do not seek for anything; do not perform anything; do not intend anything. *Simply accept the fact that you are accepted!*" If that happens to us, we experience grace. After such an experience we may not be better than before, and we may not believe more than before. But everything is transformed. In that moment, grace conquers sin, and reconciliation bridges the gulf of estrangement. And nothing is demanded of this experience, no religious or moral or intellectual presupposition, nothing but *acceptance.*

PAUL TILLICH, "You Are Accepted"

                   Then think
what a storm, what a towering wave of ruin
         rushes down on you!
You can't escape it.
First, the Father will flash
         lightning and thunder down, and pound

this jagged ravine into an avalanche
to bury your body in it.
Arms of stone will hug and hold you.
And so, you'll travel through the vast tracts
   of time. And at last
come back up into sunlight.
      Then
Zeus's feathered hound, the blood red golden EAGLE
will tear your flesh
      into flapping rags.
It won't be invited, but it will come:
all day
      feasting, its beak
            stabbing your liver black.
Blood black.

At no point can you expect
an end to that anguish.
      Until perhaps
a God comes, willing to suffer
your pain for you,
willing to sink
      down into lightless Hades and the dead dark
            hollows of Tartaros.

AESCHYLUS, *Prometheus Bound*

My poor sister followed me to the door and begged me for Heaven's sake to go to the priests at St Peter's and implore one of them to come to Mozart—a chance call, as it were. I did so, but for a long time they refused to come and I had a great deal of trouble to persuade one of those clerical brutes to go to him. Then I ran off to my mother who was anxiously awaiting me. It was already dark. Poor soul, how shocked she was! I persuaded her to go and spend the

night with her eldest daughter, the late Josepha Hofer. I then ran
back as fast as I could to my distracted sister. Süssmayr was at
Mozart's bedside. The well-known Requiem lay on the quilt and
Mozart was explaining to him how, in his opinion, he ought to finish it, when he was gone. Further, he urged his wife to keep his death
a secret until she should have informed Albrechtsberger, who was in
charge of all the services [at St Stephen's Cathedral]. A long search
was made for Dr Closset, who was found at the theatre, but who had
to wait for the end of the play. He came and ordered cold poultices
to be placed on Mozart's burning head, which, however, affected
him to such an extent that he became unconscious and remained so
until he died. His last movement was an attempt to express with his
mouth the drum passages in the Requiem. That I can still hear.

FROM LETTER OF MOZART'S SISTER-IN-LAW SOPHIE

———————

Peace, and be at peace with your thoughts and visions.
These things had to come to you and you to accept them.
This is your share of the eternal burden,
The perpetual glory. This is one moment,
But know that another
Shall pierce you with a sudden painful joy
When the figure of God's purpose is made complete.
You shall forget these things, toiling in the household.
You shall remember them, droning by the fire,
When age and forgetfulness sweeten memory
Only like a dream that has often been told
And often been changed in the telling. They will seem unreal.
Human kind cannot bear very much reality.

T. S. ELIOT, *Murder in the Cathedral*

———————

The daimon of creativity has ruthlessly had its way with me. The
ordinary undertakings I planned usually had the worst of it—

though not always and not everywhere. By way of compensation, I think, I am conservative to the bone. I fill my pipe from my grandfather's tobacco jar and still keep his alpenstock, topped with a chamois horn, which he brought back from Pontresina after having been one of the first guests at that newly opened *Kurort.*

I am satisfied with the course my life has taken. It has been bountiful, and has given me a great deal. How could I ever have expected so much? Nothing but unexpected things kept happening to me. Much might have been different if I myself had been different. But it was as it had to be; for all came about because I am as I am. Many things worked out as I planned them to, but that did not always prove of benefit to me. But almost everything developed naturally and by destiny. I regret many follies which sprang from my obstinacy; but without that trait I would not have reached my goal. And so I am disappointed and not disappointed. I am disappointed with people and disappointed with myself. I have learned amazing things from people, and have accomplished more than I expected of myself. I cannot form any final judgment because the phenomenon of life and the phenomenon of man are too vast. The older I have become, the less I have understood or had insight into or known about myself.

I am astonished, disappointed, pleased with myself. I am distressed, depressed, rapturous. I am all these things at once, and cannot add up the sum. I am incapable of determining ultimate worth or worthlessness; I have no judgment about myself and my life. There is nothing I am quite sure about. I have no definite convictions—not about anything, really. I know only that I was born and exist, and it seems to me that I have been carried along. I exist on the foundation of something I do not know. In spite of all uncertainties, I feel a solidity underlying all existence and a continuity in my mode of being.

The world into which we are born is brutal and cruel, and at the same time of divine beauty. Which element we think outweighs the other, whether meaninglessness or meaning, is a matter of temperament. If meaninglessness were absolutely preponderant, the meaningfulness of life would vanish to an increasing degree with each step in our development. But that is—or seems to me—not the case. Probably, as in all metaphysical questions, both are true: Life is—or has—meaning and meaninglessness. I cherish the anxious hope that meaning will preponderate and win the battle.

When Lao-tzu says: "All are clear, I alone am clouded," he is expressing what I now feel in advanced old age. Lao-tzu is the example of a man with superior insight who has seen and experienced worth and worthlessness, and who at the end of his life desires to return into his own being, into the eternal unknowable meaning. The archetype of the old man who has seen enough is eternally true. At every level of intelligence this type appears, and its lineaments are always the same, whether it be an old peasant or a great philosopher like Lao-tzu. This is old age, and a limitation. Yet there is so much that fills me: plants, animals, clouds, day and night, and the eternal in man. The more uncertain I have felt about myself, the more there has grown up in me a feeling of kinship with all things. In fact it seems to me as if that alienation which so long separated me from the world has become transferred into my own inner world, and has revealed to me an unexpected unfamiliarity with myself.

C. G. JUNG, *Memories*

———————

Serving soul implies letting it rule; it leads, we follow. Here we adapt Jung's famous dictum that analysis is dreaming the myth onward, transposing it to "pathologizing the myth onward." By following the peculiar disordered activity itself as one of our guides, therapy will have room for the bizarre, decayed, and fantastic. As our model of thought is that "like has an affinity with like," therapy for the abnormal would have to be abnormal as well. Since our occupation is primarily with the failed aspects of life, we would have to put away all ideas of therapeutic success. Since pathologizing is frightening, we are obliged to follow fear, not with courage, but as a path that leads deeper into awe for what is at work in the depths of the soul. Here we must keep from seizing up in panic and coagulating the frightening peculiarities with a literal interpretation of them, giving them a diagnosis that demands treatment. "Pathologizing the myth onward" means staying in the mess while at the same time regarding what is going on from a mythical perspective. We try to follow the soul wherever it leads, trying to learn what the imagination is doing in its madness. By staying with the mess, the morbid, the fantastic, we do not abandon method itself, only its medical model. Instead we adopt the method of the imagination. By following pathologizing onward we are attempting to discover precisely the methods and laws of the imaginal in distinction to the rational and the physical. Madness teaches the method.

Before any attempt to treat, or even understand, pathologized phenomena we meet them in an act of faith, regarding them as authentic, real, and valuable *as they are*. We do not decrease their value by considering them as signs of medical sickness or inflate their value by considering them as signs of spiritual suffering. They are ways of the psyche and ways of finding soul.

JAMES HILLMAN, *Re-Visioning*

Admit the void; accept loss forever. Not to admit the void is the trouble with those schizophrenics who treat words as real things. Schizophrenic literalism equates symbol and original object so as to retain the original object, to avoid object-loss. Freedom in the use of symbolism comes from the capacity to experience loss. Wisdom is mourning; blessed are they that mourn.

NORMAN O. BROWN, *Love's Body*

The hour had waited till Mars or Jupiter had returned angrily in their courses to where they had set out from, with the outcome that Anfortas was abandoned to the pain of his wound, suffering such agony that knights and maidens both heard his frequent cries and saw the doleful glances he gave them with his eyes. His wound was beyond all cure: there was nothing they could do for him. Nevertheless, the story says true help was now on its way to him. They took hold of heartfelt grief.

When sharp and bitter anguish inflicted severe discomfort on Anfortas they sweetened the air for him to kill the stench of his wound. On the carpet before him lay spices and aromatic terebinth, musk, and fragrant herbs. To purify the air there were also theriac and costly ambergris: the odour of these was wholesome. Wherever people trod on the carpet, cardamom, cloves and nutmeg lay crushed beneath their feet for the sake of the fragrance—as these were pounded by their tread the evil stench was abated. Anfortas's fire was a wood of aloes, as I have told you before. His bedposts were of viper's horn. To give relief from the poison, the powder of various spices had been dusted over the counterpane. The cushions on which he reclined were of brocade of Nourient, quilted, not just sewn, and his mattress was of palmat-silk. His bed was further adorned with precious—no other!—stones. The tensed crossropes on which the bed beneath him rested were of salamander. On every side it was luxurious, this bed of a man beggared of joy! . . .

Parzival wept. "Tell me where the Gral is," he said. "If the goodness of God triumphs in me, this Company here shall witness it!" Thrice did he genuflect in its direction to the glory of the Trinity, praying that the affliction of this man of sorrows be taken from him. Then, rising to his full height, he added: "Dear Uncle, what ails you?" . . .

He Who for St Sylvester's sake bade a bull return from death to life and go, and Lazarus stand up, now helped Anfortas to become whole and well again. The lustre which the French call "fleur" entered his complexion—Parzival's beauty was as nothing beside it, and that of Absalom son of David, and Vergulaht of Ascalun, and of all who were of handsome race, and the good looks conceded to Gahmuret when they saw the delightful sight of him marching into Kanvoleiz—the beauty of none of these was equal to that which Anfortas carried out from his illness. God's power to apply his artistry is undiminished today.

WOLFRAM VON ESCHENBACH, *Parzival*

One must be natural and easy,
Take the happy with the sad,
Feel as one who looks,
think as one who walks,
And, when it's time to die, remember the day dies too,
And the sunset is beautiful, and beautiful too the
enduring night. . . .
That's how it is, and so be it. . . .

FERNANDO PESSOA

He only can create the greatest imaginable beauty
who has endured all imaginable pangs.

W. B. YEATS, "Anima Hominis"

One could call every illness an illness of the soul.

NOVALIS, *Pollen and Fragments*

Problems linked to illness, such as psychic crises, but also pains of
a physiological nature (fever, migraines, rheumatic pains) can be
assumed to be just so many initiatory trials. Uncovering the religious
significance of illness and physical pain constitutes in effect shamanism's essential contribution to the history of the spirit.

MIRCEA ELIADE, *Journals*

Similarly, man and remedy derive from the same substance, and
both together form a whole, that is to say, a whole man. . . . In this

sense, the disease desires its wife, that is, the medicine. The medicine must be adjusted to the disease, both must be united to form a harmonious whole, just as in the case of man and woman. If the physician finds such a remedy, he is complete.

PARACELSUS

Each illness is a musical problem—the healing a musical solution. The shorter and more complete the solution—the greater the musical talent of the physician.

NOVALIS, *Pollen and Fragments*

MRS. SMITH: Yogurt is excellent for the stomach, the kidneys, the appendicitis, and apotheosis. It was Doctor Mackenzie-King who told me that, he's the one who takes care of the children of our neighbors, the Johns. He's a good doctor. One can trust him. He never prescribes any medicine that he's not tried out on himself first. Before operating on Parker, he had his own liver operated on first, although he was not the least bit ill.

MR. SMITH: But how does it happen that the doctor pulled through while Parker died?

MRS. SMITH: Because the operation was successful in the doctor's case and it was not in Parker's.

MR. SMITH: Then Mackenzie is not a good doctor. The operation should have succeeded with both of them or else both should have died.

MRS. SMITH: Why?

MR. SMITH: A conscientious doctor must die with his patient if they can't get well together. The captain of a ship goes down with his ship into the briny deep, he does not survive alone.

MRS. SMITH: One cannot compare a patient with a ship.

MR. SMITH: Why not? A ship has its diseases too; moreover, your

doctor is as hale as a ship; that's why he should have perished at
the same time as his patient, like the captain and his ship.

MRS. SMITH: Ah! I hadn't thought of that . . . Perhaps it is true . . .
And then, what conclusion do you draw from this?

MR. SMITH: All doctors are quacks. And all patients too.

EUGÈNE IONESCO, *The Bald Soprano*

"There are sicknesses worse than sicknesses"

There are sicknesses worse than sicknesses,
There are pains that do not ache, not even in the soul,
Yet are more painful than all the others.
There are anxieties dreamed of more real
Than those life brings us, sensations
Felt only by imagining them,
More our own than life itself.
So many things exist without existing,
Exist, and linger on and on,
And on and on belong to us, and are us . . .
Over the turbid green of the wide-spreading river
The white circumflexes of the gulls . . .
Over and above the soul, the useless fluttering
Of what never was, nor ever can be, and that's all.

Let me have more wine, life is nothing.

Note

My soul came apart like an empty jar.
It fell overwhelmingly, down the stairs.
Dropped from the hands of a careless maid.
It fell. Smashed into more pieces than there was china in the jar.

FERNANDO PESSOA

Man is released from bonds made by man himself; for there are no
eternally established situations or absolute elements which man must
accept as part of existence. The person who accepts the emptiness-
teaching regards life's sorrows as his own construction and knows
that he must desist from constructing them in order to be released
from sorrow.

FREDERICK STRENG, *Emptiness*

The alchemists insisted that two things must happen before the cure
can be extracted from the disease: The problem must be kept in a
closed container, and it must be reduced to its original state through
a process of breakdown. The limitations and immobility of illness
provide the closed container that enables this transformation, precisely because there is no way out. Early on in my illness my dreams
offered the image of a snarl of snakes stuck in a bottle for my situation; alchemical texts are filled with images of dangerous animals—
lions or wolves—trapped in the chemist's flask. Alice James called
herself "bottled lightning . . . a geyser of emotions, sensations, spec-
ulations, and reflections fermenting . . . in my poor old carcass"
when she was dying of cancer. The isolation and lack of sympathy or
understanding that sick people often endure may even be necessary
to secure the walls of the container, so that nothing is spilled or
shared and the matter inside will reach the point of transmutation.
The walled space of illness, like therapy, intensifies the brooding and
incubates the egg.

KAT DUFF, *The Alchemy of Illness*

Cheating belongs to a God. All the Gods are important, but the God
of cheaters and cheating is particularly crucial in the legacy of

Jungian psychology. Jung wrote a great deal about Hermes/Mercury, so he is of capital importance in his psychology.

Throughout our discussion of cheating, I want to keep very close to the imagery of Hermes first cheating his brother and then cheating his father. We should not move into those worn-out notions of a society that demands the truth, the whole truth, and nothing but the truth, notions coming from other archetypal traditions in Western culture. It is only by connecting to the imagery—Hermes cheating his brother, Apollo, and his father, Zeus—that we can gain any profitable idea about cheating. Hermes showed an art and shamelessness in his cheating, both facets being very much part of his nature. He convinced his father to the point of laughing, and his brother Apollo to go on dealing with him until, later in the story, this dealing together clearly demarcates their two different natures.

I would like to present my own thoughts about this episode. Both Zeus and Apollo have accepted Hermes' cheating because Hermes, by introducing himself so barefacedly as a cheater, reflects to them a life-style very remote from their own. We cannot think of Zeus and Apollo as cheating in the way Hermes cheats, but this does not mean that they never do it. Apollo is more connected with searching for the truth, with moderation, ritual cleanliness, etc.: he is Zeus' consciousness. Zeus, the Rainmaker, is *Pater Familias,* the ruling principle, the balancer of the personality and of life; he alone carries the principle of monotheism as far as the Greeks conceived it. These two Gods belong to the archetypal carriers of collective consciousness to the Establishment, to the spirit of an epoch, reflecting a great deal of the collective morality.

Hermes, as we have said before following Jung, is the archetype of the unconscious, and he is also a cheater. He is the God who propitiates psychic movement, therefore we can postulate too that his cheating belongs to the complexities of psychic movement. Hermes, as Otto writes: ". . . is the spirit of a constellation which recurs in most diverse conditions and which embraces loss as well as gain, mischief as well as kindliness. Though much of this must seem questionable from a moral point of view, nevertheless it is a configuration which belongs to the fundamental aspects of living reality . . ." And we can add cheating to loss and gain, mischief and kindliness. Hermes introduces himself as a cheater accepting such a reality, a reality very different from that of his brother Apollo. If we take their dialogue and convey it into modern psychological terms, we can see it as a dialogue between the collective consciousness or super-ego and the unconscious. The gracefulness of the old Hymn enables us to catch a glimpse into these two sides of the psyche long before they appeared as the tremendous split that necessitated the study of modern psychology. The conflict between ruling consciousness (equivalent to Zeus and Apollo) and the unconscious (equivalent to Hermes) is well known as being at the core of psychotherapy. The Hymn gives us a lesson in how these two psychic forces can come together again without any uniting symbol, which would be that these two Gods, these two forces, accept each other's reality, each other's differences, and yet go on talking, bartering, and cheating.

RAFAEL LOPEZ-PEDRAZA, *Hermes and His Children*

Primarily out of trust in the alliance with the "Devil," archetypal medicine's verbal therapy seeks to "redeem" that which has metamorphosed into physical disease. We can envision the process as a "resublimation" of something that has fallen victim to materialization. *Sublim* can be understood as "floating," a complementary condition to that which in Latin is designated *gravis* ("heavy," "severe") and, in English, "gravitation."

Precisely by means of its almost ironic, quasi-masochistic position toward disease, its tendency to a mystique of suffering, and its love relationship—bordering on the perverse—with illness, archetypal medicine attempts to draw spirit from matter. The process does not occur without a kind of *Todeshochzeit* (marriage with death). Suppose the asthmatic became aware that Nature intended to strangle him because of his leanings to expiratory grandeur. Then it might also occur to him that his inner suffocation could only be lifted out of the physical realm when suffocation in the form of self-limitation enters into a liaison with his tendencies to "greatness." He may realize that he has no choice but to "marry" the monster, to enter upon a *Todeshochzeit*. The term is perhaps a bit grandiloquent but certainly applies. Furthermore, it evokes the general mythologem of something particularly desirable joining with something dreadful and, thereby, "dying"—a monster containing something of hidden value. A *Todeshochzeit* is only superficially such since death plays but a very minor actual role and then only from a distance. Usually it is but the specter of the *Todeshochzeit* which arouses horror, disbelief, laughter, or indignation.

The unusual conjunction with "death" results in a sense of expanding horizons—as if the sufferer experienced "eternity." It is as if the individual's life for the first time acquired unmistakable and incorruptible uniqueness, particular limitation and freedom simultaneously. It is as if this recognition conferred an unassailable security amid the hustle and bustle of human existence.

The moment of this "mystical marriage" may also carry bliss or ecstasy with it. Just as eternity is not solely a realm we enter at the close of our lives, an empire in which the ravages of time no longer affect us, so is ecstasy not solely a condition which begins with eternity. Ecstasy may occur with every marriage. Certainly not the least of marriages would be the *Todeshochzeit*, as long as we do not understand ecstasy as a euphoric exuberance but rather as an inner sense of security and well-being. The terms we usually associate with religion reoccur in medicine in conjunction with the manner and form in which we experience health and disease.

What applies to eternity and eternal ecstasy applies to "resurrection" as well. We need not understand resurrection exclusively as a posthumous ascent of an astral body. That is but the religious version of a completely realistic event, what medicine refers to as "reconvalescence." Whenever life continues following those experiences we have called *Todeshochzeit*, something akin to a resurrection has taken

place. When an infarct patient's condition improves after he has
been released from the sinister *machine infernale* of an intensive care
unit, he shows all the signs of having experienced a *Todeshochzeit*. He
may resolve no longer to invest so much "heart" in things once felt to
be important—until an unheeded hate literally attacks him. If he
adopts the perhaps naïve-seeming attitude of not taking things so
seriously anymore, he is headed for a *status quo ante*, albeit one in
which a certain reserve has taken its place. Reconvalescence, in other
words, is a reconstituting in which we take something previously
regarded as unworthy or useless and join with it in a kind of sacra-
mental marriage.

Reconvalescence, therefore, resembles those resurrection images
of Christian origin in which the resurrected Christ is afflicted with all
the signs of his recent agonizing ordeal. The risen Christ of Grune-
wald's "Isenheim Altarpiece" emanates not only a sense of the eternal
as He hovers before the backdrop of the universe, not only a sense
of ecstasy as illumination transforms the materiality of His body
into something pneumatic. Rather, He carries also the marks of His
wounds emitting a phosphorescent glow surpassing all profane, first
aid/emergency surgery. Christ appears like the martyrs of Christianity in general. Charity and piety, belief in a hereafter and eternal
peace, and a condemnation of all brutality force brutality to realize
itself in martyrs physically. Correspondingly, saints are, as a rule,
mutilated. Had they perceived their existence from a less idealistic,
more morbid point of view, they would probably not as often have
found such glorious and heroic ends.

ALFRED ZIEGLER, *Archetypal Medicine*

The moon, it is said, once sent an insect to men, saying, "Go to men
and tell them, 'As I die, and dying live; so you shall also die, and
dying live.'"

The insect started with the message, but, while on his way, was overtaken by the hare, who asked, "On what errand are you bound?"

The insect answered, "I am sent by the Moon to men, to tell them that as she dies and dying lives, so shall they also die and dying live."

The hare said, "As you are an awkward runner, let me go." With these words he ran off, and when he reached men, he said, "I am sent by the Moon to tell you, 'As I die and dying perish, in the same manner you also shall die and come wholly to an end.'"

The hare then returned to the Moon and told her what he had said to men. The Moon reproached him angrily, saying, "Do you dare tell the people a thing which I have not said?"

With these words the moon took up a piece of wood and struck the hare on the nose. Since that day the hare's nose has been slit, but men believe what Hare had told them.

[*Hottentot*]

PAUL RADIN, *African Folktales*

There are Sweets of Pathos, when Sweets of Mirth have passed away—

EMILY DICKINSON, *Letters*

PATHOS. that which happens to a person or thing. 2. What one has experienced. In a bad sense, misfortune, calamity. II. of the soul, emotion, passion. III. state, condition. 2. incidents of things, changes or happenings occurring in them. 3. properties, qualities of things. IV. modification in form. passivity.

LIDDELL-SCOTT, *Greek Lexicon*

Pleasure and Pain represent as twins, since there never is one without the other; and as if they were united back to back, since they are contrary to each other.

LEONARDO DA VINCI, *Notebooks*

What shall we do my darling, when trial grows more, and more, when the dim, lone light expires, and it's dark, so very dark, and we wander, and know not where, and cannot get out of the forest— whose is the hand to help us, and to lead, and forever guide us, they talk of a "Jesus of Nazareth," will you tell me if it be he?

EMILY DICKINSON, *Letters*

Do not be afraid of the past. If people tell you that it is irrevocable, do not believe them. The past, the present and the future are but one moment in the sight of God, in whose sight we should try to live. Time and space, succession and extension, are merely accidental conditions of thought. The imagination can transcend them, and more in a free sphere of ideal existences. Things, also, are in their essence what we choose to make them. A thing is, according to the mode in which one looks at it. "Where others," says Blake, "see but the dawn coming over the hill, I see the sons of God shouting for joy." What seemed to the world and to myself my future I lost irretrievably when I let myself be taunted into taking the action against your father: I had, I dare say, lost it in reality long before that. What lies before me is my past. I have got to make myself look on that with different eyes, to make the world look on it with different eyes, to make God look on it with different eyes. This I cannot do by ignoring it, or slighting it, or praising it, or denying it. It is only to be done fully by accepting it as an inevitable part of the evolution of my life and character: by bowing my head to everything that I have suffered. How far I am away from the true temper of soul, this letter in its changing uncertain moods, its scorn and bitterness, its aspirations and its failures to realize those aspirations, shows you quite clearly. But do not forget in what a terrible school I am sitting at my task. And incomplete, imperfect, as I am, yet from me you may have still much to gain. You came to me to learn the pleasure of life and the pleasure of art. Perhaps I am chosen to teach you something much more wonderful—the meaning of sorrow and its beauty.

Your affectionate friend,

Oscar Wilde

OSCAR WILDE, *De Profundis*

20.

SOLITUDE, LONELINESS, DEPRESSION

Depression may appear with all the clinical signs and may ask for severe forms of treatment, or it may seem no more than an ordinary, if painful, quality of daily life. In either case, it is a human condition suffered by humans, and so we must consider it as an aspect of the soul. Traditionally, it has been called melancholy and seen as one of the fundamental "humors" in human life, and it has also been associated with exceptional creative talent and with reading and scholarship. These traditional understandings of depression help us extend our imagination of it, rather than treating it as a medical condition alone, requiring medication.

Depression in its many manifestations—sadness, withdrawal, heaviness, dispiritedness, and loneliness—forces a person into solitude and away from the pursuit of happiness. Some traditions suggest that when depressed we might deepen the depression and give its gray or dark colors a place in ordinary living. Instead of curing depression, we might realign our lives for the better by following the lead of the depressive qualities. We could find ways to give solitude and withdrawal a place in lives that are usually full of events, people, and activities.

In medieval and Renaissance literature, depression lies in the province of the god Saturn, poisonous patron of sadness and creative source of insight and philosophical vision.

Omnes omnium laudes referantur in deum,
principium omnium atque finem

*All praise of all things should be given back
unto God, the beginning and the end of all*

Marsilio Ficino to his unique friend Giovanni Cavalcanti: greetings.

I praise God within myself especially on this account: that, because of a certain eternal gift of His, I have very little desire for mortal goods, since I am in truth too fearful of the surrounding evils, which you reprove in me from time to time. I accuse a certain melancholy disposition, a thing which seems to me to be very bitter unless, having been softened, it may in a measure be made sweet for us by frequent use of the lyre.

Saturn seems to have impressed the seal of melancholy on me from the beginning; set, as it is, almost in the midst of my ascendant Aquarius, it is influenced by Mars, also in Aquarius, and the Moon in Capricorn. It is in square aspect to the Sun and Mercury in Scorpio, which occupy the ninth house. But Venus in Libra and Jupiter in Cancer have, perhaps, offered some resistance to this melancholy nature.

MARSILIO FICINO, *Letters*

Hymn III: To Artemis

ARTEMIS
　　　　(not lightly do poets forget her)
we sing
　　　　who amuses herself on mountains
　　　　with archery and hareshoots
　　　　　and wide circle dances.

When she was still just a slip of a goddess,
she sat on her father's knee and said:
        "I want to be a virgin forever,
Papa, and I want to have as many names
as my brother Phoibos, and please, Papa,
give me a bow and some arrows—please?—
not a big fancy set: the Cýclopês can make me
some slender arrows and a little, curved bow.

"And let me be Light Bringer
and wear a tunic with a colored
border down to the knee, loose
for when I go hunting wild game.

"And give me sixty dancing girls,
        daughters of Ocean,
   all nine years old
      all little girl seanymphs,
and twenty woodnymphs from Amnísos for maids
to take care of my boots and tend my swift hounds
when I'm done shooting lynx and stag, and

"Give me all the mountains in the world, Papa,
and any old town, I don't care which one:
Artemis will hardly ever go down into town.
I'll live in the mountains, and visit men's cities
only when women, struck with fierce labor pang
call on my name.

CALLIMACHUS

———————

To Know the Dark

To go in the dark with a light is to know the light.
To know the dark, go dark. Go without sight,

and find that the dark, too, blooms and sings,
and is traveled by dark feet and dark wings.

WENDELL BERRY, *Collected Poems*

I never felt so lonely as in that particular hour when I was surrounded by people but suddenly realized my ultimate isolation. I became silent and retired from the group in order to be alone with my loneliness. I wanted my external predicament to match my internal one.

Loneliness can be conquered only by those who can bear solitude. We have a natural desire for solitude because we are men. We want to feel what we are—namely, alone—not in pain and horror, but with joy and courage. There are many ways in which solitude can be sought and experienced. And each way can be called "religious," if it is true, as one philosopher said, that "religion is what a man does with his solitariness."

PAUL TILLICH, *Eternal Now*

The nature and destiny of the man born under Saturn, even when, within the limits of his condition, his lot was the most fortunate, still retained a basis of the sinister; and it is on the idea of a contrast, born of darkness, between the greatest possibilities of good and evil, that the most profound analogy between Saturn and melancholy was founded. It was not only the combination of cold and dryness that linked black bile with the apparently similar nature of the star; nor was it only the tendency to depression, loneliness and visions, which the melancholic shared with the planet of tears, of solitary life and of soothsayers; above all, there was an analogy of action. Like melancholy, Saturn, that demon of the opposites, endowed the soul both with slowness and stupidity and with the power of intelligence and contemplation. Like melancholy, Saturn menaced those in his power, illustrious though they might be, with depression, or even

madness. To quote Ficino, Saturn "seldom denotes ordinary characters and destinies, but rather people set apart from the rest, divine or
bestial, blissful, or bowed down by the deepest sorrow."

KLIBANSKY, SAXL & PANOFSKY, *Saturn and Melancholy*

Demeter consciousness becomes depressed, and within this depression we can see many classically psychiatric attributes: she ceases to
bathe, ceases to eat, disguises her beauty, denies the future (her possibilities of rejuvenation and productivity), regresses to menial tasks
beneath her ability (or sees her tasks as menial), becomes narcissistic
and self-concerned, sees (and actually engenders) worldwide catas-
trophe, and incessantly weeps. The depression of Demeter consciousness manifests itself with a certain dry asceticism (no bathing,
no eating, no sensuality) and self-denial. But alongside this dryness,
she weeps with "vain and insatiate anger." So her wetness is in effect
dry, an excess of tears that neither moistens nor makes for flow or
connection. There is no anima in this wetness. It is a kind of contin-
uous downpour that erodes rather than replenishes the soil, making
it ever more dry and less fertile.

Another peculiarity of Demeter depression is her tendency to seek
refuge among man, the social world, the city. She doesn't go off alone
into the woods as might Artemis, or try to prove her self-sufficiency
as might Hera, or rush into a love affair as might Aphrodite. Rather
she breaks her connection with the Gods and seeks refuge in the
polis, the world of everyday events, "reality." Thus she may defend
herself from the needs of her own deepening with "reality excuses."
It becomes "impractical" to tend to her soul. She has no time. It is
not her business. She must take care of the children and the household (which chances are she is doing inadequately, with only the surface of herself, anyway). Indeed then the needs of Demeter's soul
begin to cast themselves in ways that actually *are* impractical and
anti-social. She perhaps expresses these needs in suicide attempts
(literalizing death as Hades), in religious conversion (portraying her

need for spirit), or by leaving her family, breaking her marriage, and living out in desperation some fling or affair (in a displaced enactment of her daughter Persephone).

As it is Persephone's narcissism (the flower Narcissus), in the Homeric tale, which brings Hades rushing up upon her, so Demeter's narcissism helps connect, and yet depotentiate, underworld forces. One way we see this is in the ceaseless, self-indulgence of much of her suffering. Her dry tears erode the soil, her suffering engenders suffering for all the world, her mourning, mourning. On and on, as though her suffering fed upon itself—and yet where is the sustenance for such feeding, since everyday life gets worse and worse? It is as though this repetition were mimetic to another underworld characteristic—the endless cycle by which essence is expressed (e.g., Ixion on the wheel, Sisyphus and his stone, etc.). In the upper world, this endless, cyclical essence is expressed as repetition. Apparently meaningless emotions are compelled to repeat again and again fruitlessly as though to connect to the essence beneath themselves, the Hades realm.

PATRICIA BERRY, "The Rape of Demeter / Persephone"

Exile gives the imagination its power to perceive with the instruments of the senex structure. Exile reflects the idea that human life itself is cast out of its origins in Kronos' Golden Age, the lost *terre celeste* of archetypal forms. We are each in exile; but senex consciousness, cooped in its cabin of winter desiccation, bridges beyond by spatial imagination, by measure and music, or with a "dying" awareness of decline. It sees through, sees out with insight. The melancholy temperament, never bled nor purged, never transformed, is nonetheless satisfied by seeing to the end where impenetrable darkness is penetrated by the darkening intellect and blackened psyche of a "being whose thoughts have reached the limit."

Such is our vision of Ficino's vision. His solution in the Renaissance is worth our contemporary notice, since he resolved a question for each of us struggling with the "negative senex" not only in our natures, but also in our culture. The inbuilt contradiction and the inherent need in senex consciousness for negation were transmuted by him into a profound process of soul-making. His work on the senex archetype made his own soul and had effect on the psychic constellation of his time. This time was the Renaissance.

JAMES HILLMAN, "The Negative Senex"

One might argue that the best, the highest, is imposed on all in monasteries. Far from it: St. Benedict's principle is that the Rule should be moderate, so that the strong may desire to do more and the weak may not be overwhelmed and driven out of the cloister.

You must be free, and not involved. Solitude is to be preserved, not as a luxury but as a necessity: not for "perfection" so much as for simple "survival" in the life God has given you.

Hence, you must know when, how, and to whom you must say "no." This involves considerable difficulty at times. You must not hurt people, or want to hurt them, yet you must not placate them at the price of infidelity to higher and more essential values.

People are constantly trying to use you to help them create the particular illusions by which they live. This is particularly true of the collective illusions which sometimes are accepted as ideologies. You must renounce and sacrifice the approval that is only a bribe enlisting your support of a collective illusion. You must not allow yourself to be represented as someone in whom a few of the favorite daydreams of the public have come true. You must be willing, if necessary, to become a disturbing and therefore an undesired person, one who is not wanted because he upsets the general dream. But be careful that you do not do this in the service of some other dream that is only a little less general and therefore seems to you to be more real because it is more exclusive!

THOMAS MERTON, *Conjectures*

I find it wholesome to be alone the greater part of the time. To be in company, even with the best, is soon wearisome and dissipating. I love to be alone. I never found the companion that was so companionable as solitude. We are for the most part more lonely when we go abroad among men than when we stay in our chambers. A man thinking or working is always alone, let him be where he will. Solitude is not measured by the miles of space that intervene between a man and his fellows. The really diligent student in one of the crowded hives of Cambridge College is as solitary as a dervis in the desert. The farmer can work alone in the field or the woods all day, hoeing or chopping, and not feel lonesome, because he is employed; but when he comes home at night he cannot sit down in a room alone, at the mercy of his thoughts, but must be where he can "see the folks," and recreate, and as he thinks remunerate, himself for his day's solitude; and hence he wonders how the student can sit alone in the house all night and most of the day without ennui and "the blues"; but he does not realize that the student, though in the house, is still at work in *his* field, and chopping in *his* woods, as the farmer in his, and in turn seeks the same recreation and society that the latter does, though it may be a more condensed form of it.

I have heard of a man lost in the woods and dying of famine and exhaustion at the foot of a tree, whose loneliness was relieved by the grotesque visions with which, owing to bodily weakness, his diseased imagination surrounded him, and which he believed to be real. So also, owing to bodily and mental health and strength, we may be continually cheered by a like but more normal and natural society, and come to know that we are never alone.

HENRY DAVID THOREAU, *Walden*

The virginal may appear in another pattern of image work. The virgin Narcissus reflects endlessly, purely upon himself. As the clear pool of this reflection ripples in death, Narcissus raptures ever deeper. The movement is profound. Narcissistic reflection is deeply self-revealing and self-contained, alchemically enclosed within the narrow limits of the pond. But despite this depth of vertical reflection, or perhaps because of it, the horizontal world of Echo is ignored. In the tale, Echo pines away, longing for the narcissistic reflection that excludes her. Let us say that Echo is the echoing of what is "out-there"—objects, the daily, others, the lateral. Narcissus ignores these reverberations from surfaces, things around. Attempting to find insight and meaning within oneself, one becomes deaf to surroundings.

Image work seems to invite this narcissistic virginity. Because reflection and depth are so vitally important, image tends to draw one into "vertical" rather than "horizontal" reflection. But the Lopez maxim, "stick to the image," does not necessitate a mesmerized downward stare. Depth can also mean a depth within, a penetration of the immediate, across and through surfaces.

Although narcissistic virginity denies the horizontal, Narcissus unlike other virgins does not flee from the physical; rather, he flees into it. It is the less physical realm of sounds and echoes that he fears. As sound, Echo cannot be touched, cannot be concretized. The essence of Echo is precisely in the reverberations, the hiatus, the space between. Whereas the image can remain virginal if it is held—narcissistically—too close, Echo requires distance, breadth.

Dreams in which one is rejected, betrayed, made jealous, failed, create the distance needed for echo to sound. In these dreams, emptiness is created, room established, attachments dissolved, sensuality irrelevant. The movement is one of echoing out of oneself, beyond physical attachments, and attachments to the physical, into a broader, more substantial, wider-ranging world.

PATRICIA BERRY, "Virginities of Image"

———————

There is another related element which was to have a profound effect on the development of the pleasure garden in England and that is melancholy. The late Elizabethan and early Stuart preoccupation with melancholy has already received considerable attention from literary historians but no one as far as I know has commented upon its influence on the development of landscape gardening.

Melancholy is one of the four humours. The Renaissance inherited two traditions concerning it: the first, the Galenic, in which melancholy, because of its cold and dry qualities, is inimical to life; and the Aristotelian, in which melancholy of the right kind is favourable to the imaginative and intellectual powers. During the late fifteenth and early sixteenth centuries in Italy this latter concept was revived, principally by the Florentine Humanist and neoplatonist, Marsilio Ficino, whose book *De vita libri tres* sums up this revaluation. By following Aristotle's statement that all the intellectually brilliant were melancholic by temperament, he fused the *furor melancholicus* with the platonic *furor divinus*. In this way he transformed what in the Middle Ages had been regarded as the most inimical of all the humours into that which was a mark of genius. Gradually the attributes and attitudes of melancholy became an indispensable adjunct of any Renaissance man with artistic or intellectual pretensions.

All this arrived with force in late Elizabethan England when the generation of Elizabeth's favourite, Essex, adopted the pose. Portraits depict these fashionable young men negligently attired in black with their arms folded and wearing large floppy hats falling over their eyes. What was an affection in its extreme form reflects an accepted truth, as enunciated above all by Burton in his *Anatomy of Melancholy* (1621):

> . . . melancholy men of others are most witty, causeth many times divine ravishment, and a kind of *enthiasmus* . . . which stirreth them up to be excellent Philosophers, Poets, Prophets, &c.

Such men seek the shade of the greenwood tree and *not* the walks of a formal garden. The contrast is epitomized beautifully in a portrait by Isaac Oliver of an unknown gallant dressed in black with a large hat sitting in a "dump" beneath a tree meditating, while in the distance can be seen an Elizabethan formal garden. In other words melancholy man requires a quite different setting, one at first glance totally naturalistic but which could and would eventually be simulated.

The melancholy man, Sir Thomas Overbury writes, will "seldom be found without a shade of some grove, in whose bottome a river dwels." Burton develops this:

> What is more pleasant than to walke alone in some solitary grove betwixt Wood and Water, by a Brook side, to meditate upon some delightsome and plesant subject. . . .

Or, to take a final even more famous text, Milton's *Il Penseroso:*

> There in close covert by som Brook,
> Where no profaner eye may look,
> Hide me from Day's garish eie,
> While the Bee with Honied thie,
> That at her flowry work doth sing.
> And the waters murmuring
> With such consort as they keep,
> Entice the dewy-feather'd Sleep;
> And let some strange mysterious dream,
> Wave at this Wings in Airy stream. . . .

We need only turn to Oliver's portrait of the black Lord Herbert of Cherbury reclining in a wood by a babbling brook to see its visual equivalent.

That this must have had a profound effect on the development of gardens is obvious. John Evelyn is a convenient starting-point because he specifically describes creating such a place of solace for melancholic meditation at his brother's house at Wotton in 1643:

> . . . I made . . . the stews & receptacles for Fish, and built a little study over a Cascade, to passe my Melencholy houres shaded there with Trees.

This statement surely means that we must regard the whole development of the naturalistic garden outside the formal parterres—it being such a marked feature of the early Stuart period with its shady walks, islands and artificial streams—as, at least in one of its aspects, the deliberate creation of settings conducive to the melancholic mood.

ROY STRONG, *Renaissance Gardens*

21.

KNOWING AND UNKNOWING

We live in an age that values information, and so it is at odds with the ancient religious traditions that value an empty mind. Wisdom, these old sources say, arrives at the point where we become profoundly aware of our ignorance and when we have given up the futile attempt to understand ourselves. Even the famous utterance of the Delphic Oracle, "Know thyself," could refer to something other than a mental understanding. We come to know who we are over a lifetime, and any passing sensation that the soul has been revealed is ephemeral and provisional.

It's important to stand deep in our ignorance, enjoying an unending exploration of the world's secrets and the mysteries of our own hearts. Anything more than that leads to a superior place of illusion. Today we have astounding resources for knowledge, but we also desperately need the means of forgetting and letting go what we know. We are so full of humanly packaged learning that we have no room for the influx of the muse and the inspirations that flow from sources beyond the human ego. As a result, the imagination and the religious sensibility suffer. We don't know who we are because who we are lies so deep that it requires revelation rather than explanation.

The new pond,
a frog jumps in,
—no sound!

RYOKAN

Several things dovetailed in my mind, & at once it struck me, what quality went to form a Man of Achievement especially in Literature & which Shakespeare possessed so enormously—I mean *Negative Capability,* that is when a man is capable of being in uncertainties, Mysteries, doubts, without any irritable reaching after fact & reason—Coleridge, for instance, would let go by a fine isolated verisimilitude caught from the Penetralium of mystery, from being incapable of remaining content with half knowledge. This pursued through Volumes would perhaps take us no further than this, that with a great poet the sense of Beauty overcomes every other consideration, or rather obliterates all consideration. . . .

It has been an old Comparison for our urging on—the Bee hive—however it seems to me that we should rather be the flower than the Bee—for it is a false notion that more is gained by receiving than giving—no the receiver and the giver are equal in their benefits—The fower I doubt not receives a fair guerdon from the Bee—its leaves blush deeper in the next spring—and who shall say between Man and Women which is the most delighted? Now it is more noble to sit like Jove that to fly like Mercury—let us not therefore go hurrying about and collecting honey-bee like, buzzing here and there impatiently from a knowledge of what is to be arrived at: but let us open our leaves like a flower and be passive and receptive—budding patiently under the eye of Apollo and taking hints from every noble insect that favors us with a visit—sap will be given us for Meat and dew for drink—

JOHN KEATS, *Letters*

Floral muscle,
Little by little open
Morning meadow's anemone
Til in her lap
The polyphonous light

Of sounding skies
Radiates.

In the quiet blossom's star, flexed,
Muscle of infinite receptivity
Often so overwhelmed with fullness
That the sunset's call to rest

Can hardly return to you
The wide-relaxed petals:
You, the firmness and fortitude
Of many worlds.

We are violent
And stay around longer
But when, in which of all our lives,
will we finally open up
and become receptive?

RAINER MARIA RILKE, *Sonnets to Orpheus*

———————————

Poems are a corrupt version of some text in nature with which they ought to be made to tally. A rhyme in one of our sonnets should not be less pleasing than the iterated nodes of a seashell, or the resembling difference of a group of flowers. The pairing of the birds in an idyl, not tedious as our idyls are; a tempest is a rough ode, without falsehood or rant; a summer, with its harvest sown, reaped and stored, is an epic song, subordinating how many admirably executed parts. Why should not the symmetry and truth that modulate these, glide into our spirits, and we participate the invention of nature?

This insight, which expresses itself by what is called Imagination, is a very high sort of seeing, which does not come by study, but by the intellect being where and what it sees; by sharing the path or circuit of things through forms, and so making them translucid to others. The path of things is silent. Will they suffer a speaker to go with them? A spy they will not suffer; a lover, a poet, is the transcendency of their own nature,—him they will suffer. The condition of true naming, on the poet's part, is his resigning himself to the divine *aura* which breathes through forms, and accompanying that.

It is a secret which every intellectual man quickly learns, that beyond the energy of his possessed and conscious intellect he is capable of a new energy (as of an intellect doubled on itself), by abandonment to the nature of things; that beside his privacy of power as an individual man, there is a great public power on which he can draw, by unlocking, at all risks, his human doors, and suffering the ethereal tides to roll and circulate through him; then he is caught up into the life of the Universe, his speech is thunder, his thought is law, and his words are universally intelligible as the plants and animals. The poet knows that he speaks adequately then only when he speaks somewhat wildly, or "with the flower of the mind"; not with the intellect used as an organ, but with the intellect released from all service and suffered to take its direction from its celestial life; or as the ancients were wont to express themselves, not with intellect alone but with the intellect inebriated by nectar.

RALPH WALDO EMERSON, *The Poet*

———————

Yen Hui said, "I have made some progress."

"What do you mean?" asked Confucius.

"I have forgotten humanity and righteousness," replied Yen Hui.

"Very good, but that is not enough," said Confucius.

On another day Yen Hui saw Confucius again and said, "I have made some progress."

"What do you mean?" asked Confucius.

"I have forgotten ceremonies and music," replied Yen Hui.

"Very good, but that is not enough," said Confucius.

Another day Yen Hui saw Confucius again and said, "I have made some progress."

"What do you mean?" asked Confucius.

Yen Hui said, "I forget everything while sitting down."

Confucius' face turned pale. He said, "What do you mean by sitting down and forgetting everything?"

"I cast aside my limbs," replied Yen Hui, "discard my intelligence, detach from both body and mind, and become one with Great Universal (Tao). This is called sitting down and forgetting everything."

CHUANG TZU

Amor intellectualis quo Murphy se ipsum amat.

It is most unfortunate, but the point of this story has been reached where a justification of the expression "Murphy's mind" has to be attempted. Happily we need not concern ourselves with this apparatus as it really was—that would be an extravagance and an impertinence—but solely with what it felt and pictured itself to be. Murphy's mind is after all the gravamen of these informations. A short section to itself at this stage will relieve us from the necessity of apologising for it further.

Murphy's mind pictured itself as a large hollow sphere, hermetically closed to the universe without. This was not an impoverishment, for it excluded nothing that it did not itself contain. Nothing ever had been, was or would be in the universe outside it but was already present as virtual, or actual, or virtual rising into actual, or actual falling into virtual, in the universe inside it.

This did not involve Murphy in the idealist tar. There was the mental fact and there was the physical fact, equally real if not equally pleasant.

He distinguished between the actual and the virtual of his mind, not as between form and the formless yearning for form, but as between that of which he had both mental and physical experience and that of which he had mental experience only. Thus the form of kick was actual, that of caress virtual.

The mind felt its actual part to be above and bright, its virtual beneath and fading into dark, without however connecting this with the ethical yoyo. The mental experience was cut off from the physical experience, its criteria were not those of the physical experience, the agreement of part of its content with physical fact did not confer worth on that part. It did not function and could not be disposed according to a principle of worth. It was made up of light fading into dark, of above and beneath, but not of good and bad. It contained forms with parallel in another mode and forms without, but not right forms and wrong forms. It felt no issue between its light and dark, no need for its light to devour its dark. The need was now to be in the light, now in the half light, now in the dark. That was all.

Thus Murphy felt himself split in two, a body and a mind. They had intercourse apparently; otherwise he could not have known that they had anything in common. But he felt his mind to be bodytight and did not understand through what channel the intercourse was effected nor how the two experiences came to overlap. He was satisfied that neither followed from the other. He neither thought a kick because he felt one nor felt a kick because he thought one. Perhaps the knowledge was related to the fact of the kick as two magnitudes to a third. Perhaps there was, outside space and time, a non-mental non-physical Kick from all eternity, dimly revealed to Murphy in its correlated modes of consciousness and extension, the kick *in intellectu* and the kick *in re.*

SAMUEL BECKETT, *Murphy*

———

. . . Since the desire [to know] within us is not in vain, we desire to know that we are ignorant. If we shall be able to fully attain this, then we shall attain learned ignorance. Indeed, nothing more perfect will happen to even the man most devoted to learning than to be found most learned in that ignorance itself which is peculiar to him; and he will become more learned to the extent that he knows his own ignorance.

. . . The human mind is dark and nightlike, the angelic mind is clear like the dawn, and the divine mind is like the sun, since it illumines every person coming into the world.

NICHOLAS OF CUSA, *On Learned Ignorance, Sermon*

The Tao that can be told is not the eternal Tao.
The name that can be named is not the eternal name.
The nameless is the beginning of heaven and earth.
The named is the mother of ten thousand things.
Ever desireless, one can see the mystery.
Ever desiring, one can see the manifestations.
These two spring from the same source but differ in name;
    this appears as darkness.
Darkness within darkness.
The gate to all mystery.

LAO TZU, *Tao Te Ching*

Furthermore, the Zen experience is more of a conclusion than a premise. It is never to be used as the first step in a line of ethical or metaphysical reasoning, since conclusions draw to it rather than from it. Like the Beatific Vision of Christianity, it is a "which than which there is no whicher"—the true end of man—not a thing to be used for some other end. Philosophers do not easily recognize that there is a point where thinking—like boiling an egg—must come to a stop. To try to formulate the Zen experience as a proposition—"everything is the Tao"—and then to analyze it and draw conclusions from it is to miss it completely. Like the Crucifixion, it is "to the Jews [the moralists] a stumblingblock and to the Greeks [the logicians] foolishness." To say that "everything is the Tao" almost gets the point, but just at the moment of getting it, the words crumble into nonsense. For we are here at a limit at which words

break down because they always imply a meaning beyond themselves—and here there is no meaning beyond.

ALAN WATTS, The Way of Zen

The somebodies will be nobodies
and
the nobodies will be somebodies

JOHN DOMINIC CROSSAN, The Essential Jesus

I speak of ordinary men, of whom none are born without their
imperfections, and happy is he that is prest with the least: for among
wise Princes there is either no friendship at all, or if there be, 'tis
unpleasant and reserv'd, and that too but amongst a very few, 'twere
a crime to say none. For that the greatest part of mankind are fools,
nay there is not any one that dotes not in many things; and friendship, you know, is seldome made but amongst equalls. . . .

Do but observe our grim Philosophers that are perpetually beat-
ing their brains on knotty Subjects, and for the most part you'll find
'em grown old before they are scarce young. And whence is it, but
that their continual and restless thoughts insensibly prey upon their
spirits, and dry up their Radical Moisture? Whereas, on the contrary,
my fat fools are as plump and round as a Westphalian Hogg, and
never sensible of old age, unless perhaps, as sometimes it rarely happens, they come to be infected with Wisdom; so hard a thing it is for
a man to be happy in all things. And to this purpose is that no small
testimony of the Proverb, that says, "Folly is the onely thing that
keeps Youth at a stay, and Old age afar off"; as it is verifi'd in the
Brabanders, of whom there goes this common saying, "That Age,
which is wont to render other Men wiser, makes them the greater
Fools."

ERASMUS, In Praise of Folly

PROFESSOR: We can't be sure of anything, young lady, in this world.

PUPIL: The snow falls in the winter. Winter is one of the four seasons. The other three are . . . uh . . . spr . . .

PROFESSOR: Yes?

PUPIL: . . . ing, and then summer . . . and . . . uh . . .

PROFESSOR: It begins like "automobile," miss.

PUPIL: Ah, yes, autumn . . .

PROFESSOR: That's right, miss, that's a good answer, that's perfect. I am convinced that you will be a good pupil. You will make real progress. You are intelligent, you seem to me to be well informed, and you've a good memory.

PUPIL: I know my seasons, don't I, Professor?

PROFESSOR: Yes, indeed, miss . . . or almost. But it will come in time. In any case, you're coming along. Soon you'll know all the seasons, even with your eyes closed. Just as I do.

PUPIL: It's hard.

PROFESSOR: Oh, no. All it takes is a little effort, a little good will, miss. You will see. It will come, you may be sure of that.

PUPIL: Oh, I do hope so, Professor. I have a great thirst for knowledge. My parents also want me to get an education. They want me to specialize. They consider a little general culture, even if it is solid, is no longer enough, in these times.

PROFESSOR: Your parents, miss, are perfectly right. You must go on with your studies. Forgive me for saying so, but it is very necessary. Our contemporary life has become most complex.

PUPIL: And so very complicated too . . . My parents are fairly rich, I'm lucky. They can help me in my work, help me in my very advanced studies.

PROFESSOR: And you wish to qualify for . . . ?

PUPIL: Just as soon as possible, for the first doctor's orals. They're in three weeks' time.

PROFESSOR: You already have your high school diploma, if you'll pardon the question?

PUPIL: Yes, Professor, I have my science diploma and my arts diploma, too.

PROFESSOR: Ah, you're very far advanced, even perhaps too advanced for your age. And which doctorate do you wish to qualify for? In the physical sciences or in moral philosophy?

PUPIL: My parents are very much hoping—if you think it will be possible in such a short time—they very much hope that I can qualify for the total doctorate.

PROFESSOR: The total doctorate? . . . You have great courage, young lady, I congratulate you sincerely. We will try, miss, to do our best. In any case, you already know quite a bit, and at so young an age too.

PUPIL: Oh, Professor.

PROFESSOR: Then, if you'll permit me, pardon me, please, I do think that we ought to get to work. We have scarcely any time to lose.

EUGÈNE IONESCO, *The Lesson*

All rational beings, angels and men, possess two faculties, the power of knowing and the power of loving. To the first, to the intellect, God who made them is forever unknowable, but to the second, to love, he is completely knowable, and that by every separate individual. So much so that one loving soul by itself, through its love, may know for itself him who is incomparably more than sufficient to fill all souls that exist. This is the everlasting miracle of love, for God always works in this fashion, and always will. Consider this, if by God's grace you are able to. To know it for oneself is endless bliss; its contrary is endless pain. . . .

If ever you are to come to this cloud and live and work in it, as I suggest, then just as this cloud of unknowing is as it were above you, between you and God, so you must also put a cloud of forgetting beneath you and all creation. We are apt to think that we are very far from God because of this cloud of unknowing between us and him, but surely it would be more correct to say that we are much farther from him if there is no cloud of forgetting between us and the whole created world. Whenever I say "the whole created world" I always mean not only the individual creatures therein, but everything connected with them. There is no exception whatever, whether you think of them as physical or spiritual beings, or of their states or actions, or of their goodness or badness. In a word, everything must be hidden under this cloud of forgetting.

THE CLOUD OF UNKNOWING

ENCHANTMENT

I'm not certain that he distinguishes between the natural
and the supernatural very clearly.

W. B. YEATS

ENCHANTMENT IS BOTH *the capacity of the world to charm us and the spell that comes upon us when we open ourselves to the magic in everyday experiences. An enchanted world is alive and rich in personality. It reveals itself to us in its beauty and poetic presence. Both the realm of nature and the world of manufactured things have their magic that can stun us and ultimately make life feel worth living.*

Especially in the past century, we have taken such pride in our scientific and technological achievements that we have come to imagine our entire lives as mechanical. We prize our rationality and quantifying methods, believing that they offer unmatched reliability. We have even introduced them into our arts and our psychological studies and therapies.

But we pay a price for this kind of progress. We have lost much that quickens the heart and nurtures the imagination. Our arts are marginalized as never before. Education has been reduced to information gathering and training. Medicine neglects the soul and spirit, and focuses exclusively on the purely physical dimensions of the person, using only mechanical and chemical means of healing. Politics appears obsessed with power and money instead of genuine needs of communities. All of these aspects of modern life wound the soul and therefore decrease our humanity.

It's tempting to respond to these serious problems with remedies that remain within the paradigm of modern culture instead of imagining an altogether different way of life. A philosophy of enchantment turns current values upside down and asks that we step outside the boundaries of contemporary wisdom. Instead of rushing into the future, we might profoundly appreciate the past, and instead of treating nature as an inert, inanimate substance, a resource for making the merely physical world, we might grant it its soul and personality. We become enchanted when we open our senses and our imaginations to the song and speech of the world.

To live in an enchanting world we also have to assume a receptive posture rather than an exclusively active one. We can become skilled at allowing the world in, taking its secrets to heart and finding power outside of ourselves. This is the chief teaching of the magus, that neglected visionary who has explored the secret potentialities of nature and human ingenuity in every period of history and in every culture. When, emptied of the hubris of modernism, we enjoy the role of being a conduit for the powers that lie outside us, the world floods us with its wisdom and support.

In an enchanted state, we speak with a voice far deeper than that of the scheming ego and the work we do is the product of many hands— those of the figures of one's own soul and of nature, depicted enchantingly in religion and art as angels, little people, daimons, and spirits.

22.

DIVINATION AND MAGIC

There is nothing wrong with living in a world charmed by technology, information, machinery, and telecommunications. What is wrong is to limit the pleasures and purposes of human life to the worldview created by the technological vision. While there is undoubtedly a kind of magic in technology, and while I'm certain that my Renaissance heroes would go to almost any length to own a computer, the mechanical, rational world we have developed leaves out an ingredient of utmost importance to the human heart—enchantment.

Sometimes we can know important items through deep intuition, psychic sensitivity, and simple forms of divination. Opening a book at random and reading the line found blindly by your finger can be more revealing and offer sounder guidance than searching through tables of statistics and pages of scientific studies. Reading the book of nature, becoming acquainted with nature's patterns by watching the sun, the moon, and the stars, can educate a person in the mysteries of the body and soul. The byproduct of this kind of education of the heart is a life full of warmth, charm, and meaning.

Magic has two forms. One consists wholly in the operations and powers of demons, and this consequently appears to me, as God is my witness, an execrable and monstrous thing. The other proves, when thoroughly investigated, to be nothing else but the highest realization of natural philosophy.

Just as that first form of magic makes man a slave and pawn of evil powers, the latter makes him their lord and master. That first form of magic cannot justify any claim to being either an art or a science

while the latter, filled as it is with mysteries, embraces the most profound contemplation of the deepest secrets of things and finally the
knowledge of the whole of nature. This beneficent magic, in calling
forth, as it were, from their hiding places into the light the powers
which the largess of God has sown and planted in the world, does
not itself work miracles, so much as sedulously serve nature as she
works her wonders. Scrutinizing, with greater penetration, that harmony of the universe which the Greeks with greater aptness of terms
called συμπάθεια (sympathy) and grasping the mutual affinity of
things, she applies to each thing those inducements, called the ίύγγεσ
(charms) of the magicians, most suited to its nature. Thus it draws
forth into public notice the miracles which lie hidden in the recesses
of the world, in the womb of nature, in the storehouses and secret
vaults of God, as though she herself were their artificer. As the farmer
weds his elms to the vines, so the "magus" unites earth to heaven, that
is, the lower orders to the endowments and the powers of the higher.

GIOVANNI PICO DELLA MIRANDOLA, *Oration on the Dignity of Man*

The physician does not learn everything he must know and master
at high colleges alone; from time to time he must consult old
women, gypsies, magicians, wayfarers, and all manner of peasant
folk and random people, and learn from them; for these have more
knowledge about such things than all the high colleges.

PARACELSUS

Infinite nature, which is boundless Spirit, unutterable, not intelligible, outside of all imagination, beyond all essence, unnameable,
known only to the heart.

ROBERT FLUDD, *History of the Macrocosm*

Life is a spell so exquisite that everything conspires to break it.

EMILY DICKINSON, *Letters*

Melancholy students who have used up their vital powers in their studies, and the old in whom these forces are in any case declining, are therefore advised to avoid as far as possible plants, herbs, animals, stones, and the like belonging to Saturn, and to use and surround themselves with plants, herbs, animals, stones, people, belonging to the more fortunate, cheerful, and life-giving planets, of which the chief are Sol, Jupiter, and Venus. Ficino has many enthusiastic passages on the valuable "gifts" making for health and good spirits to be obtained from these planets, which he poetically describes more than once as "the Three Graces." The equation of beneficent astral influences with the Three Graces may be derived from a passage in the Emperor Julian's Hymn to the Sun. Gold is a metal full of Solar and Jovial spirit and therefore beneficial in combating melancholy. Green is a health-giving and life-giving colour, and the reader is urged to come to "Alma Venus" and to walk in the green fields with her, plucking her flowers, such as roses, or the crocus, the golden flower of Jupiter. Ficino also gives advice on how to choose a non-Saturnian diet, and thinks that the use of pleasant odours and scents is beneficial. We might be in the consulting room of a rather expensive psychiatrist who knows that his patients can afford plenty of gold and holidays in the country, and flowers out of season.

FRANCES A. YATES, *Giordano Bruno*

While talismans are generally similar to amulets in purpose and in mode of employment, historians sometimes treat them separately. The distinguishing feature is that talismans, unlike amulets, have written words or at least letters inscribed on them. The power of

such inscriptions is at least as great as that of plants and animals.
Many in medieval society, including the noted medical authority
Bernard Gordon (d. ca. 1320), believed one could ward off epileptic
attacks by carrying the names of the biblical magi on one's person,
written on a slip of parchment. One manuscript gives series of letters
from the alphabet which, if written out and carried, will have wondrous effect: one series, to be hidden under the right foot, will
silence the bearer's enemies; another, to be held in the left hand, will
win favors from potential benefactors. Another manuscript gives a
series of names for God which, if borne on one's person, will protect
against fire, water, arms, and poison. If a pregnant woman has this
formula on her she will not die in childbirth. Then the author hedges,
adding a condition: whoever carries such a sequence of divine names
and looks at them each day will not die by sword, fire, or water, and
will remain unvanquished in battle.

RICHARD KIECKHEFER, *Magic in the Middle Ages*

The Rune casters of the Teutons and Vikings wore startling garb that
made them easily recognizable. Honored, welcomed, feared, these
shamans were familiar figures in tribal circles. There is evidence that
a fair number of runic practitioners were women. The anonymous
author of the thirteenth-century *Saga of Erik the Red* provides a vivid
description of a contemporary mistress of runecraft:

> She wore a cloak set with stones along the hem. Around her neck
> and covering her head she wore a hood lined with white catskins.
> In one hand, she carried a staff with a knob on the end and at her
> belt, holding together her long dress, hung a charm pouch.

To pre-Christian eyes, the earth and all created things were alive.
Twigs and stones served for Runecasting since, as natural objects,
they were believed to embody the sacred. Runic symbols were carved
into pieces of hardwood, incised on metal or cut into leather that
was then stained with pigment into which human blood was sometimes mixed to enhance the potency of the spell. The most common

Runes were smooth flat pebbles with symbols or glyphs painted on one side. The practitioners of *runemal* would shake their pouch and scatter the pebbles on the ground; those falling with glyphs upward were then interpreted.

The most explicit surviving description of this procedure comes from the Roman historian Tacitus. Writing in A.D. 98 about practices prevalent among the Germanic tribes, he reports:

> To divination and casting of lots they pay attention beyond any other people. Their method of casting lots is a simple one: they cut a branch from a fruit-bearing tree and divide it into small pieces which they mark with certain distinctive signs (*notae*) and scatter at random onto a white cloth. Then, the priest of the community, if the lots are consulted publicly, or the father of the family, if it is done privately, after invoking the gods and with eyes raised to heaven, picks up three pieces, one at a time, and interprets them according to the signs previously marked upon them.

RALPH BLUM, *The Book of Runes*

Why not make a universal image, that is, an image of the universe itself? The ancients seem to have expected benefits from such an image. One who is a follower of these might be the sculptor then; he could make a kind of archetypal form of the whole world, if you want, in the air, imprinting it in silver on gold plate.

When is the best time to imprint it? When the Sun has touched the first minute of Aries. The astrologers say this is, as it were, where the universe was when it first started, and they predict from here the fortune of the world for at least a year. The sculptor then could imprint a figure of the whole world on this, its birthday.

So let us return to our purpose, that one should not carve his world on a day or in an hour of Saturn, but rather in an hour of the Sun. He should draw it on the year's birthday, especially if Jupiter and Diana are happily approaching.

The ancients thought it was best, by the way, if you colored all the features of the work. There are three universal and singular colors of the world: green, gold, and sapphire, and they are dedicated to the three Graces of heaven. Green, of course, is for Venus and the Moon, moist, as it were, for the moist ones, and appropriate to things of birth, especially mothers. There is no question that gold is the color of the Sun, and no stranger to Jove and Venus either. But we dedicate the sapphire color especially to Jove, to whom the sapphire itself is said to be consecrated. This is why lapis lazuli was given its color (sapphire), because of its Jovial power against Saturn's black bile. It has a special place among doctors, and it is born with gold, distinct with gold marks, so it is a companion of gold just as Jupiter is the companion of the Sun. The stone ultramarine has a similar power, possessing a similar color with a little green.

The ancients decided, therefore, that it was a big help, if you wanted to capture the gifts of the heavenly Graces, to look at these three powerful colors frequently, and to color in, on the little wall-map of the universe that you are making, the sapphire color for the spheres of the world. They thought it was worthwhile, too, to add the color gold to the spheres of the heavens and the stars, and to dress Vesta herself, or Ceres, that is, earth, in a green mantle. In this way a follower of these ancients would either wear this little form of the universe, or look at it on the wall.

It would be useful, too, to look at a sphere with its motions, as Archimedes once did, and which recently a certain Florentine by the name of Lorenzo has made. Not just to look at it, but to reflect on it in the soul.

Deep inside your house you might set up a little room, one with an arch, and mark it all up with these figures and colors, especially the room where you spend most of your time and where you sleep. When you leave your house, do not pay so much attention to the spectacle of individual things, but look at the shape and colors of the universe.

MARSILIO FICINO, *Book of Life*

Literalism does not get rid of the magical element in scriptural or historical interpretation. The Holy Spirit, instead of a living spirit in the present, becomes the Holy Ghost, a voice from the past, enshrined in the book. The restriction of meaning to conscious meaning makes historical understanding a personal relation between the personality of the reader and the personality of the author, now dead. Spiritual understanding (*geistiges Verstehen*) becomes a ghostly operation, an operation with ghosts (*Geisteswissenschaft*). The document starts speaking for itself; the reader starts hearing voices. The subjective dimension in historical understanding is to animate the dead letter with the living reader's blood, his "experience"; and simultaneously let the ghost of the dead author slide into, become one with, the reader's soul. It is necromancy, or shamanism; magical identification with ancestors; instead of living spirit, to be possessed by the dead.

NORMAN O. BROWN, *Love's Body*

———————

Reenchantment, as I understand it, means stepping beyond the modern traditions of mechanism, positivism, empiricism, rationalism, materialism, secularism and scientism—the whole objectifying consciousness of the Enlightenment—in a way that allows for a return of soul. Reenchantment implies a release from the affliction of nihilism, which David Michael Levin has called "our culture's cancer of the spirit." It also refers to that change in the general social mood toward a new pragmatic idealism and a more integrated value system that brings head and heart together in an ethic of care, as part of the healing of the world.

SUZI GABLIK, *The Reenchantment of Art*

———————

The effects of a prayer are real because one part [of the universe] is in sympathy with a[nother] part, as [one may observe] in a properly tuned string [on a lyre]. When it has been struck in its lower part, the upper part vibrates as well. And it often happens that when one string has been struck, another one, if I may say so, feels this, because they are in unison and have been tuned to one and the same pitch. If the vibration travels from one lyre to another, [one can see] how far the sympathetic element extends. In the universe, too, there is one universal harmony [or, tuning?], even though it is made up of discordant notes. It is also made up of similar notes, and all are related, even the discordant ones. Everything that is harmful to men—passionate impulses, for instance, that are drawn, along with anger, into the nature of the liver [i.e., the liver as their physical organ and center]—did not come [into the world] to be harmful [to men]. If, for example, one were to take fire from fire and hurt someone, yet without approaching him with any evil intention he who took the fire [would be] responsible, because, you know, he delivered, as it were, something from one place to another, and it [i.e., the accident] happened because the person to whom the thing was transferred was unfit to receive it.

For this very reason the stars will need no memory—our whole discussion leads up to this point—nor any sense perceptions transmitted to them. Hence they have no power of conscious assent to [our] prayers, but one must admit that with or without prayer their influence is real, since they [like us] are part of the One. Since there are many powers that are not guided by a conscious will, some spontaneously, some through a technique, and since this is happening in one living organism [the universe], some elements are helpful, some harmful, to one another, according to their nature. Medical art and magic art compel one element to surrender part of its own specific power to another element. In the same way, the universe also distributes something of itself to its parts, both spontaneously and because it feels the attraction of something else to part of itself which is essential to its own parts, because they share the same nature. After all, he who demands [something from the universe] is no stranger [to it].

PLOTINUS, *Enneads*

So precious stones are engendered by fire and by water, and therefore they contain fire and moisture within themselves. They possess many virtues and great efficacy so that many benefits can be brought about by their means. These are good and worthy effects and useful to mankind—not effects of corruption, fornication, adultery, hatred, murder, and similar things that lead to sin and are inimical to man. For the nature of precious stones procures the worthy and the useful, and wards off the perverse and evil, just as virtues cast down vices and just as the vices cannot operate against the virtues. . . .

The emerald is formed in the morning of the day and in the sunrise, when the sun is powerfully situated in its sphere and about to set forth on its journey. Then the greenness of the earth and the grasses thrives with the greatest vigor. For the air is still cold and the sun is already warm. The plants suck the green life-force as strongly as a lamb sucks its milk. The heat of the day is just beginning to be adequate for this—to cook and ripen the day's green life-force and nourish the plants so that they will be fertile and able to produce fruit.

It is for this reason that the emerald is powerful against all human weaknesses and infirmities; because the sun engenders it and because all of its matter springs from the green life-force of the air.

Therefore, whoever suffers a malady of the heart, the stomach, or the side, let that person carry an emerald so that the body's flesh may be warmed by it, and the sick one will be healed. But if diseases so overwhelm the patient that their tempest cannot be resisted, then let the patient place an emerald in the mouth so that it may be wetted by the saliva. Let the body frequently absorb the saliva, warmed by the stone, and then spit it out. The sudden attack of those diseases will then in all likelihood cease.

If a person falls down, stricken by epilepsy, place an emerald in the patient's mouth while he is still lying down, and presently the spirit will revive. After the patient is raised up and the emerald is removed from the mouth, let the patient look attentively and say, "Just as the spirit of the Lord fills up the earthly sphere, so let his mercy fill the house of my body so that it may never again be shaken." Let the patient do this for nine consecutive days, in the morning, and the cure will follow. But the patient should always keep the same emerald and gaze at it daily in the morning, all the while saying these words. And the sick person will be made well.

Anyone who suffers especially from headache should hold the emerald before the mouth and warm it with his breath, so that the breath moistens it. The sufferer should then rub the temples and forehead with the moisture. Let it be placed in the mouth and held there for a little while, and the patient will feel better.

HILDEGARD OF BINGEN

The prophetess at Delphi gives oracles to people from a thin, firelike spirit that rises from somewhere through a crevice, or she makes predictions sitting in the sanctuary on a bronze tripod or on a four-footed stool that is sacred to the god. In any case she gives herself entirely to a divine spirit, and she shines with a ray from the divine fire. An intense, concentrated fire comes up through the crevice and surrounds her on all sides, filling her with divine radiance. When she takes her place on the seat of the god, she adapts and conforms herself to his firm divinatory power. As a result of both preliminaries she becomes completely the possession of the god. He then appears to her and illuminates her as a separate entity, because he is different from the fire, the spirit, his own seat, and from all the normal and sacred apparatuses that are visible.

IAMBLICHUS, *On the Mysteries of Egypt*

Insofar as divination is not strictly bound to mechanical procedures—and many mechanical procedures themselves manipulate
multivocal symbolic elements subject to variable interpretation—
there is a figurative process going on in divination that is well cap-
tured in a number of these essays. This is a process by which the
diviner and the client often enough together "figure out" (with figures of speech in mind) a pattern of knowing that will meet the existential anomalies and ambiguities, the aleatory and inchoate qualities, of the social situation that has brought them together. This "figuring out" in my view is largely accomplished in primary process
language rich in dreamlike images, metaphors, metonyms, synech-
doches, and other figurative devices which are put forth as relevant to
the divinatory problem but whose relevance has to be subsequently
"figured out" in a more straightforward cognitive fashion.

In some respects I could have been informed, to be sure, more than
a decade and a half ago. Richard Werbner alerted us to the figurative,
if enigmatic and innuendo laden, richness of Kalanga domestic divination, the "superabundance of understandings" it offered through
its language of metaphors about the "common occult." Indeed, as
Werbner showed, the divinatory apparatus of the Kalanga, the four
two-sided pieces of ivory, could be regarded as a matrix of metaphors, a comprehensive concordance of divination that conditioned
the play of verbal art at seances. These ivory metaphors, as cast, offer
to the diviner and congregation a "superabundance" of possibilities
of interpretation as they reason together about the plausible patterns
of meaning before them. This metaphoric matrix enables the diviner
to avoid falling into too easy error. It enables him—frees him up—
to fit his pattern discovery subtly but suitably into the social and personal intricacies of the case at hand.

. . . The diviner offers a more acceptable world for his client to live
in, more acceptable than the troubled social world that brought the
diviner and the client together in the first place. At the heart of this
world creation, this therapeutic cosmogony, is, as many of these
essays demonstrate, the play of metaphor. Though the reader may

already have divined that I, with my long-term interest in the tropes, would have come to metaphor as the final word in my afterword, I simply reiterate Levin's argument that the putting forth of a metaphor is always the imaginative assertion of a different possible world than the one in which we literally live. There is surely that imaginative assertiveness in much divination.

JAMES W. FERNANDEZ, *African Divination Systems*

The Emerald Tablet

It is true, without fabrication, certain, and reliable:

What is below is as that which is above,
and what is above is as that which is below
to create the miracles of one thing.

And just as everything has come from one thing,
by the contemplation of the one,
so everything born is from this very one thing
by elaboration.

Its father is the Sun, its mother is the Moon.
The wind carried it in its lap.
The earth is its nurse.
The father of every object in the world is here.
Its power is pristine if it is directed toward the earth.

Separate earth from fire, the subtle from the gross,
Gently, and with great intelligence.

It ascends from earth to heaven,
and then it descends again to earth,
and it receives power from above and from below.
Then you have the glory of the entire world.

Then all darkness will vanish from you.
This is the powerful power of all power,
because it overcomes every subtle thing,
and penetrates everything solid.

This is how the world was created. From this there will be
wonderful elaborations
for this is the model.
And so I am called Hermes Trismegistus,
having the three parts of the philosophy of the entire universe.

What I have said about the working of the Sun is complete.

ANONYMOUS

———————

But why do we think that Love is a *magician*? Because the whole
power of magic consists in love. The work of magic is the attraction
of one thing by another because of a certain affinity of nature. But
the parts of this world, like the parts of a single animal, all deriving
from a single author, are joined to each other by the communion of
a single nature. Therefore just as in us the brain, lungs, heart, liver,
and the rest of the parts draw something from each other, and help
each other, and sympathize with any one of them when it suffers, so
the parts of this great animal, that is all the bodies of the world, similarly joined together, borrow and lend natures to and from each
other. From this common relationship is born a common love; from
love, a common attraction. And this is the true magic. Thus fire is
drawn upward by the concavity of the sphere of the moon, because
of a congruity of nature; air, by the concavity of fire; earth is drawn
downward by the center of the world; water also is drawn by its
region. Thus also the lodestone draws iron, amber draws chaff, and
sulphur, fire; the sun turns many flowers and leaves toward itself, and
the moon, the waters; Mars is accustomed to stir the winds, and the
various plants also attract to themselves various kinds of animals. In

human affairs also, "his own pleasure draws each." Therefore the works of magic are works of nature, but art is its handmaiden. For where anything is lacking in a natural relationship, art supplies it through vapors, numbers, figures, and qualities at the proper times. Just as in agriculture, nature produces the crops, but art makes the preparations. The ancients attributed this art to daemons because the daemons understand what is the inter-relation of natural things, what is appropriate to each, and how the harmony of things, if it is lacking anywhere, can be restored. Some are said to have been either friends, through some similarity of nature, such as Zoroaster and Socrates, or their beloveds, through worship, such as Apollonius Tyaneus and Porphyry. For this reason signs, voices, and portents from daemons are said to have come to them, when they were awake, or oracles and visions when they were asleep. They seem to have become magicians through the friendship of the daemons, just as the daemons are magicians through understanding the friendship of things themselves. And all nature, because of mutual love, is called a magician. Moreover, anyone who is beautiful bewitches us with his youthful eyes. Men charm and win men over to themselves through the powers of eloquence and the measures of songs, as if by certain incantations. Moreover, they drug and capture them with worship and gifts exactly as though with enchantments. Therefore no one can doubt that love is a magician, since the whole power of magic consists in love, and the work of love is fulfilled by bewitchments, incantations, and enchantments.

MARSILIO FICINO, *Commentary on Plato's Symposium*

The date of the façade of S. Maria Novella has often been a matter for discussion. Relying on documentary indications some scholars date the beginning in 1448, others in 1456. The latter date is much nearer the truth, for according to a document in the Rucellai Archives the façade was begun in 1458. The inscription in the upper entablature dates its completion in 1470, but the portal was still unfinished in 1478. The entrance to S. Francesco, designed in 1450, is only the first step leading up to the fully developed classical composition displayed in that of S. Maria Novella.

It is characteristic that for the entrance of S. Maria Novella Alberti followed closely the main features of a work of classical antiquity, the entrance to the Pantheon. Here, too, there occurs the motif of the two pilasters placed at right angles to the doorway at each side of a deep niche; here also we find a large door with the entablature and arch above.

It is clear, then, that Alberti imbued his additions to the old façade with motifs directly derived from ancient buildings. This was for him consistent with his professed belief that it was possible to maintain continuity between the old and the new parts while at the same time improving upon the work of his predecessors—"vuolsi aiutare quello ch'è fatto."

All the new elements introduced by Alberti in the façade, the columns, the pediment, the attic, and the scrolls, would remain isolated features were it not for that all-pervading harmony which formed the basis and background of his whole theory. Harmony, the essence of beauty, consists, as we have seen, in the relationship of the parts to each other and to the whole, and, in fact, a single system of proportion permeates the façade, and the place and size of every single part and detail is fixed and defined by it. Proportions recommended by Alberti are the simple relations of 1:1, 1:2, 1:3, 2:3, 3:4, etc., which are the elements of musical harmony and which Alberti found in classical buildings. The diameter of the Pantheon, for instance, corresponds exactly to its height, half its diameter corresponds to the height of the substructure as well as to that of the dome, and so forth.

Such simple ratios were used by Alberti. The whole façade of S. Maria Novella can be exactly circumscribed by a square. A square of half the side of the large square defines the relationship of the two storeys. The main storey can be divided into two such squares, while one encloses the upper storey. In other words, the whole building is related to its main parts in the proportions of one to two, which is in musical terms an octave, and this proportion is repeated in the ratio of the width of the upper storey to that of the lower storey.

The same ratio of 1:2 recurs in the sub-units of the single storeys. The central bay of the upper storey forms a perfect square, the sides of which are equal to half the width of the whole storey. Two squares of that same size encase the pediment and upper entablature which together are thus exactly as high as the storey under them. Half the side of this square corresponds to the width of the upper side bays and is also equal to the height of the attic. The same unit defines the proportions of the entrance bay. The height of the entrance bay is one and a half times its width, so that the relation of width to height is here two to three. Finally the dark square incrustations of the attic are one third of the height of the attic, and these squares are related to the diameter of the columns as 2:1. Thus the whole façade is geometrically built up of a progressive duplication or, alternatively, a progressive halving of ratios. It is clear then that Alberti's theoretical precept that the same proportion be kept throughout the building has here been fulfilled. It is the strict application of an unbroken series of ratios that marks the unmediaeval character of this pseudo-Proto-Renaissance façade and makes it the first great Renaissance example of classical *eurythmia*.

RUDOLF WITTKOWER, *Architectural Principles*

———————

I cannot now think symbols less than the greatest of all powers whether they are used consciously by the masters of magic, or half unconsciously by their successors, the poet, the musician and the artist.

W. B. YEATS, *Essays*

———————

Magic has power to experience and fathom things which are inaccessible to human reason. For magic is a great secret wisdom, just as reason is a great public folly. Therefore it would be desirable and good for the doctors of theology to know something about it and to understand what it actually is, and cease unjustly and unfoundedly to call it witchcraft.

PARACELSUS

Even a brief shock (say, for example, when discovering the moon over city roofs or hearing a sharp bird cry at night) can yield an experience of the order of no-mind: that is to say, the poetical order, the order of art. When this occurs, our own reality-beyond-meaning is awakened (or perhaps better: *we* are awakened to our own reality-beyond-meaning), and we experience an affect that is neither thought nor feeling but an interior impact. The phenomenon, disengaged from cosmic references, has disengaged ourselves, by that principle, well known to magic, by which like conjures like. In fact, both the magic of art and the art of magic derive from and are addressed to experiences of this order. Hence the power of the meaningless syllables, the mumbo jumbo of magic, and the meaningless verbalizations of metaphysics, lyric poetry, and art interpretation. They function evocatively, not referentially; like the beat of a shaman's drum, not like a formula of Einstein.

JOSEPH CAMPBELL, *Flight of the Gander*

The world as a work of art could be the title of all Ficino's philosophy—the figured, animated, living world of the astrologers and the magicians. The world, indeed, which he wanted to reconstruct in its archetype when the Sun touches the first minute of Aries, or in that fatal hour which seals the fate of a world which is being reborn—when *sors quaedam quasi renascentis mundi revolvitur* (a certain destiny of the world as though being born again returns), as Ficino emphasises in an important passage. It is neither enough to build a perfect model of the world nor only to look at it: we must also bring it within ourselves through intense meditation ("not only contemplating but also refuting it in the mind") and the contemplation of its painted image in the rooms in which we live. Man the microcosm, that is, must adapt himself to the macrocosm through the technique of images, he must synthesise himself and so realise perfect harmony by identifying himself with the life and with the power of everything. Art and magic meet together.

EUGENIO GARIN, *Astrology in the Renaissance*

23.

ANGELS, DEVILS, SPIRITS, AND DREAM FIGURES

In modern times we have reduced the internal life to a mental world of ideas and thoughts, and at the same time we've shrunk the outer world to anything that can be weighed and measured. When conversation turns to angels, dream figures, and other spirits, either we witness thoughtlessly to our irrational beliefs or from an excessively rational position we demand proof. Perhaps in reaction to what we perceive as superstition, we sometimes explain these figures away as metaphors and symbols.

In an enchanted world, I would rather learn how to live on many levels at once than to reduce experience either to naive belief or superior skepticism. I'd rather discover ways to live both with my modern intelligence and with my awareness of a spiritual or preternatural order. The gift of such openness to imagination is the rich, warm, inspiring presence of a world alive with soul.

The shadow figures or shades we meet in dreams are not the people themselves (Jung's objective level), nor even are they their characterologic essence (Jung's subjective level), that is, my own traits that I can integrate. My brother with whom I worry about my father's business in a dream is neither my actual objective brother nor the older, sombre, responsible traits that slow and weigh me down. My dream-brother, because he is now a shade in the underworld, is an *eidola,* a purely psychic form, and our interpretation of him must also make this move from the everyday to the mythic.

Dare I say it loud and clear? The persons I engage with in dreams are neither representations (*simulacra*) of their living selves nor parts of myself. They are shadow images that fill archetypal roles; they are personae, masks, in the hollow of which is a *numen*.

There is a somewhat similar idea in the Egyptian cult of the dead, where the shadow soul is also the image of one or another God. So these shadow images were spoken of as Hathor, Chnum, Ity, etc. In the realm of death, that is, at the psychic level of existence, the essential image of our personal self, who is our shadow soul, is at the same time the image of a God. Our human person is shadowed by an archetypal image in the likeness of a God, and the God appears as the shade of a human person. The dream image of a human person cannot be taken in terms of his actuality, since the image in a dream belongs to the underworld shades and therefore refers to an archetypal person in human shape.

In the example above, the male triplicity of two brothers and a father, even an absent father, their being worried about the father business, the connection through worry to the father, and the other intricacies of this very simple image reach toward configurations that not only sustain but require mythic reflection. Something archetypal is going on, as in every image.

The former teacher, or my professor, in a dream is not only some intellectual potential of my psychic wholeness. More deeply, this figure is the archetypal mentor, who, for now, in this dream, wears the robes of this schoolteacher or that professor. The childhood love in my dreams is not only a special feeling tone that I may rediscover and unite with now as I age. More deeply this youth from then, living in remembrance, is the archetypal *kore* or *puer* who comes in the shape of this or that personal memory. In dreams, we are visited by the *daimones,* nymphs, heroes, and Gods shaped like our friends of last evening.

JAMES HILLMAN, *Dream and the Underworld*

In the meantime the more I tried to concentrate on Angels the more snakes appeared. I had a rattlesnake skin that Roxy Gordon had given me and some old wooden cigar boxes that I had started making little tableaux with snakes, birds and eggs in. & God knows making Art beats thinking any day. I kept making them & the snakes were becoming wilder, redder, fierier. Then it was Christmas which I spent in New Jersey drinking Jack Daniels and watching my sister's huge television. After a couple of weeks of New Jersey, Jack Daniels, and television, I was ready again for Angels but only snakes were waiting. I made more boxes. It wasn't till I was reading a book that dealt with Coleridge and his Angels that I ran across something that made everything click into place. Seraphim are flying, fiery serpents. The Hebrew word S'R'PH could signify either a serpent or an angelic being. Then Wilkins translates from the Sanskrit: ". . . describing this luxuriant paradise of Eendra, so remarkable for being guarded by serpents breathing fire, the flaming seraphim of Scripture, for saraph means a serpent." & as Rabbi Bechai observes: "this is the mystery of our holy language that a serpent is called a saraph, as an angel is called seraph." And I was someplace like in the bodhimandala of my soul. That place I'd read about in *The Vimalakirti Nirdesa Sutra*—"a circle, holy site or place of enlightenment; a place where a Bodhisattva" or an Angel appears and you get a glimpse of it. & this One that appears is a hot one, on fire. The Hebrew root of seraphim being "to burn." These burn with Love. They are on fire and their sword burns and they are extremely dangerous. That fiery, flying serpent that Isaiah saw above the throne of God. The one who guards the gates of Paradise & the Way to The Tree of Life. One puts a hot coal to the lips of Isaiah. They are Hell. Satan was one. & they purify. Seraphim burn out spiritual impurities & they do it with Love. Their planet is Mars. They burn out of us accumulations of useless mental and spiritual rubbish. They purify, and if we have failed to correct our faults by other means they will not let us into Paradise without using their fiery swords on us. The only way we can prevent this is to let go, to become truly detached from all within ourselves that is spiritually useless. Angelsnakes, plumed serpents

like Quetzalcoatl. & after these angelsnakes have purified us the true
spiritual waters are freed. These same waters are released in the Rig
Veda when the hero Indra slays the dragon/snake with his
Thunderbolt. As in Yahweh's victory over Leviathen & Zeus' over
Typhon.

Now what interested me was how I got to this Angel or how this
seraphim was getting to me. The more I tried to use my conscious,
rational mind, the more I looked to Heaven, the further away, the
further underground I drove the angel until there was no deeper to
go and the winged serpent forced its way up and out, bursting like a
rocket.

ROBERT TRAMMELL, *Angels*

────────

Our task is to stamp this provisional, perishing earth into ourselves
so deeply, so painfully and passionately, that its being may rise again,
"invisibly," in us. WE ARE THE BEES OF THE INVISIBLE. NOUS BUTI-
NONS ÉPERDUMENT LE MIEL DU VISIBLE, POUR L'ACCUMULER DANS
LA GRANDE RUCHE D'OR DE L'INVISIBLE. The "Elegies" show us at
this work, this work of the continual conversion of the dear visible
and tangible into the invisible vibration and agitation of our own
nature.

The earth has no other refuge except to become invisible: IN US,
who, through one part of our nature, have a share in the Invisible, or,
at least, share-certificates, and can increase our holding in invisibility
during our being here,— only IN US can this intimate and enduring
transformation of the visible into an invisible no longer dependent
on visibility and tangibility be accomplished, since our own destiny
is continually growing at once MORE ACTUAL AND INVISIBLE
within us.

The Angel of the ELEGIES is the creature in whom the transformation of the visible into the invisible we are performing already
appears complete . . . The Angel of the Elegies is the being who

vouches for the recognition of a higher degree of reality in the invisible.—Therefore "terrible" to us, because we, its lovers and transformers, still depend on the visible.—All the worlds of the universe are plunging into the invisible as into their next-deepest reality; SOME STARS HAVE AN IMMEDIATE WAXING AND WANING IN THE INFINITE CONSCIOUSNESS OF THE ANGEL,—OTHERS ARE DEPENDENT ON BEINGS THAT SLOWLY AND LABORIOUSLY TRANSFORM THEM, IN WHOSE TERRORS AND RAPTURES THEY ATTAIN THEIR NEXT INVISIBLE REALISATION. WE, let it be once more insisted, WE, IN THE MEANING OF THE ELEGIES, ARE THESE TRANSFORMERS OF THE EARTH, OUR WHOLE EXISTENCE, THE FLIGHTS AND PLUNGES OF OUR LOVE, ALL FIT US FOR THIS TASK (in comparison with which there is, essentially, no other).

RAINER MARIA RILKE, *Letters*

When characters are encouraged to speak to us as they desire, when they are allowed to share their versions of things, dreams cease to be the only place of *explicit* imaginal dialogue. Within the ebb and flow of thought and experience, one can begin to distinguish voices as they enter and suggest their presence. The "purpose of poetry," as Czeslaw Milosz describes it, becomes a telos of our work with thought itself.

> The purpose of poetry is to remind us
> How difficult it is to remain just one person
> for our house is open, there are no keys to the doors
> and invisible guests come in and out at will.

MARY WATKINS, *The Characters Speak*

The great advantage of the concepts "daimon" and "God" lies in making possible a much better objectification of the *vis-à-vis*, namely, a *personification* of it. Their emotional quality confers life and effectuality upon them. Hate and love, fear and reverence, enter the scene of the confrontation and raise it to a drama. What has merely been "displayed" becomes "acted." The whole man is challenged and enters the fray with his total reality. Only then can he become whole and only then can "God be born."

C. G. JUNG, *Memories*

Angel Surrounded by Paysans

One of the countrymen:
                                                    There is
            A welcome at the door to which no one comes?
The angel:
            I am the angel of reality,
            Seen for a moment standing in the door.

            I have neither ashen wing nor wear of ore
            And live without a tepid aureole,

            Or stars that follow me, not to attend,
            But, of my being and its knowing, part.

            I am one of you and being one of you
            Is being and knowing what I am and know.

            Yet I am the necessary angel of earth,
            Since, in my sight, you see the earth again,

            Cleared of its stiff and stubborn, man-locked set,
            And, in my hearing, you hear its tragic drone

            Rise liquidly in liquid lingerings,
            Like watery words awash; like meanings said

            By repetitions of half-meanings. Am I not,
            Myself, only half of a figure of a sort,

A figure half seen, or seen for a moment, a man
Of the mind, an apparition apparelled in

Apparels of such lightest look that a turn
Of my shoulder and quickly, too quickly, I am gone?

WALLACE STEVENS, *Collected Poems*

———————————

Soon after this fantasy another figure rose out of the unconscious. He developed out of the Elijah figure. I called him Philemon. Philemon was a pagan and brought with him an Egypto-Hellenistic atmosphere with a Gnostic coloration. His figure first appeared to me in the following dream.

There was a blue sky, like the sea, covered not by clouds but by flat brown clods of earth. It looked as if the clods were breaking apart and the blue water of the sea were becoming visible between them. But the water was the blue sky. Suddenly there appeared from the right a winged being sailing across the sky. I saw that it was an old man with the horns of a bull. He held a bunch of four keys, one of which he clutched as if he were about to open a lock. He had the wings of the kingfisher with its characteristic colors.

Since I did not understand this dream-image, I painted it in order to impress it upon my memory. During the days when I was occupied with the painting, I found in my garden, by the lake shore, a dead kingfisher! I was thunderstruck, for kingfishers are quite rare in the vicinity of Zürich and I have never since found a dead one. The body was recently dead—at the most, two or three days—and showed no external injuries.

Philemon and other figures of my fantasies brought home to me the crucial insight that there are things in the psyche which I do not produce, but which produce themselves and have their own life. Philemon represented a force which was not myself. In my fantasies I held conversations with him, and he said things which I had not consciously thought. For I observed clearly that it was he who spoke, not I. He said I treated thoughts as if I generated them myself, but in his view thoughts were like animals in the forest, or people in a room, or birds in the air, and added, "If you should see people in a room, you would not think that you had made those people, or that you were responsible for them." It was he who taught me psychic objectivity, the reality of the psyche. Through him the distinction was clarified between myself and the object of my thought. He confronted me in an objective manner, and I understood that there is something in me which can say things that I do not know and do not intend, things which may even be directed against me.

Psychologically, Philemon represented superior insight. He was a mysterious figure to me. At times he seemed to me quite real, as if he were a living personality. I went walking up and down the garden with him, and to me he was what the Indians call a guru.

C. G. JUNG, *Memories*

———————

Then a Voice said: "Behold this day, for it is yours to make. Now you shall stand upon the center of the earth to see, for there they are taking you."

I was still on my bay horse, and once more I felt the riders of the west, the north, the east, the south, behind me in formation, as before, and we were going east. I looked ahead and saw the mountains there with rocks and forests on them, and from the mountains flashed all colors upward to the heavens. Then I was standing on the highest mountain of them all, and round about beneath me was the whole hoop of the world. And while I stood there I saw more than I can tell and I understood more than I saw; for I was seeing in a sacred manner the shapes of all things in the spirit, and the shape of all shapes as they must live together like one being. And I saw that the sacred hoop of my people was one of many hoops that made one circle, wide as daylight and as starlight, and in the center grew one mighty flowering tree to shelter all the children of one mother and one father. And I saw that it was holy. . . .

First they sent a crier around in the morning who told the people to camp in a circle at a certain place a little way up the Tongue from

where the soldiers were. They did this, and in the middle of the circle Bear Sings and Black Road set up a sacred tepee of bison hide,
and on it they painted pictures from my vision. On the west side they
painted a bow and a cup of water; on the north, white geese and the
herb; on the east, the daybreak star and the pipe; on the south, the
flowering stick and the nation's hoop. Also, they painted horses,
elk, and bison. Then over the door of the sacred tepee, they painted
the flaming rainbow. It took them all day to do this, and it was
beautiful. . . .

My bay horse had bright red streaks of lightning on his limbs, and
on his back a spotted eagle, outstretching, was painted where I sat. I
was painted red all over with black lightning on my limbs. I wore a
black mask, and across my forehead a single eagle feather hung.

When the horses and the men were painted they looked beautiful;
but they looked fearful too.

The men were naked, except for a breech-clout; but the four
maidens wore buckskin dresses dyed scarlet, and their faces were
scarlet too. Their hair was braided, and they had wreaths of the sweet
and cleansing sage, the sacred sage, around their heads, and from the
wreath of each in front a single eagle feather hung. They were very
beautiful to see.

JOHN G. NEIHARDT, *Black Elk Speaks*

Spirits (Kongo). The Bakongo believe that every person has a body,
nitu, and a spirit, *moyo.* When life ends, the spirit leaves the body
and lives on in or near the water, preferably the rivers in the forest. A
person also has a soul, *mtumu-kutu,* literally, the king of the ear,
because one can hear it whispering in one's ear. When someone
faints or swoons, they say: his soul has gone away. A sleeping person's
soul wanders about. What he sees is what we call his dreams. Meanwhile his body may have marital relations while asleep. The soul is
the cause of a person's shadow.

JAN KNAPPERT, *African Mythology*

Whoever is born of sound mind has been naturally intended by heaven for some honest work and some kind of life. Whoever, therefore, wishes heaven to be nice to him, will go after this work and this kind of life, and doggedly pursue it. For heaven favors things it has itself begun. You were made by nature for this purpose beyond anything else. What you do from your tender years on, what you talk about, mould, fit, dream, imitate, what you try very often, what you can do easily, what you are most of all good at, what you love beyond all else, what you would be unwilling to leave—this is clearly what heaven and the rector of heaven bore you for.

To this extent, therefore, heaven will favor your beginnings and will smile on your life, as much as you pursue the signs of this creator, especially if that Platonic saying is true (in which all antiquity agreed), that there is a certain daemon guardian of life for everyone who is born, bound by one's own star itself. In order for him to help someone in this duty of life, the heavenly beings assign him to each person being born.

Whoever, therefore, scrutinizes his mind, through the kind of discussions we have just described, will find his own natural work, and will find likewise his own star and daemon, and following their beginnings he will thrive and live happily. Otherwise, he will find fortune to be adverse, and he will feel that heaven hates him.

MARSILIO FICINO, *Book of Life*

She wasn't wee at all when I think of it, for all we called her the Wee Woman. She was bigger than many a one, and yet not tall as you would say. She was like a woman about thirty, brown-haired and round in the face. She was like Miss Betty, your grandmother's sister, and Betty was like none of the rest, not like your grandmother, nor any of them. She was round and fresh in the face, and she never was married, and she never would take any man; and we used to say that the Wee Woman—her being like Betty—was, maybe, one of their own people that had been took off before she grew to her full height, and for that she was always following us and warning and foretelling. This time she walks straight over to where my mother was standing. "Go over to the Lough this minute!"—ordering her like that—"Go over to the Lough, and tell Joseph that he must change the foundation of this house to where I'll show you fornent the thorn-bush. That is where it is to be built, if he is to have luck and prosperity, so do what I'm telling ye this minute." The house was being built on "the path," I suppose—the path used by the people of Faery in their journeys, and my mother brings Joseph down and shows him, and he changes the foundation, the way he was bid, but didn't bring it exactly to where was pointed, and the end of that was, when he come to the house, his own wife lost her life with an accident that come to a horse that hadn't room to turn right with a harrow between the bush and the wall. The Wee Woman was queer and angry when next she come, and says to us, "He didn't do as I bid him, but he'll see what he'll see." My friend asked where the woman came from this time, and if she was dressed as before, and the woman said, "Always the same way, up the field beyant the burn." It was a thin sort of shawl she had about her in summer, and a cloak about her in winter; and many and many a time she came, and always it was good advice she was giving to my mother, and warning her what not to do if she would have good luck. There was none of the other children of us ever seen her unless me; but I used to be glad when I seen her coming up the burn, and would run out and catch her by the hand and the cloak, and call to my mother, "Here's the Wee Woman!" No man-body ever seen her. My father used to be wanting to, and was angry with my mother and me, thinking we were telling lies and talking foolish-like. And so one day when she had come, and was sitting by the fireside talking to my mother, I slips out to the field where he was digging. "Come up," says I, "if ye want to see her. She's sitting at the fireside now, talking to mother." So in he comes with me and looks round angry-like and sees nothing, and he up with a broom that was near hand and hits me a crig with it. "Take that now!" says he, "for making a fool of me!" and away with him as fast as he could, and queer and angry with me. The Wee Woman says to me then, "Ye got that now for bringing people to see me. No manbody ever seen me, and none ever will."

W. B. YEATS, The Celtic Twilight

24.

LOVE, BEAUTY, AND THE TASTE OF ETERNITY

The human soul cannot be equated with the brain, consciousness, or behavior. The soul is the very breath of our vitality and the unfathomable source of our identity. It is not a problem to be solved, but rather our very life that needs food and nurturing. The best food for the soul is a mixture of love, beauty, and excursions out of time where we glimpse the eternal.

We need love, we need beauty, and we need at least passing acquaintance with eternity. To the soul these are absolutes, and yet in modern life these three graces of life are values largely neglected. We reduce love to interpersonal relationship and then treat relationship as an emotional problem. We seem numb to ugliness and allow our world to be shaped and adorned according to the exclusive principle of function. Even religions seem to have forgotten the central place of the eternal in the development of reverence, ritual, and contemplation.

The soul longs for love that is unconditional, unending, and without a tangible object. Beauty relieves us of the limitation of functionality and pragmatism—dehumanizing signals of a loss of soul. And eternity is the proper time frame of the soul, whose immortality is ever present and whose endurance knows no limitation.

By beauty we do not mean beautifying, adornments, decorations. We do not mean aesthetics as a minor branch of philosophy concerned with taste, form and art criticism. We do not mean "disinterestedness"—the lion asleep. Nor can beauty be held in museums, by maestros at the violin, a profession of artists. Indeed we must cleave beauty altogether away from art, art history, art objects, art appreciation, art therapy. These are each positivisms: that is, they posit beauty into an instance of it: they position *aisthesis* in aesthetic events such as beautiful objects.

In pursuing what we mean by beauty we are obstructed by the word beauty itself. It strikes the ear as so effete, so ineffectual, lovely and etheric, so far removed from the soul's desperate concerns. Again we see how our notions are determined by archetypal patterns, as if beauty had become relegated only to Apollo, the examination of invisible forms like music, belonging to collectors and subject to disputes in journals of aesthetics. Or, beauty has been given over wholly to the soft hands of Adonis and Paris, beauty as violets, mutilation and death. In Plato and Plotinus, however, beauty does not have this glabrous, passive and ungenerative sense at all, and it is rarely brought into relation with art. In fact beauty is not "beautiful" and Socrates' person is witness. Rather, the beautiful in Platonic thought can only be understood if we can enter an Aphroditic cosmos and this in turn means penetrating into the ancient notion of *aisthesis* (sense-perception) from which aesthetics derives.

We must press beyond our usual ideas of beauty that have held the imagination captive to heavenly notions only, Aphrodite Urania, and away from the world of sense in which Aphrodite was always immanent. Hence, her nakedness has been pornographized by denigrating the visibility of physical appearance. As well, these lofty ideas have mystified revelation into an eschatological expectation: revelation comes as an epiphany that must shatter the sensate world only when we cannot sense the revelation in the immediate presentation of things as they are.

As Corbin writes: Beauty is that great category which specifically refers to the *Deus revelatus,* "the supreme theophany, divine self-revelation." As the Gods are given with creation so is their beauty in creation, and is the essential condition of *creation as manifestation.* Beauty is the manifest anima mundi—and do notice here it is neither transcendent to the manifest or hiddenly immanent within, but refers to appearances as such, created as they are, in the forms with which they are given, sense data, bare facts, Venus Nudata. Aphrodite's beauty refers to the luster of each particular event; its clarity, its particular brightness; that particular things appear at all and in the form in which they appear.

JAMES HILLMAN, *Thought of the Heart*

With his venom

Irresistible
and bittersweet

that loosener
of limbs, Love

reptile-like
strikes me down

SAPPHO

I imagine a far finer and more comprehensive task for ψA than alliance with an ethical fraternity. I think we must give it time to infiltrate into people from many centres, to revivify among intellectuals a feeling for symbol and myth, ever so gently to transform Christ back into the soothsaying god of the vine, which he was, and in this way absorb those ecstatic instinctual forces of Christianity for the *one* purpose of making the cult and the sacred myth what they once were—a drunken feast of joy where man regained the ethos and holiness of an animal. That was the beauty and purpose of classical religion, which from God knows what temporary biological needs has turned into a Misery Institute. Yet what infinite rapture and wantonness lie dormant in our religion, waiting to be led back to their true destination! A genuine and proper ethical development cannot abandon Christianity but must grow up within it, must bring to fruition its hymn of love, the agony and ecstasy over the dying and resurgent god, the mystic power of the wine, the awesome anthropophagy of the Last Supper—only *this* ethical development can serve the vital forces of religion.

C. G. JUNG, Freud / Jung Letters

I believe that the recovery of beauty is important as a movement toward healing the wound in the modern psyche caused by the separation of appearance and being. The symptom of this separation, Cartesian doubt of the world, reveals the anxiety of consciousness without a home. Without a sense of dwelling, the modern mind is constantly on a journey, incessantly focused upon the horizon in search of meaning. The purpose of the recovery would be to bring consciousness back to dwelling. When meaning is seen in appearance at hand, then beauty provides a habitat for consciousness.

Likewise, in beauty psychology finds its home. Without an aesthetic foundation, psychology loses its ground and becomes an endeavor of perpetual journey: research chases its own tail in never-ending circles of statistical analysis; psychoanalysis becomes interminable as a therapeutic endeavor, striving incessantly to recover hidden meaning; and the psychologist can never become impressed, in-formed, or touched by necessity outside of his or her preconceptions. . . .

Henri Corbin refers to beauty as the "supreme theophany, divine self-revelation." The Neoplatonists regard beauty as simply manifestation, the display of phenomena, appearances as such, created as they are, in the forms that they are given. If all creatures, things, and events exist to be perceived, the aesthetic psychologist would see beauty as the shining through of the suprasensuous in the simple bare facts—the raw data. To paraphrase Heidegger, things thing, occurrences occur, worlds world because they are beautiful.

James Hillman declares finally that beauty and soul are inherently connected. "Soul is born in beauty, and feeds on beauty and requires beauty for its life." The aesthetic psychologist is of necessity a psychological aesthete because he or she sees the soul's essence as beauty. When psyche appears, then beauty is revealed; where the voluptuous eye is attracted, there is soul.

RONALD SCHENK, *The Soul of Beauty*

Art is man's embodied expression of interest in the life of man; it springs from man's pleasure in his life; pleasure we must call it, taking all human life together, however much it may be broken by the grief and trouble of individuals . . .

neutrality is impossible in man's handiwork: a house, a knife, a cup, a steam engine . . . anything that is made by man and has form, must either be a work of art or destructive to art.

WILLIAM MORRIS, "The Socialist Idea in Art"

The almost religious reverence for wood is, fortunately for us, among the many traditions that have stood the test of time. A tree, like other natural phenomena, is believed to possess a spirit, and a carpenter, when he cuts down a tree, incurs a moral debt. One of the themes that runs throughout Japanese culture is the belief that nature exacts from man a price for coexistence. A carpenter must put a tree to uses that assure its continued existence, preferably as a thing of beauty to be treasured for centuries. There is a prayer that Nishioka recites before laying a saw to a standing tree. It goes in part, "I vow to commit no act that will extinguish the life of this tree."

S. AZBY BROWN, *The Genius of Japanese Carpentry*

It is one of the amiable traits in Ficino's character that he began his literary career as an Epicurean. Although he claimed to have burned these youthful essays, and even stoutly denied their authorship when he was teasingly reminded of them by Politian, he always retained, even while posing as a Platonic high priest, an air of tolerant worldly benevolence which he could hardly claim to have acquired from Plato. A picture of the smiling Democritus, defying the tears of Heraclitus, continued to decorate his study, and reminded him and his visitors that ευθυμια (cheerfulness) was a quality becoming a philosopher. Among his early compilations was one with the title *De voluptate*, which clearly foreshadowed his later attempts to redefine the nature of Pleasure with such care that it could become the highest good of a Platonist. In an *Apologus de voluptate*, for example, he invented a fable by which to explain why Pleasure, originally residing on earth, was transferred to heaven where she is still to be found, while her place on earth is occupied by a deceptive double. Distrust of the false *Voluptas*, however, should not deceive us into believing that knowledge is a higher good than pleasure. The fruition of knowledge is in pleasure, and therefore pleasure and joy, in a philosophical lover, are superior to inquiry and vision. This hedonistic conclusion, so unexpected by the common standards of Platonism, was firmly asserted by Ficino in his *Epistola de felicitate*, an important little treatise addressed to Lorenzo de' Medici.

EDGAR WIND, *Pagan Mysteries*

Ficino is the only thinker in modern times who has tried to found a philosophical school as an intellectual and moral communion between master and pupils. And in so far as love and friendship between men are based on the individual's love for God, in other words, on the spiritual wakefulness of the individual friends, the school, as a field of activity and as a community, is directly connected through its bond of friendship with the essence of the philosophical system and with the basic phenomenon of inner experience.

Conversely, the inner certainty of consciousness and the metaphysical doctrine acquire a concrete form in the philosophical communion of friends and so are realized not only as a propagated doctrine, but as a living part of reality.

This love between friends, which is the foundation for the communion of the Florentine Platonists and is itself based on the love of the Soul for God, is called "divine" love (*amor divinus*) by Ficino, in opposition to the vulgar concept of love. And since he develops this concept essentially in accordance with Plato's *Symposium*, he states explicitly that he is following the model of Socrates and Plato on this point, and occasionally he speaks of Socratic or Platonic love, that is, of love conceived in the sense of Socrates and Plato. For instance, one of the last chapters of the *De amore* is entitled: "How Useful Socratic Love Is." It begins with the following words: "You ask what the utility of Socratic love (*amor Socraticus*) is." In the Preface to Plato's *Phaedrus* he mentions "Socratic and Platonic love." The most explicit passage is found in the important letter to Alamanno Donati from which we quoted the definition of friendship.

> What kind [of friendship] will ours be called, oh Alamanno? Since it began from nothing else than from Platonic love (*amore Platonico*), we must call it nothing else than Platonic [friendship]. For when we recently explained our commentary *De amore* composed on Plato's *Symposium*, we began meanwhile to love each other, so that apparently we have realized and perfected in ourselves that Idea of true love which Plato formulates in that work. From this Platonic love therefore a Platonic friendship arises. . . . So why do you doubt, oh Alamanno, whether Plato believed that there were several Souls in one body? There are not several in one, but the contrary seems frequently to be true when we see that one Soul exists in the bodies of several friends as the result of the Platonic love.

This remarkable passage, which has no analogies in Ficino's works, deserves our full attention. Here for the first time in the history of philosophy and literature, as far as I am aware, we have the term "Platonic love.". . . So the term "Platonic love" in Ficino has its clear and precise meaning: it is intellectual love between friends; love which unites the members of the Academy into a community, which is based on the individual's love for God, and is called, with reference to Plato's *Symposium,* "Platonic love"—that is, love conceived in the sense of Plato. . . .

With the concept of Platonic love Ficino enters into a large historical perspective, comprising not only philosophy and theology but also poetry and literature. In his concept of love he combines the will of St. Augustine, the charity of St. Paul, the friendship of Aristotle and the Stoics with love in Plato's sense of the term into a new and fertile idea. Moreover, Ficino's speculation on love was foreshadowed (as has been repeatedly observed) by the old Provençal and Tuscan lyric to which he himself consciously refers. In this respect the explicit quotation of Guido Cavalcanti in the *De amore* is of great importance, and in other points also the influence of the old poets is clearly visible in Ficino. The physiological theory concerning the genesis of love which makes the so-called spirit pass from the heart of the beloved person through its eyes to the eyes and the heart of the lover and the whole technical language of love which exchanges the Souls of the lovers and transforms them into each other are evidently taken from poetry and developed into a more precise system.

PAUL OSCAR KRISTELLER, *The Philosophy of Marsilio Ficino*

The Wild Horse

Again trapped
chained by
his love
all struggle
to escape
vain.

Love
an ocean
with invisible
shores,
        with
no shores.
If you
are wise
you will
not swim
in it.
To reach
the end
of love
you must
suffer many
unpleasantries
and think
it good,
drink poison
and find
it sweet.
I acted
like a
wild horse
not knowing:
to struggle
draws the
noose tighter.

RĀBI'AH BENT KA'B

All things
are too small
to hold me,
I am so vast

In the Infinite
I reach
for the Uncreated

I have
touched it,
it undoes me
wider than wide

Everything else
is too narrow

You know this well,
you who are also there

HADEWIJCH

_____

AUTHOR INDEX

COPYRIGHT ACKNOWLEDGMENTS

Every effort has been made by the author to contact the sources of the selections in this book. Grateful acknowledgment is made for permission to reprint excerpts from:

Aeschylus. *Prometheus Bound,* James Scully and C. J. Harrington, translators. © 1975. Oxford University Press, Inc., New York, NY.

Alexander, Christopher. *A Pattern Language.* © 1977. Oxford University Press, Inc., New York, NY.

Atwood, Margaret. "Axiom," from *The Animals of That Country.* © 1968. Oxford University Press, Inc., New York, NY.

Bachelard, Gaston. *Poetics of Space,* Maria Jolas, translator. © 1969. Viking Penguin, New York, NY.

Beckett, Samuel. From *Murphy, Stories and Texts for Nothing,* and *Ends and Odds. Murphy* © 1938 by Samuel Beckett. *Stories and Texts for Nothing* © 1967 by Samuel Beckett. *Ends and Odds* © 1973 by Samuel Beckett. Used by permission of Grove/Atlantic, Inc.

Berry, Patricia. *Echo's Subtle Body.* © 1982 by Patricia Berry.

———. "The Rape of Demeter/Persephone and Neurosis," from *Spring 1975: An Annual of Archetypal Psychology and Jungian Thought.* © 1975. Spring Publications, Woodstock, CT 06281.

———. "Virginities of the Image," from *Images of the Untouched: Virginity in Psyche, Myth, and Community,* Joanne Stroud and Gail Thomas, editors. © 1982. Spring Publications, Woodstock, CT 06281.

———. *The Shadow in America.* © 1994 by Patricia Berry.

Berry, Wendell. "To Know the Dark," from *Farming: A Hand Book.* © 1970 by Wendell Berry. Reprinted by permission of Harcourt Brace & Company, Orlando, FL.

Bishop, Peter. *The Greening of Psychology: The Vegetable World in Myth, Dream, and Healing.* © 1990. Spring Publications, Woodstock, CT 06281.

———. *Sphinx 1.* © 1988. *Sphinx,* the annual journal of the London Convivium for Archetypal Studies, London, England.

———. *Spring 1984: An Annual of Archetypal Psychology and Jungian Thought.* © 1984. Spring Publications, Woodstock, CT 06281.

Bly, Robert. "A Doing Nothing Poem," from *Jumping Out of Bed.* © 1987. Reprinted by permission of White Pine Press, 10 Village Square, Fredonia, NY 14063.

Brown, Norman O. *Love's Body.* © 1966. Random House, New York, NY.

Burkert, Walter. *Ancient Mystery Cults.* © 1987. Harvard University Press, Cambridge, MA.

————. *Greek Religion,* John Raffan, translator. © 1955. Harvard University Press, Cambridge, MA.

Cage, John. *Silence.* © 1961. Wesleyan University Press, Middletown, CT.

Chuang Tzu. *The Mystical Way of Chuang Tzu,* Thomas Merton, translator. © 1965. New Directions, New York, NY.

Cousins, Norman. *Anatomy of an Illness as Perceived by the Patient: Reflections on Healing and Regeneration.* © 1979 by W. W. Norton & Company, Inc. Reprinted by permission of W. W. Norton & Company, Inc., New York, NY.

Cowan, Louise. *Stirrings of Culture: Essays from the Dallas Institute,* R. J. Sardello and G. Thomas, editors. © 1986. Dallas Institute of Humanities and Culture, Dallas, TX.

Eliade, Mircea. *Journals I,* MacLinscott Ricketts, translator. © 1990. University of Chicago Press, Chicago, IL.

————. *Journals II,* Fred H. Johnson Jr., translator. © 1977. University of Chicago Press, Chicago, IL.

————. *Journals III,* Teresa Lavender Fagan, translator. © 1989. University of Chicago Press, Chicago, IL.

————. *Myths, Dreams and Mysteries,* Philip Mairet, translator. © 1957 by Librairie Gallimard. English language translation copyright © 1960 by Harville Press. Copyright renewed. Reprinted by permission of HarperCollins Publishers, Inc., New York, NY.

————. *The Myth of the Eternal Return,* Willard R. Trask, translator. © 1959. Princeton University Press, Princeton, NJ.

Eliot, T. S. *Murder in the Cathedral.* © 1935 by Harcourt Brace & Company, Orlando, FL; renewed 1963 by T. S. Eliot. Reprinted by permission of the publisher. Also © 1963 by Faber and Faber Ltd., London, England.

Erasmus. *The Correspondence of Erasmus,* vol. 7, R. A. B. Mynors, translator. © 1987. University of Toronto Press, Toronto, Canada. Reprinted by permission of University of Toronto Press Incorporated.

————. *The Erasmus Reader,* R. A. B. Mynors, D. F. S. Thomson, and Beert C. Verstraete, translators; Erika Rummel, editor. © 1990. University of Toronto Press, Toronto, Canada. Reprinted by permission of University of Toronto Press Incorporated.

Eriugena, John Scotus. *The Voice of the Eagle: The Heart of Celtic Christianity,* Christopher Bamford, translator. © 1990 by Lindisfarne Press. Reprinted by permission of Lindisfarne Press, Hudson, NY 12534.

Euripides. *Hippolytos,* Robert Bagg, translator. © 1973. Oxford University Press, New York, NY, and London, England.

Ferenczi, Sandor. *First Contributions to Psycho-Analysis,* pages 132–33 and 140, E. Jones, translator. © 1952 by Brunner/Mazel, Inc. Reprinted by permission of Brunner/Mazel, Inc., New York, NY.

————. *Thalassa,* Henry Aldin Bunker, translator. © 1968. The Psychoanalytic Quarterly, New York, NY 10010.

Ficino, Marsilio. *The Book of Life,* Charles Boer, translator. © 1980, 1994 by Charles Boer. Spring Publications, Woodstock, CT 06281.

———. *Commentary on Plato's Symposium on Love,* Sears Jayne, translator. © 1985 by Sears Jayne. Woodstock, CT: Spring Publications, 1994.

———. *The Letters of Marsilio Ficino,* vols 1, 2, & 4, translated by the Language Department of the School of Economic Science, London, England. © 1975, 1978, 1988. Shepheard-Walwyn, London, England.

———. *Three Books on Life,* Carol Kaske and John R. Clarke, translators. © 1989 by the Center for Medieval and Renaissance Studies, State University of New York at Binghamton, Binghamton, NY.

Gadelica, Carmina. *Charms of the Gaels: Hymns and Incantations,* Alexander Carmichael, editor. © 1994. Lindisfarne Press, Hudson, NY 12534.

Hadewijch. "All things," from *Women in Praise of the Sacred,* Jane Hirshfield, editor. © 1994. HarperCollins Publishers, New York, NY.

Hayum, Andrée. *The Isenheim Altarpiece.* © 1990 by Princeton University Press. Reprinted by permission of Princeton University Press, Princeton, NJ.

Hildegard of Bingen. *Writings of Medieval Women,* Marcelle Thiébaux, translator. © 1994 by Marcelle Thiébaux. Garland Publishing, New York, NY.

Hillman, James. "Alchemical Blue and the Unio Mentalis," from Spring 54: *A Journal of Archetype and Culture.* © 1993. Spring Publications, Woodstock, CT 06281.

———. "The 'Negative' Senex and a Renaissance Solution," from Spring 1975: *An Annual of Archetypal Psychology and Jungian Thought.* © 1975. Spring Publications, Woodstock, CT 06281.

———. "An Inquiry into Image," from Spring 1977: *An Annual of Archetypal Psychology and Jungian Thought.* © 1977. Spring Publications, Woodstock, CT 06281.

———. *The Dream and the Underworld.* © 1979 by James Hillman. Reprinted by permission of HarperCollins Publishers, Inc., New York, NY.

———. "Wars, Arms, Rams, Mars: On the Love of War," from *Facing Apocalypse,* V. Andrews, R. Bosnak, and K. W. Goodwin, editors. © 1987. Spring Publications, Woodstock, CT 06281.

———. "The Bad Mother: An Archetypal Approach," from *Fathers and Mothers,* Patricia Berry, editor. Second edition 1990. © 1983 by James Hillman. Spring Publications, Woodstock, CT 06281.

———. *Healing Fiction.* © 1983 by James Hillman. Spring Publications, Woodstock, CT 06281.

———. *Inter Views—Conversations with Laura Pozzo.* © 1983 by James Hillman. Woodstock CT: Spring Publications, 1992.

———. *Kinds of Power.* © 1995. Doubleday, New York, NY.

———. "Toward the Archetypal Model of the Masturbation Inhibition," from *Loose Ends: Primary Papers in Archetypal Psychology.* © 1975 by James Hillman. Spring Publications, Woodstock, CT 06281.

———. *The Myth of Analysis.* © 1972 by Northwestern University Press. © 1992 by HarperPerennial, New York, NY.

————. "Peaks and Vales—The Soul/Spirit Distinction as Basis for the Differences between Psychotherapy and Spiritual Disciplines," from *Puer Papers*, James Hillman, editor. © 1979. Spring Publications, Woodstock, CT 06281.

————. *Re-Visioning Psychology.* © 1975 by James Hillman. Reprinted by permission of HarperCollins Publishers, Inc., New York, NY.

————. "A Contribution to Soul and Money," from *Soul and Money.* © 1982. Spring Publications, Woodstock, CT 06281.

————. "Souls Take Pleasure in Moisture," from *Stirrings of Culture: Essays from the Dallas Institute,* R. J. Sardello and G. Thomas, editors. © 1986 by James Hillman. Dallas Institute of Humanities and Culture, Dallas, TX.

————. *The Thought of the Heart and the Soul of the World.* © 1982 by James Hillman. Spring Publications, Woodstock, CT 06281.

Hirshfield, Jane. "Autumn," from *The October Palace.* © 1994 by Jane Hirshfield. Reprinted by permission of HarperCollins Publishers, Inc., New York, NY.

Homer. *Homeric Hymns,* Charles Boer, translator. © 1970 by Charles Boer. Ohio University Press, Athens, OH.

Jung, C. G. *Collected Works of C. G. Jung,* vol. 7, R. F. C. Hull, translator. © 1953. Princeton University Press, Princeton, NJ.

————. *Collected Works of C. G. Jung,* vol. 9, R. F. C. Hull, translator. © 1959. Princeton University Press, Princeton, NJ.

————. *Collected Works of C. G. Jung,* vol. 12, R. F. C. Hull, translator. © 1953. Princeton University Press, Princeton, NJ.

————. *Collected Works of C. G. Jung,* vol. 13, R. F. C. Hull, translator. © 1967. Princeton University Press, Princeton, NJ.

————. *Collected Works of C. G. Jung,* vol. 14, R. F. C. Hull, translator. © 1965. Princeton University Press, Princeton, NJ.

————. *Collected Works of C. G. Jung,* vol. 17, R. F. C. Hull, translator. © 1954. Princeton University Press, Princeton, NJ.

————. *The Freud/Jung Letters,* Ralph Manheim and R. F. C. Hull, translators. © 1974. Princeton University Press, Princeton, NJ.

————. *Letters,* vol. 2, R. F. C. Hull, translator. © 1975 by Princeton University Press. Reprinted by permission of Princeton University Press, Princeton, NJ.

————. *Memories, Dreams, Reflections,* Richard and Clara Winston, translators. Translation copyright © 1961, 1962, 1963; copyright renewed 1989, 1990, 1991 by Random House, Inc. Reprinted by permission of Pantheon Books, a division of Random House, Inc., New York, NY.

Kristeller, Paul Oskar. *Philosophy of Marsilio Ficino.* © 1970. Peter Smith Publisher, Inc., Gloucester, MA.

Lao Tzu. *Tao Te Ching,* English and Feng, translators. © 1972 by Jane English and Gia-fu Feng. Reprinted by permission of Alfred A. Knopf, Inc., New York, NY, and by Crown Publishing, Ltd., Aldershot, Hampshire, England.

Lattimore, Richmond. *The Odyssey of Homer.* © 1965, 1967 by Richmond Lattimore.

Copyright renewed. Reprinted by permission of HarperCollins Publishers, Inc., New York, NY.

Lawrence, D. H. "Things Men Have Made," from *Complete Poems*. © 1971. Penguin Books, New York, NY.

Li Po. "Zazen on the Mountain," Sam Hamill, translator, from *A Drifting Boat: Chinese Zen Poetry*, J. P. Seaton and Dennis Maloney, editors. © 1994. Translation copyright © 1994 by Sam Hamill. Reprinted by permission of White Pine Press, 10 Village Square, Fredonia, NY 14063.

Lopez-Pedraza, Rafael. *Cultural Anxiety*. © by Rafael Lopez-Pedraza. Reprinted by permission of Daimon Verlag, Einsiedeln, Switzerland.

———. *Hermes and His Children*. © 1977 by Rafael Lopez-Pedraza. Reprinted by permission of Daimon Verlag, Einsiedeln, Switzerland.

Mackey, Mary. "The Kama Sutra of Kindness: Position No. 2," from *The Dear Dance of Eros*. © 1987. Fjord Press, Seattle, WA.

Merton, Thomas. *Conjectures of a Guilty Bystander*. © 1966 by the Abbey of Gethsemani. Reprinted by permission of Doubleday, a division of Bantam Doubleday Dell Publishing Group, Inc., New York, NY.

Miller, David. *Gods and Games*. © 1973 by David Miller. Augsburg Fortress Publishers, Minneapolis, MN.

———. *Three Faces of God*. © 1986 by David Miller. HarperCollins Publishers, New York, NY.

Neihardt, John G. *Black Elk Speaks*. © 1961. Simon & Schuster, New York, NY.

Oliver, Mary. "In Blackwater Woods," from *American Primitive*. © 1992 by Mary Oliver. First appeared in *Yankee* magazine. Reprinted by permission of Little, Brown and Company, Boston, MA.

———. "Some Questions You Might Ask," from *House of Light*. © 1990 by Mary Oliver. Reprinted by permission of Beacon Press, Boston, MA.

———. "Entering the Kingdom," from *Twelve Moons*. © 1974 by Mary Oliver. First appeared in *Commonweal*. Reprinted by permission of Little, Brown and Company, Boston, MA.

Olson, Charles. "The Ring of," from *Selected Writings*. © 1950. New Directions, New York, NY.

Ovid. *Ovid's Metamorphoses,* Charles Boer, translator. © 1989 by Charles Boer. Spring Publications, Woodstock, CT 06281.

Paracelsus. *Selected Writings,* Norbert Guterman, translator. © 1979. Princeton University Press, Princeton, NJ.

Pessoa, Fernando. "Note" and "There are Sicknesses worse than sicknesses" from *Poems of Fernando Pessoa*, Edwin Honig and Susan M. Brown, translators and editors. © 1986 by Edwin Honig and Susan M. Brown. First published by The Ecco Press in 1986. Reprinted by permission.

Plato. *The Collected Dialogues of Plato*. © 1961. Princeton University Press, Princeton, NJ.

————. *Republic,* H. D. P. Lee, translator. © 1955. Penguin Books Ltd., London, England.

Rabi'ah bent Ka'b. "The Wild Horse," from *The Drunken Universe: An Anthology of Persian Sufi Poetry,* Peter L. Wilson and Nasrollah Pourjavady, translators. © 1987. Reprinted by permission of Phanes Press, Grand Rapids, MI.

Rilke, Rainer Maria. *Duino Elegies,* J. B. Leishman and Stephen Spender, translators. Translation © 1939 by W. W. Norton & Company, Inc.; renewed 1967 by Stephen Spender and J. B. Leishman. Reprinted by permission of W. W. Norton & Company, Inc., New York, NY.

————. *Letters to a Young Poet,* Stephen Mitchell, translator. © 1984 by Stephen Mitchell. Reprinted by permission of Random House, Inc., New York, NY.

————. *The Selected Poetry of Rainer Maria Rilke,* Stephen Mitchell, translator and editor. Copyright © 1982 by Stephen Mitchell. Reprinted by permission of Random House, Inc., New York, NY.

Rimbaud, Arthur. "Vigils I," from *Illuminations,* Louise Varese, translator. © 1957. New Directions, New York, NY.

Ryokan. "A quiet night behind my grass hut," and "The new pond," Dennis Maloney and Hide Oshiro, translators, from *Between the Floating Mist: Poems by Ryokan.* © 1992. Translation copyright © 1992 by Dennis Maloney and Hide Oshiro. Reprinted by permission of White Pine Press, 10 Village Square, Fredonia, NY 14063.

Saint Patrick. "The Rune of Saint Patrick," from *Celtic Christianity,* William Marsh and Christopher Bamford, editors; Christopher Bamford, translator. © 1987. Reprinted by permission of the Lindisfarne Press, Hudson, NY 12534.

Sappho. "With His Venom" from *Sappho: A New Translation,* Mary Barnard, translator. © 1958 by The Regents of the University of California; renewed 1984 by Mary Barnard. The University of California Press, Berkeley, CA.

Sardello, Robert. *Money and the Soul of the World.* © 1983. Dallas Institute of Humanities, Dallas, TX.

————. "Taking the Side of Things," from Spring 1984: *An Annual of Archetypal Psychology and Jungian Thought.* © 1984. Spring Publications, Woodstock, CT 06281.

Scully, Vincent. *The Earth, the Temple, and the Gods.* © 1962 by Yale University. Revised edition © 1969 by Frederick A. Praeger Inc. Revised edition © 1979 by Yale University. Yale University Press, New Haven, CT.

————. *Household Gods and Sacred Places.* © 1988. Little, Brown and Company, Boston, MA.

Simpson, Louis. "Ed," from *Collected Poems.* © 1988. Paragon House, New York, NY.

Snyder, Gary. "For the Children," from *Turtle Island.* © 1969. New Directions, New York, NY.

Stevens, Wallace. *Collected Poems.* © 1954 by Wallace Stevens. Reprinted by permission of Alfred A. Knopf Inc., New York, NY, and by Faber and Faber Ltd., London, England.

———. *Opus Posthumous.* © 1989 Alfred A. Knopf Inc., New York, NY.

Stravinsky, Igor. *The Poetics of Music.* © 1947. Harvard University Press, Cambridge, MA.

Strong, Roy. *The Renaissance Garden in England.* © 1979 by Thames and Hudson. Reprinted by permission of Thames and Hudson, New York, NY.

Tedlock, Dennis. *Finding the Center: Narrative Poetry of the Zuni Indians.* © 1972 by Dennis Tedlock. Bantam Doubleday Dell, New York, NY.

Tillich, Paul. *The Courage to Be.* © 1952 by Paul Tillich. © 1952 by Yale University Press. Thirty-third printing November 1969. Yale University Press, New Haven, CT.

———. *The Eternal Now.* © 1963 by Paul Tillich. Reprinted by permission of Scribner, a division of Simon & Schuster, New York, NY, and by SCM Press Ltd., London, England.

———. *The Shaking of the Foundations.* © 1948 by Charles Scribner's Sons; renewed 1976 by Hannah Tillich. Reprinted by permission of Scribner, a division of Simon & Schuster, New York, NY, and by SCM Press Ltd., London, England.

Wind, Edgar. *Pagan Mysteries of the Renaissance,* revised and enlarged edition. © 1958, 1968 by Edgar Wind. Reprinted by permission of W. W. Norton & Company, Inc., New York, NY.

Wittkower, Rudolf. *Architectural Principles in the Age of Humanism.* © 1988. Academy Editions Press, Paris, France.

Yeats, William Butler. *Essays and Introductions.* © 1961 by Mrs. W. B. Yeats. Reprinted by permission of Simon & Schuster, New York, NY. Permission also granted by A. P. Watt Ltd., London, on behalf of Michael Yeats.

———. *Mythologies.* © 1959 by Mrs. W. B. Yeats. Reprinted by permission of Simon & Schuster, New York, NY. Permission also granted by A. P. Watt Ltd., London, on behalf of Michael Yeats.

Ziegler, Alfred J. *Archetypal Medicine.* © 1983. Spring Publications, Woodstock, CT 06281.